IMAGINING NATURE

IMAGINING NATURE

Practices of Cosmology and Identity

Edited by
Andreas Roepstorff, Nils Bubandt & Kalevi Kull

AARHUS UNIVERSITY PRESS

Graphic Design: Jørgen Sparre

Cover illustration: Kirstine Roepstorff, 'Lost Virginity'
from series 'Wonders of Life' printed collage, 2002

Photos:

Le Corbusier's Villa Savoye, 1929.
© Fondation Le Corbusier

Fallingwater. Photograph by Thomas A. Heinz.
Courtesy of Western Pennsylvania Conservancy

Printed in Denmark by Scanprint, Aarhus

ISBN 87 7288 945 4

AARHUS UNIVERSITY PRESS

Langelandsgade 177

8200 Aarhus N

Denmark

Fax (+ 45) 8942 5380

www.unipress.dk

73 Lime Walk

Headington, Oxford OX3 7AD

United Kingdom

Fax (+ 44) 1865 750 079

Box 511

Oakville, Conn. 06779

USA

Fax (+ 1) 860 945 9468

Preface

This book grew out of a Baltic–Scandinavian research workshop *Uses of Nature – towards an Anthropology of the Environment,* held in Estonia in May 1998. During a few sunny days in Tartu and in the former cottage of Jakob von Uexküll on the Baltic shore near the wooded meadows of Puhtu, researchers from social anthropology, biology, geography, semiotics and philosophy came together in lively interactions. The discussions fused Scandinavian styles of phenomenological ethnography, Baltic styles of structural semiotics, continental philosophy of science, ecosemiotics and social anthropology into a highly inspiring melange.

Over the next years, selected papers from the workshop were rewritten and reworked to form the core of the current publication. As further contributions were invited, the focus shifted from 'use' to 'imagining', and, in the end, the current volume emerged. It endeavours to make a cross-disciplinary examination of how to find one's bearings in dealing with imagined natures, conflicting identities and contested cosmologies, both in this corner of the world and on a global scale.

Financial support from NorFA and from the Danish Research Council for the Humanities allowed for the 1998 workshop to take place. The publication and language revision of this book was made possible by generous grants from the Danish Research Council for the Humanities and from the University of Aarhus Research Foundation. However, money does not do the work alone: the workshop could not have taken place without the great organisational competence and amazing spirit of Ehte Puhang and Peter Toorop in Estonia and Poul Pedersen and Aake Norborg in Denmark. The completion of this volume would not have been possible without the gentle and effective work of Mary Waters Lund at Aarhus University Press in her capacity as general editor and language reviser.

Aarhus and Tartu, September 2003
Andreas Roepstorff, Nils Bubandt & Kalevi Kull

Contents

General introduction:
The critique of culture and
the plurality of nature

Andreas Roepstorff & Nils Bubandt

Nature is no longer what it used to be. But neither is culture. The former is being deconstructed, the latter is being naturalised, and yet the two antagonists in themselves appear as important and foundational as ever. It may be that the bearings of this dichotomy are simply in the midst of a reconfiguration. Coming to grips with this complex condition, however, calls for novel analytical approaches. We believe that this collection of essays breaks new ground by arguing that recent reconceptualisations of the processes of practice and imagining can act as a useful starting point from which to understand the complex ways in which nature emerges as a human reality.

The emphasis on the dual perspective of practices and processes of imagining arises from a concern to capture how nature is simultaneously real and really imagined. From different theoretical points of departure, the contributors to this volume all seek to describe the multifarious forms which the dialectic between nature as 'fact' and nature as 'imagined' may take and to show how this seeming dichotomy is a constantly shifting whole. Thus we maintain that the arguments of 'constructivists' and 'primordialists' need to be refashioned and reconciled rather than accepted as each other's opposites. Nature is neither 'just' made up nor 'just' there to begin with as an innate fact; rather its 'constructedness' has real effects that need to be taken seriously, while its 'facticity' has a history that needs to be traced. We suggest that both of these perspectives may be appreciated by paying attention to the ways 'nature' is engaged through human varieties of practice and imagination.

While all human forms of practices and imaginings are constantly changing, they do so in tangible, traceable ways because they arise and are reproduced within specific social and institutional settings. By emphasising the way 'practices and imaginings of nature' are part of particular historical and institutional circumstances we hope to avoid the latent mentalism of much recent academic thinking, in which 'nature' appears primarily as a matter of 'classification', 'perception' or 'invention'.

After briefly tracing how this 'shift towards classification' has come about, the introduction lays out in detail the arguments and implications of the anthology. It is argued that detailed attention to human practices highlights how 'nature' is at the same time real and constructed, simultaneously independent and full of human agency.

Understanding Nature 'in the active'

Within the past ten years of anthropological, sociological and philosophical writings, 'nature' has emerged as a firmly established *problematique*. The backdrop of this emergence of 'nature' as a conceptual and scientific problem is the increased political focus on environmental issues that has placed 'nature' centre stage far beyond the academic theatre (Sachs 1993; United Nations 1993; Kalland this volume). In response to the sharp social and political focus on matters of nature, the overall trend within the social sciences has been to 'denaturalise' nature as an academic concept and to relativise or historicise it as a cultural category (Milton 1996). The emphasis has thus been on showing that nature is not an eternal constant but inherently an unstable concept, prone to change dependent on the cultural and historical context. 'Nature', it is argued, is a historical, cultural and social construct with powerful emotional, moral and political associations.

A brief glance at the recent academic bibliography on 'nature' suggests the outlines of this – dare one term it 'constructivist'? – trend. There have been calls for a 'redefinition' (Ellen & Fukui 1996) and a 'reconstruction' of nature (Dickens 1996). Others have set out to demonstrate that nature is a cultural construction (Eder 1996; Simmons 1993), an invention (Bargatzky & Kuschel 1994; Cronon 1995), a social or historical creation (Evernden 1992; Teich et al. 1997); while still others have stressed how differently other cultural perceptions of and attitudes towards nature are constructed (Bruun & Kalland 1995; Croll et al. 1992; Holm & Bowker 1994). What nature is, has in other words been thrown fundamentally into question. The following essays set out to explore some of the implications of and lacunae in this recent push to 'denaturalise nature'. If we accept that 'nature' is constructed, perceived, and classified according to social, historical and cultural context, this means rethinking the processes through which this construction, perception or classification is established. Rather than following the recent trend and asking 'what is nature? (Soper 1995), the contributors to this volume provide specific answers to the question of 'how nature is established' as an entity. While the constructed nature of 'nature' may now have become accepted dogma, the volume attempts to go one step further and inquire into the processuality of this construction. This is done through a range of analyses which focuses on 'the practices of nature', that is, human practices that depend upon or are involved in generating particular perceptions and categories of nature. These practices of nature are in a 'feedback' or 'looping' relationship with their environment making them both producers of 'nature' and products of nature. Paradoxical as it may initially seem, detailed attention to these 'practices of nature' in fact problematises the whole issue of the constructedness of 'nature'.

Anthropologists have now for some time criticised the 'constructivist' stance for not allowing 'the environment' to play an active role (Descola & Pálsson 1996a: 11; Ingold 1992a; Milton 1996: 214), but constructivism has, we will argue, a way of reproducing itself in new and unexpected ways, as evidenced in the many recent attempts to 'reconstruct' our understanding of 'nature'. We believe the solution is not to discard the issue of construction, but rather to take it much more seriously. Thus pointing to the cultural constructed-ness of nature should not blind us analytically to its imposing productive reality. It is as an inescapable reality that 'nature' is constantly engaged, practised, semiotised, and reproduced – hence, constructed as a category (at least within a Western tradition, see Ingold 1992b). In turn, it is as a practised and semiotised reality that nature constrains, affects, and shapes human 'being and doing'. As Michael Taussig suggests, we need to come to grips analytically with the dialectic between the real and the really made-up. Only then can we 'gain some release from the hold of "constructivism" no less than the dreadfully passive view of nature it upholds' (Taussig 1993: xix). We believe that the best way to engage this epistemological paradox of the constructed, yet real – which may be a problem unique to the modern Western tradition but with which we are nevertheless forced to contend – is through a practice-oriented approach which seeks to understand the processes that gird the variety of human relations with 'nature'.

The following chapters all present case studies that depart from the passive view of nature shared by many culturalist and 'constructivist' approaches to 'nature' without succumbing to the naive realism evinced by some sections within sociobiology

(Escobar 1999; Ingold, this volume). Without wanting to exaggerate the homogeneity of the varied selection of approaches and research focus of the contributions to this volume, we wish to highlight some of the commonalities in the contributions by suggesting a number of concepts that might help reconfigure our understanding of nature 'into the active mode'. We will do this by first outlining what we take to be the underlying logic behind the recent 'constructivist turn', namely a parallel shift in the anthropological understanding of 'nature' and of 'culture'. We will then clarify in a piecemeal fashion the concepts that go into the title of this volume: *practice, imagining, nature, cosmology,* and *identity.*

The critique of culture – and the consequences for nature

The trend in the theoretical understanding of nature outlined above appears to parallel and to some extent incorporate the shift that has happened to the concept of 'culture'. Within anthropology and associated disciplines, the validity of 'culture' as an analytical concept thus came under increasing attack during the 1980s and 1990s (Clifford 1988; Clifford & Marcus 1986; Dirks 1994; Gupta 1992; Herbert 1991). The critique of the concept of culture meant that many – especially in the British and French tradition, both with a long history of suspicion against the concept (Barth 1992; Kuper 1996; Kuper 1999) – argued for the abandonment of 'culture' as a valid analytical concept. Others suggested being attentive to the processual character of cultural processes and using the concept cautiously and only in its adjectival form (Keesing 1994). Despite various suggestions for a cure, the overall effect of the critical diagnoses was that the concept of 'culture' was displaced from its formerly paradigmatic position as a master trope.

It is the same theoretical trend emphasising an epistemological reconsideration and deconstruction of central concepts of the social sciences that has allowed for an increasing pluralism in the academic understanding of nature. A consequence of the criticism of the concept of culture was that the opposition between 'culture' and 'nature', which had acted as a baseline for much anthropological research, became increasingly untenable. As noted by Descola and Pálsson (1996a: 2-3), the nature-culture dualism used to be the structural backbone for several widely differing schools of thought, although it performed this function in remarkably different ways. On the one hand, materialist interpretations such as Marxism, cultural ecology and sociobiology all regarded 'culture' as an epiphenomenon for underlying environmental or genetic realities. On the other hand, symbolic and structuralist anthropology used a nature–culture dichotomy as a basic classificatory device enabling the interpretation and understanding of various types of cultural phenomena. While the former strove to establish 'the naturalistic ordering of culture', the latter advocated an understanding of 'the cultural order of nature' (see Sahlins 1976: 100). Although the 1980s and 1990s experienced a paradigmatic break with both of these theoretical approaches within anthropology and frequent calls to avoid such contrastive thinking by not positing 'culture' and 'nature' as opposing monolithic entities, the contrast held its ground. Moreover, as structuralism turned into post-structuralism and symbolism into postmodernism, 'culture' became fragmented and with this fragmentation the other term in the equation, the concept of nature, also exploded into heterogeneity. From this process of reconsideration, 'nature' – very much like 'culture' – emerged as historical, contextual and specific. The attempt to highlight the contextuality and specificity of 'nature' mirrored, in other words, the theoretical critique of the homogeneous and static character of the concept of 'culture'.

As a reaction to the increased impossibility of maintaining the nature–culture dichotomy, some within the Continental and British tradition suggested seeing the opposition between 'culture' and 'nature' in terms of a dichotomy between 'nature' and 'society' instead (Descola & Pálsson 1996b; Teich et al. 1997). But the very notion of there being an opposition at all was by now questioned and the new terms of the dichotomy, 'nature' and 'society', were even at times set up only to ostensibly be torn down in an act of 'healthy self-criticism' (Descola & Pálsson 1996a: 12). Thus Descola showed the 'dualist paradigm' to be inadequate to describe the Jivaro world view, since the modes of social engagement with animals followed much the same rules as those organising social conduct among humans (Descola 1994).

Whether one prefers to see the 'dualist paradigm' in terms of a nature–culture or a nature–society dichotomy is probably a matter of individual idiosyncrasy as much as theoretical affiliation. Whatever the terms of the opposition, however, most anthropologists have displayed an unwavering distrust towards it, preferring to see it dissolve into a monism (Descola & Pálsson 1996a: 7), even as the difficulty of escaping the opposition, once it was posited, was acknowledged (Pálsson 1996). Descola and Pálsson suggest that a demolition by decree of the nature–culture dichotomy is necessary for further insight:

Going beyond dualism opens up an entirely different intellectual landscape, one in which states and substances are replaced by processes and relations; the main question is not any-more how to objectify closed systems, but how to account for the very diversity of the processes of objectification. (Descola & Pálsson 1996a: 12)

As tempting as this suggestion may appear at first blush, we are not convinced that the dualism − whether understood as 'nature' opposed to 'society' or 'culture' − is easily demolished and replaced by a monist explanation. While we acknowledge the problems involved in allowing the dichotomy to be an unreflected backdrop to one's argument, as structural, symbolical, materialist and socio-biological studies in each their way have done, we doubt it is possible to simply discard the opposition. The fact that this opposition has persevered despite the long history of critique sug-gests that the critique itself may be as much part of its mode of reproduction as its destruction. We agree, however, with Descola and Pálsson's point that it is necessary to 'account for the very diversity of the processes of objectification', especially if this also includes the processes by which 'nature', 'society' and 'culture' are objectified both in the Western discourse and increasingly also in global political discourse (see Kalland, this volume Milton 1996; Pedersen 1995). Examining the creation and critical reproduction of this distinction as well as the ways in which it appears both to give meaning and to be meaningful in itself is only possible, we argue, by attend-ing to the level of practice.

The framework: practice

A central part of the critique of culture has been what Sherry Ortner already in 1984 termed a 'practice turn' (Ortner 1984). An attention to the unfolding of actual practice over time, which highlighted the plurality and historicity of human agency involved in making communities, has thus increasingly replaced the static, systemic understanding of culture as a community bound by rules and norms. We are not using culture as an analytical concept in this introduction, and we do not have an overarching notion that will replace it one to one. We prefer instead to discuss human practices as a complex multitude of activities out of which certain emerging features arise that one might attempt to study, understand and classify.

As a pragmatic header, 'practice' is attractive for two reasons. Firstly, it is an open term that allows for the focus on a number of interrelated phenomena, from knowledge, perception and meaning to power, identity and money. Secondly, the heading allows for and indeed encourages close empirical study that is open to the phenomenological processes of doing and being, while also maintaining an analytical understanding of structure, power, and meaning.

It is this attention to the level of practices and processes of establishment that we find missing from the recent critique of the concept of 'nature'. Although the critique of culture has been acknowledged, the consequences have not been thoroughly incorporated into the understanding of how 'nature' emerges out of a dialectic between human perception and human practice at the same time as human practice and perception are shaped by their history of engagement with 'nature'.

If 'nature', then, is shown to be like 'culture', at the same time as 'culture' is no longer taken to be a homogenous and static entity but a heterogeneous and dynamic set of practices, what does this do to our understanding of 'nature'? This volume suggests that paying attention to the practical as well as the discursive engagement with 'nature' – what we call 'practices of nature' – is necessary to get at the processuality, heterogeneity, and contextuality of imaginings of 'nature'.

The metaphor: imagining

The human activity of *imagining* acts as the overarching metaphor for the practices of nature analysed in this volume. But the process of imagining is more than a metaphor; it is a particular form of practice. Imagining is not just the grasping or the conceptualisation of that which is 'out there', it also implies an attempt to render an idea real by making it the model for future action. In other words, imagining entails a model *of* as well as a model *for* reality, to paraphrase Geertz' famous dictum (1966: 93-94). As the contributions to this volume show, imaginings of nature are established through the bodily internalisation of habitual practice (Ingold, Bjerkli and Pedersen). Inversely, once established, particular imaginings of nature become moral realities that affect local practices of identity as well as scientific knowledge-practices (Kalland, Witoszek, Roepstorff, and Hornborg).

The dialectical relationship between practice and imagining has been explored in detail by Benedict Anderson who, in his highly acclaimed book *Imagined Communities* (1991), set a new agenda for the study of nations. Anderson demonstrated that the idea of the nation was historical, and that it coincided with the development of specific institutional practices and technologies, which made it possible and feasible for very large groups of people to conceive of themselves in a new way. They became part of a national collective: an imagined community of anonymous individuals whose relative homogeneity was guaranteed by their sharing of a common past, present and future within a common territory defined by fixed boundaries. This new symbolic universe was made possible by new reproductive technologies and media as well as by new institutional forms of communication that Anderson labels 'print-capitalism'.

The fact that the nation is a historical construction and the outcome of certain practices and imaginings does not, however, detract from its contemporary reality. Once established, nations are real and they further come to produce reality in several ways: the nation-system is a universal classificatory system for dividing up the world; the nation has become a spatial, political and historically given entity; and it is now an important field of action for human practice for its citizens. As such, it is part of the 'nature of nations' that they exist in an interplay between the historically given and the constant practice of imagining (Billig 1995, Roepstorff and Simoniukstyte, in press). Anderson's notion of the imagined community allowed for a careful and subtle understanding of how nations could be at the same time real and constructed. He showed how imagining oneself as part of a national community arose as a possibility with the transformation of a whole series of institutional, technological and scientific practices. Once established as an entity, the imagined community changed the parameters for action by instituting a new sense of self, space, and time. In a similar if more humble vein, the contributions to this volume suggest an approach to the entity of 'nature' that captures the dialectics of practice and imagining, and that explains how 'nature' acts simultaneously as the product and source of practice.

The title of this volume, *Imagining Nature,* implies an extension, in two directions, of Anderson's original concept of 'imagined communities'. First, it entails a shift from the passive *imagined* to the active procedural *imagining,* and this shift is central for the practice perspective advocated. Second, the inclusion of the term 'nature' means an expansion of the entirely social entity 'the community' to a more inclusive term that encompasses all relations in which humans are implicated. Such relations exist not only between social human actors, but also as relations to non-human actors such as spirits, landscapes, resources, machines, or animals. The French philosopher and anthropologist of science Bruno Latour has proposed the term 'collective' to encompass this interrelated amalgam of humans and non-humans

(Latour 1999a). At the level of ideology, then, 'imagining nature' describes the way 'nature' is established in institutional, scientific, and political discourse as an entity 'out there'. Rather than describing 'imagined communities' the contributions to this volume therefore analyse 'the imagining of collectives'.

The case studies in the section entitled 'Cosmology' contribute to an understanding of these processes of imagining. The segregation of things 'natural' from things 'social' or 'cultural' is one of the characteristics of the modern constitution, as several contributors point out. Entailed by this argument is, however, a simultaneous attention to the level of practice: it is after all only through scientific, institutional or other discursive practices that the dichotomy is maintained. This attention to the complex ways in which practice engages nature is shared by the contributors to the section called 'Identity'. Thus, while the dichotomy might be maintained at the level of ideology and ideal conceptions of 'practice', the dichotomy between things social and things natural collapses 'in actual practice' as actors and entities assume a hybrid form as at once social and natural, moral and factual. This goes for the modern context of science and politics in the West, as Hornborg, Ingold and Kalland show, as much as it applies to the coevalness of the human and the non-human spheres in Mongolia or in Greenland as demonstrated by Pedersen and Roepstorff in their contributions. Thus, instead of positing an imagined community faced with a real nature, the contributions to *Imagining Nature* describe the way collectives, understood as an amalgam of people and non-humans, are organised, practised and imagined in a variety of settings. In this sense, 'nature' becomes an aspect of and agent in the constitution of 'imagined collectives'.

Nature – and nations

Our extension of Benedict Anderson's metaphor is furthermore supported by the fact that the terms 'nation' and 'nature' share more than a few similarities. Etymologically both are derived from the latin *nasci* (to be born) (Bargatzky 1994: 16) or *natio* (something born) (Greenfeld 1992: 4), indicating that they share a common semantic history of being associated with origin and emergence. The two notions also appear to assume their contemporary semantic form in Western Europe sometime around the turn of the eighteenth century (Bargatzky 1994: 9-10; Greenfeld 1992: 24), although the exact where and when is as contentious and disputed as all other issues related to the origin of modernity. It is, however, not only at an etymological and semantic level that 'nation' and 'nature' are connected. Ties are also clearly discernible in the historical emergence of nationalist ideology. As shown by Witoszek in her analysis of German and Scandinavian nationalism (Witoszek, this volume), notions of 'nature' are frequently tailored to fit the constitution of specific national ideologies, while emotive themes related to conceptions of nature come to have a bearing on the shaping of the nation and ideas about the nation. Nations seem, in other words, to demand specific natures.

Finally and most importantly for our purposes, 'nation' and 'nature' appear to share some of the same properties from a general, analytical perspective. Anderson's analysis of nationalism introduced an important mediation between two positions on the origin of the nation. The so-called 'primordialist' interpretation, defended by most nationalists, claimed that the nation was a manifestation of eternal commonalities founded upon a primordial attachment to the soil, the mother-tongue, blood or ethnic origin (Smith 1986). Conversely, the critical stance, found for example in orthodox Marxist-Leninist thought (Connor 1984), saw nations as inventions of the eighteenth century. As an invention, the nation was created and, thus, was but an ideational fetish that would in due course be superseded by history. Rather than being mutually exclusive truths about the origin of the nation, the two positions combined in Anderson's approach into a synthetic explanation. Nations were indeed constructed, historical entities, as the constructivists claimed, but nations were also factually existing agents in the modern world order whose significance could hardly be underestimated. The constructedness of the nation had, in other words, to be taken seriously by understanding how nationalism was a real institutional and political agent. As the contributions to this volume argue, 'nature' occupies the same interstice between the real and the really made-up and defies any unilateral relegation to the domain of the 'purely constructed' or the 'really real'.

Nature as *factish*

Anthropological phenomena are arguably always located epistemologically between the real and the really made-up, but by what concepts might the interstitial character of these phenomena be highlighted? In his call for a non-modern conceptual order, Bruno Latour (1999a) has proposed a new name for such hybrids; namely *factish*, a word that in itself is a hybrid between fact and fetish. 'Nature' and 'nation' both appear to belong to this awkward class of phenomena that one for lack of a better word may call factishes: phenomena that are at once constructed and real, processual and independent entities. The most comprehensive understanding of the conditions of production and being of 'factishes' is achieved, we argue, by the application of a dynamic practice perspective.

Bruno Latour was led to the notion of factish through his anthropological and philosophical studies of scientific practice. A central issue in the philosophy and anthropology of science in the last decade has been the 'social constructionism' debate (Hacking 1999). In its strong version, this discussion asks whether results in the natural sciences are 'real'; that is, unaffected by human agency and intentionality, or whether they were 'socially constructed'; that is, mere reflections of ideology and interests among the scientists producing them. This discussion reflects a central difference between the sciences devoted to nature and culture respectively, Latour claims. Particularly, it reflects different ways of handling human agency analytically. Setting up a no doubt simplified dichotomy that nevertheless captures a significant difference, Latour argues that the natural sciences strive to eliminate the intervention of human agency into scientific inquiry in order to ensure the 'truth' of its facts. The social sciences, on the other hand, far from trying to eliminate it, tend to take human action as their object of study. In its critical form, social science thus seeks to unmask what appears to be solid entities (such as facts, nature or nation) as instances of human agency. As a rule, the social sciences do so by demonstrating that the presumed fact is 'really' a fetish: an ideological effect of a strategic endeavour by some segment of society or an unintentional outcome of 'epistemic' preferences. This epistemological conflict between two scientific cultures that has dogged the sciences for at least a century is, according to Latour, an instance of the so-called 'modern constitution' – a certain conceptual division of the world that relegates phenomena into distinct categories: nature on one side, society on the other. The ideational construct wherein 'facts' belong to nature while 'fetishes' belong to society thus organises the scientific division of labour but is also related to the nature-culture dichotomy, the dialectical relationship of which has been the bone of academic contention for decades. Latour even suggests that the epistemological conflict between nature and culture is an organising principle in the modern constitution (Latour 1993).

While the epistemological opposition between nature and culture may seemingly achieve its congruent social form in the scientific division of labour, the opposition between the social and natural sciences appears less clear when one studies carefully the actual scientific practices, as Latour and his colleagues did. The entities popping up as a result of the practice of the natural sciences are thus undoubtedly real but also human-made and full of agency. In fact, it is precisely because they are made that they may get an independent existence. This finding has a very different message than the much criticised bogus of universal constructionism (see Hacking, 1999: 24) which states that scientific knowledge is only human agency, therefore it is constructed and by implication it is relative, fetishistic and false ideology. In Latour's analysis, then, the epistemological opposition between the real and the made up, which both types of science have agreed to uphold, also dissolves. This opposition as well as the dichotomy between the natural and the social sciences are only valid as long as human agency is not factored into the equation. We wish to apply the same logic to the dichotomy within anthropology between culture and nature. Instead of advocating for the abolition of the dichotomy, we suggest looking at its mode of reproduction by beginning, simply, where anthropologists have always begun: with human practice.

It was the study of actual scientific practice that allowed Latour and his colleagues to show that scientific facts were simultaneously full of human agency and yet reliable, independent entities. In a similar vein it was through the careful and detailed analysis of how nations came into being not as abstract ideas, but as concrete, imagined communities, that Anderson and others (e.g. Cubitt 1998) could demonstrate how nations came to be at the same time real and constructed. Their seemingly different projects of analysing the 'natural fact' as a real but constructed scientific entity and the nation as a constructed but real institutional entity overlapped, in that their objects of study, the nation and the scientific fact, were central to the constitution of modernity. Latour's research in the science lab thus led him to identify the blind opposition between nature and culture as the basic opposition organising modernity (Latour 1993), a modernity, which as Anderson highlighted, has nations as the most general principle of social organisation. We think that the overall take-home message from this volume can be formulated along the same lines: that it is through the careful study of human practices that it becomes clear how 'nature' is at the same time real and constructed, simultaneously independent and full of human agency. Additionally, if the contributions succeed in pointing to some of the ways that 'nature', real yet mediated and constructed by human practice, is related to 'the period formerly known as modernity', we feel the volume has achieved its aim. Certainly, Witoszek's analysis of the entanglement of nature and nation in Scandinavia suggest such a link, as does Hornborg's examination of the modern, rationalist economy of the environment. In both cases, we see how 'nature' is a symbolic, if real, effect of 'modern' human practice. Once institutions are set up within nations to alter 'their' nature to fit a specific ideal, the relationship between human practice and natural change within modernity becomes even more apparent. We have by now become accustomed to the 'tristes tropes' of this relationship: environmental degradation, pollution, deforestation. But human practice shapes nature in other ways, too, often creating the supposedly 'pristine nature', nations and environmentalists seek to preserve. This is for instance suggested in the analysis by Kull et al. (this volume) of the Estonian wooded meadows: a unique type of nature with an extraordinarily high species diversity that exists only through and by a practical engagement between humans and their environment pursued over centuries. The relationship between 'nature' and human practice is, in other words, more complex than might be assumed at first blush. It needs therefore to be analysed in detail with an observant eye and keen ear for the local meanings and narratives attached to the relationship, since it is at once symbolic, moral, political, imagined and real.

Cosmology

The dialectical relationship between imaginings and practices of nature unfolds within at least two different domains, which structure this volume. One domain is related to the production of knowledge; the other is related to the production of identity. Within the first domain, 'nature' is an object of scientific and popular knowledge but, as the contributions reveal, the particular status that 'nature' has as a discursive object is intimately related to a much wider reality which includes practical ways of engagement, moral issues, institutional knowledge regimes and political dynamics; in short, an encompassing conception of the world that anthropologists have traditionally called 'cosmological'. We have therefore opted for the term 'cosmology' to denote this domain in which 'nature' is produced by and produces certain moral knowledge-practices. Cosmology is an old anthropological fad, something that anthropologists can construct as a synthesis of 'the native's' thought, an overarching narrative about sky and earth, gods and people, the right, the good and the beautiful (Barth 1987). In modern societies, the conceptual cake seems to be cut somewhat differently. In the jargon of the natural sciences, cosmology is mainly understood as an objective sub-discipline of astrophysics that deals with the origin and fate of the universe (see, however, Toulmin 1982). In the popular conception, as well as in the humanities, cosmology is the domain of the supernatural, the spiritual, the unreal, but also the unseen realm of systematicity, which governs life. As such, cosmology is distinct from the pedestrian normalcy of society, and here cosmology comes to assume the same position as society's 'other' that nature otherwise occupies. It is, to cite Coppet and Iteanu, as if

European societies have opposed two qualitatively distinct domains. One attributed lesser values, is governed by relative human laws, we call it society. It is dominated by a wider realm, understood as an intrinsic universal order and represented at different times and places by the figures of God, Nature and the Individual....This larger domain fits perfectly into the dictionary's definition of the term cosmos, as "an orderly harmonious systematic universe, a complex orderly self-inclusive system". Since the primary characteristic of a cosmos is its claim to wholeness, no higher value than those which characterise it may exist (Coppet & Iteanu 1995: 1).

One of the dichotomies underlying this idea of cosmology as an encompassing order is thus the opposition of nature and culture. In this relationship nature is frequently made to function as the ordering principle of culture. Coppet and Iteanu forcefully argue that in Oceanian societies, the cosmological distinctions are drawn differently from this Western stereotype. While the insights from Oceanic and other societies may undoubtedly be useful in questioning our own doxic ideas, we need to be sure that the ideas are really as doxic and unquestioned as is claimed. The contributors to this volume thus share a suspicion against erecting such an opposition between the West and the Rest to question the nature-culture or cosmos-society dichotomy. Even in the West, alternative orders are always possible. For instance, while 'nature' may in one view – namely that of the hard sciences, of sociobiology or cultural ecology – function as the 'cosmogenic' principle behind things 'cultural', the trend within 'constructivist' anthropology has recently been to make social classification or cultural perception the ordering principle of 'nature'. Symbolic reversal of the levels of encompassing orders is thus always possible – also in the West. Even Western scientific practice may be shown to appeal to the level of cosmology, seemingly as part of its effort to establish scientific credibility. As Hornborg's study of monetary rhetorics and Roepstorff's study of knowledge forms in contemporary Greenland demonstrate, 'hard' sciences such as economics and biology employ a particular cosmology in their approach to nature. The seemingly objective and value-neutral activities of counting fish in modern Greenland or calculating the money value of biodiversity are part of a moral universe that interrelates humans and non-humans into larger frameworks and hence have the effect of mobilising cosmologies in the classical anthropological sense.

These and other suggestions in this volume seem to lend credence to Latour's polemic statement, that 'we have never been modern' (Latour 1993). Although 'we adherents' of the modern constitution on many political, institutional and ideational levels act as if reality is rigidly divided into a 'natural' and a 'cultural' domain, numerous practically mediated connections linking the two poles appear upon closer inspection and reveal 'modernity' as more of a formal statement or creed than an accurate label for contemporary society. If that is correct, this destabilises many of the common myths about the West. The institutional rationalisation of society, characterising modernity in the Weberian optic, may fade once we attend to the specifics of institutional knowledge-practices, as Hornborg, Ingold, and Kaarhus show. The opposition between the West and the Rest, already heavily chastised, also proves tenuous from this perspective. One specific instance of this is Kalland's critique in this volume of the political opposition made between the nature-exploiting West and the 'noble savage' society living in harmony with both cosmos and nature.

Identity

The second domain in which 'practices of nature' are evident is in the production of localised identity. It is thus a well-established fact of social theory that identity is an inherent outcome of the emergence of social relationships (Barth 1969; Mead 1967). These relationships are continuously made and remade as certain connections stabilise, condense and contract, while other connections are never made or simply cut (Strathern 1996). In classical symbolic anthropology, the universe of relations – out of which identities are condensed – was conceptualised as a web of significance (Geertz 1966) and were seen to be established only between groups of real social actors. However, as the contributions to this section show, the web that establishes identity is not just a web of significance, it is also real and very material. Secondly, and following from this, the communities that form out of these condensed relations, at once mental and material, contain semantic, social connections between people as well as things, objects, technologies and non-humans (Latour 1993). The types of identity established thus cut across the ideal dichotomy between the social and the natural. They are collectives in Latour's terms, being about specific groups of humans that ascertain a specific identity, but also an involvement with highlighted sections of 'the natural world', be it trees used for firewood among the Saami (Bjerkli, this volume); mountains and rivers among the Tsaatang in Mongolia (Pedersen, this volume); or soil types in the African Sahel (Paarup-Laursen and Krogh, this volume). At the same time, however, it is crucial to maintain clear sight of the fact that although humans and the non-human are immensely connected, distinctions and the cutting of networks are continuously made as part of social practice – establishing different kinds of people and different kinds of things. These 'kinds' are continuously realigned and reconnected in particular historical matrixes of social power (Bourdieu 1984; Hacking 1992; Strathern 1996). While the resulting identities can be deconstructed, be taken apart and disconnected analytically, identity carries a real existence as focal points for actions and interpretations.

The papers in the identity section are case studies from classical ethnographic settings like Africa (Paarup Laursen and Krogh), Mongolia (Pedersen), and Sami communities in northern Norway (Bjerkli) as well as modern, complex nation states like the Scandinavian (Witoszek) and the classics of modern architecture (Brauckmann). They do, however, tell a remarkably similar story of how practically mediated relations to the environment on the one hand stabilise social identities and on the other hand turn the purely physical space into a valorised place of belonging and believing (Appadurai 1995).

Concluding perspectives

Recently, a focus on the 'politics of nature' has been advanced as an important aspect of our reconceptualisation of 'nature' (Escobar 1999; Latour 1999b). This push seeks, like the contributions to this volume, to deal with the 'factish-ness' of 'nature' as being at one and the same time a cultural construct and a reality of increasing political concern (see Anderson 2000). As already indicated by Benedict Anderson (1991), imaginings always entail a particular politics. They also entail a particular ontology, epistemology, ethics, and sense of belonging. We have therefore in this volume opted to focus on the almost old-fashioned notions of identity and cosmology. This allows for a focus on those practices of nature that engage a particular view of the world, on the one hand, and those practices of nature that deal with the place of particular groups of humans in the world, on the other. The papers in the section titled 'Cosmology' demonstrate how the engagement with nature – which is discursive as well as practical – is part of the construction of an encompassing cosmology: a moral regime of knowledge and a practical getting to know the world. The papers grouped under the heading 'Identity' tell a similar story. They examine how human identity and identities arise out of interactions not just with other humans, but also with the non-human realm. In the imagining and making of 'society', 'nature' is established simultaneously as a classificatory system for dividing up this world, as a spatial, political and historical given, and as multiple fields of action for human practice. The papers also reveal how 'practices of nature' engender a particular kind of community or 'collective'. Using either phenomenological or Batesonian concepts, several papers thus show how the corporeal engagement with the natural environment sets the standards or 'ethos' for engagements within 'the social world' (Ingold, this volume; Bjerkli, this volume; see also Ingold 1998). These studies thus suggest that 'practices of nature' are involved not only in constructing specific 'perceptions of nature' but also in establishing particular human ontologies.

As argued by Ingold (this volume) humans are living organisms who both purposely and habitually act in the world. At the same time as this activity takes shape from the contours of the life-world, the life-world is also being bent and transformed by human praxis. One of the first consequent attempts to formulate a coherent framework for biology that took as its starting point an organism's life-world was that of the German-Estonian biologist Jakob von Uexküll. In the first decades of the twentieth century, Uexküll proposed a subject-based biology that examined how each organism was surrounded by and built around itself a subjective sphere of meaning, called *Umwelt* (Ingold 1995; Uexküll 1921; Uexküll 1980). This approach did mark an interesting shift of analytical stance that is receiving renewed attention today (Kull 2001; Brauckmann this volume). Although the distinctions introduced by Uexküll may still be useful, the essentially solipsistic Umwelts do not appear to be able to describe the particular human condition (Roepstorff, 2001). People do not to live enclosed in mental soap bubbles, neither individually nor socially. On the contrary, as factishes such as nature and nation demonstrate, the human Umwelt is neither confined to the single subject nor is it satisfactorily described as a subjectively perceived 'outer world'. Rather it appears that humans establish among themselves entities that cannot be understood exclusively as states of the mind, or as entirely physical things in the world around them. An analysis along this line led the late Estonia-based Russian semiotician Jurij Lotman to propose that humans create around themselves a peculiar form of environment: a meaningful, sign-based semiosphere that adds an extra layer to the organic biosphere and the inorganic lithosphere (Lotman 1990). This wide-ranging outline for a semiotic anthropology has not received much attention outside specialists in semiotics or slavonic studies (see, however, Witoszek and Randviir, this volume; Eco 1997; Hornborg 1996), but whereas much insight into the constituency of the semiotics of culture can be gained from the semiosphere perspective, it appears to show a disinterest in the non-semantic aspects of human life (see Randviir, this volume).

Our contention is that nature is simultaneously semioticised and real. As such 'nature' is both the product of human practice and its condition of possibility. In this understanding, the notion of nature is maintained only in the context of specific and dynamic practices. Aspects of the natural world obviously fall beyond the domain of the human, but humans make it their interest through action, classification and semiotisation and they thereby draw it into the field of practice and discourse. This is not a Berkeleyan argument stating that there is nothing out there if no one pays attention to it (Berkeley 1710: §45). Many natural processes occur whether humans observe them or not and may have a determining and limiting effect on humans whether we are aware of them or not. Nature may in this sense act as the background and limitation for human practice. As a background and limit, however, 'nature' is continuously being semiotised, valorised and made to be meaningful through reflection and practice. Imagining is thus a 'semiotising practice' – a practice shaped by the very world it constantly semiotises. It is this double process of shaping and being shaped, of being real and being really made-up that characterises 'nature'. Each in their own way, the contributions seek to get at this 'factish-ness' of nature by describing the specific processes of semiotisation and imagining at stake in the 'practices of nature'.

REFERENCES

Anderson, B. 1991. *Imagined Communities. Reflections on the Origin and Spread of Nationalism* (2nd. edition). London:Verso.

Anderson, E. 2000. On an Antiessential Political Ecology. *Current Anthropology* 41, 105-6.

Appadurai, A. 1995. The Production of Locality. In *Counterworks. Managing the Diversity of Knowledge*, R. Fardon (ed.). London: Routledge.

Bargatzky, T. 1994. Introduction. In *The Invention of Nature*, T. Bargatzky & R. Kuschel (eds.). Frankfurt am Main: Peter Lang.

Bargatzky, T. & R. Kuschel (eds.) 1994. *The Invention of Nature*. Frankfurt Am Main: Peter Lang.

Barth, F. (ed.) 1969. *Ethnic Groups and Boundaries. The Social Organization of Culture Difference*. Boston: Little Brown.

– 1987. *Cosmologies in the Making*. Cambridge: Cambridge University Press.

– 1992. Towards Greater Naturalism in Conceptualizing Societies. In *Conceptualizing Society*, A. Kuper (ed.). London: Routledge.

Berkeley, G. 1710 [1962]. *Three Principles of Human Knowledge*. Glasgow: Collins.

Billig, M. 1995. *Banal Nationalism*. London: Sage Publications.

Bourdieu, P. 1984. *Distinction: A Social Critique of the Judgement of Taste*. Cambridge: Harvard University Press.

Bruun, O. & A. Kalland (eds.) 1995. *Asian Perceptions of Nature: a Critical Approach*. Richmond: Curzon Press.

Clifford, J. 1988. *The Predicament of Culture. Twentieth-Century Ethnography, Literature, and Art.* Cambridge, Massachusetts: Harvard University Press.

Clifford, J. & G. Marcus (eds.) 1986. *Writing Culture. The Poetics and Politics of Ethnography.* Berkeley: University of California Press.

Connor, W. 1984. *The National Question in Marxist-Leninist Theory and Strategy*. Princeton, New Jersey: Princeton University Press.

Coppet, D.d. & A. Iteanu 1995. Introduction. In *Cosmos and Society in Oceania*, D.d. Coppet & A. Iteanu (eds.). Berg: Oxford.

Croll, E.J., D.J. Parkin (eds.) 1992. *Bush Base, Forest Farm: Culture, Environment and Development*. London, New York: Routledge.

Cronon, W. 1995. *Uncommon Ground: Toward Reinventing Nature*. New York: W.W. Norton & Co.

Cubitt, G. 1998. *Imagining Nations*. Manchester: Manchester University Press.

Descola, P. 1994. *In the Society of Nature: A Native Ecology in Amazonia*. Cambridge: Cambridge University Press.

Descola, P. & G. Pálsson. 1996a. Introduction. In *Nature and Society. Anthropological Perspectives*, P. Descola & G. Pálsson (eds.). London: Routledge.

– (eds.) 1996b. *Nature and Society. Anthropological Perspectives*. London: Routledge.

Dickens, P. 1996. *Reconstructing Nature: Alienation, Emancipation and the Division of Labour*. London: Routledge.

Dirks, N.E., Geoff & Ortner, Sherry (eds.). 1994. *Culture/Power/History. A Reader in Contemporary Social Theory*. Princeton: Princeton University Press.

Eco, U. 1997. Universe of the Mind. A Semiotic Theory of Culture. In *Reading Eco. An Anthology*, R. Capozzi (ed.). Bloomington: Indiana University Press.

Eder, K. 1996. *The Social Construction of Nature*. London: Sage Publishers.

Ellen, R. & K. Fukui (eds.) 1996. *Redefining Nature. Ecology, Culture and Domestication*. Oxford: Berg.

Escobar, A. 1999. After Nature: Steps to an Anti-essentialist Political Ecology. *Current Anthropology* 40, 1–30.

Evernden, N. 1992. *The Social Creation of Nature*. Baltimore and London: The Johns Hopkins University Press.

Geertz, C. 1966 [1973]. Religion as a Cultural System. In *The Interpretation of Cultures*. New York: Basic Books, 87–125.

Greenfeld, L. 1992. *Nationalism. Five Roads to Modernity*. Cambridge Massachusetts: Harvard University Press.

Gupta, A.F., 1992. Beyond 'Culture': Space, Identity, and the Politics of Difference. *Cultural Anthropology* 7, 6–23.

Hacking, I. 1992. World-Making by Kind-Making: Child Abuse for Example. *How Classification Works: Nelson Goodman among the Social Sciences,* M. Douglas & D. Hull (eds.). Edinburgh, Edinburgh University Press, 180–238.

– 1999. *The Social Construction of What?* Cambridge, MA: Harvard University Press.

Herbert, C. 1991. *Culture and Anomie. Ethnographic Imagination in the Nineteenth Century*. Chicago: The University of Chicago Press.

Holm, J. & W.J. Bowker (eds.) 1994. *Attitudes to Nature*. London: Pinter Publishers.

Hornborg, A. 1996. Ecology as Semiotics: Outlines of a Contextualist Paradigm for Human Ecology. In *Nature and Society. Anthropological Perspectives*, P. Descola & G. Pálsson (eds.). London: Routledge.

Ingold, T. 1992a. Culture and the Perception of the Environment. In *Bush Base, Forest Farm*, E. Croll & D. Parkin (eds.). London: Routledge.

– 1992b. Reply to Bird-David's 'Beyond the Original Affluent Society'. *Current Anthropology* 33, 41–2.

– 1995. Building, Dwelling, Living. How Animals and People Make Themselves at Home in the World. In *Shifting Contexts: Transformations in Anthropological Knowledge*. Cambridge: Cambridge University Press.

– 1998. Culture, Nature, Environment: Steps to an Ecology of Life. In *Mind, Brain and the Environment*, B. Cartledge (ed.). Oxford: Oxford University Press.

Keesing, R. 1994. Theories of Culture Revisited. In *Assessing Cultural Anthropology*, R. Borofsky (ed.). New York: McGraw-Hill.

Kull, K. (ed.) 2001. Jakob von Uexküll: A Paradigm for Biology and Semiotics (Special Issue). *Semiotica* 134.

Kuper, A. 1996. *Anthropology and Anthropologists: The Modern British School*. London: Routledge.

– 1999. *Culture: The Anthropologists' Account*. Cambridge, Mass./London: Harvard University Press.

Latour, B. 1993. *We Have Never Been Modern*. New York: Harvester Wheatsheaf.

– 1999a. *Pandora's Hope: Essays on the Reality of Science Studies*. Cambridge, Mass.: Harvard University Press.

– 1999b. *Politiques de la Nature*. Paris, Découverte.

Lotman, J. 1990. *Universe of the Mind. A Semiotic Theory of Culture*. London: I.B. Tauris and Co.

Mead, G.H. 1967. *Mind, Self, and Society from the Standpoint of a Social Behaviourist*. Chicago: The University of Chicago Press.

Milton, K. 1996. *Environmentalism and Cultural Theory. Exploring the Role of Anthropology in Environmental Discourse*. London: Routledge.

Ortner, S.B. 1984. Theory in Anthropology since the Sixties. *Comparative Studies in Society and History* 26, 126–66.

Pálsson, G. 1996. Human-Environmental Relations. In *Nature and Society. Anthropological Perspectives*, P. Descola & G. Pálsson (eds.). London, Routledge, 63–81.

Pedersen, P. 1995. Nature, Religion and Cultural Identity. In *Asian Perceptions of Nature. A Critical Approach*, A. Kalland & O. Bruun (eds.). Richmond: Curzon Press.

Roepstorff, A. 2001. Brains in Scanners: An Umwelt of Cognitive Neuroscience. *Semiotica* 134 (1/4), 747–65.

Roepstorff, A. & Simoniukstyte, A. (in press). Cherishing Nation's Time and Space. The Tradition Maintaining Lithuanian Identity. In *Anthropology and the Revival of Tradition*, T. Otto & P. Pedersen (eds.). Aarhus: Aarhus University Press.

Sachs, W. (ed.) 1993. *Global Ecology: A New Arena of Political Conflict*. London: Zed Books.

Sahlins, M. 1976. *Culture and Practical Reason*. Chicago: The University of Chicago Press.

Simmons, I.G. 1993. *Interpreting Nature. Cultural Constructions of the Environment*. London: Routledge.

Smith, A. 1986. *The Ethnic Origin of Nations*. Oxford: Basil Blackwell.

Soper, K. 1995. *What Is Nature? Culture Politics and the non-Human*. London: Blackwell Publishers.

Strathern, M. 1996. Cutting the Network. *Royal Anthropological Institute* 2, 527-35.

Taussig, M. 1993. *Mimesis and Alterity. A Particular History of the Senses*. New York: Routledge.

Teich, M., R. Porter & B. Gustafsson (eds.) 1997. *Nature and Society in Historical Context*. Cambridge: Cambridge University Press.

Toulmin, S. 1982. *The Return to Cosmology. Postmodern Science and the Theology of Nature*. Berkeley: University of California Press.

Uexküll, J.v. 1921. *Umwelt und Innenwelt der Tiere*. Berlin: Verlag von Julius Springer.

– 1980. The Theory of Meaning. *Semiotica* 42, 25-87.

United Nations. 1993. *Report on the United Nations Conference on Environment and Development, Rio de Janeiro, 3-14 June 1992* (2 vols.). New York: United Nations.

Section I

Cosmologies

Introduction

The papers in this section investigate a variety of contemporary cases to show the distinct ways in which imaginings of nature simultaneously utilise and mobilise cognitive models of nature and normative models for nature within specific epistemic, historical or political settings. They thereby all question the tendency to view perceptions of nature as merely perceptions, and they emphasise the need to see imaginings of nature as more than neutral ways of representing reality and constructing knowledge. This appears particularly important within scientific discourses and practices where there is a need to critically re-evaluate the status of the concept of nature and to reconsider the disciplinary fault lines that have sedimented in the academic division of labour. By highlighting the multiple ways in which nature is imagined as part of the practice of science, the contributors stress how such imaginings of nature are related to a larger cosmology that encompasses the political, the ethical, the social, and the cultural.

For more than a decade, *Ingold* has laboured to pinpoint the epistemic nexus between the disciplines of biology and social anthropology, a critical project which he continues in his contribution to the present volume. Departing from an analysis of the act of walking, his contribution builds into a sweeping critique of the traditional models of knowledge used in neo-Darwinian biology, cognitive psychology and cultural theory. Ingold argues that a tacit alliance has developed between the three disciplines which produces what is arguably the dominant contemporary narrative about human nature. This narrative assumes that humans are 'hard-wired' through the genetic make-up of their body, through the psychological properties of their mind, and through their membership of a culture seen as a fixed set of ideas and values. In his overview of the three disciplines, Ingold thus identifies three core concepts. In Darwinian biology the 'genotype' is seen as harbouring the formal design specifications for the human physical traits and abilities. Within cognitive psychology, empirical research seeks to establish the innate mental structures believed to compose an architecture of the 'mind'. Finally, within traditional anthropology, 'culture' is regarded as a distinct set of rules for the representation and transmission of information.

Ingold demonstrates how these concepts all appear to describe abstract, context-free models, where interactions within the organism between the body, the mind and its programs, seem to be more important than the interaction between the organism and its environment. In conjunction, the three concepts produce a static and formalistic synthesis that fails to account for the way in which human practice, adaptation and evolution become hard-wired. In brief, in each their way the core concepts block a proper understanding of practice and the processes of change. Ingold traces the emerging critique within each of the disciplines of these three core concepts and proposes a possible counter-synthesis that provides an alternative imagination of nature, both the generic one outside of humans and of human nature. Instead of dividing the world up into different segments, *mind, culture, nature* each studied by a distinct discipline, this synthesis has a single focus of inquiry: the living cell-organism-person in its environment. This ecological approach, which draws on inspiration from developmental biology, ecological psychology and anthropological theories of practice, attempts to obviate the differences between body, mind and culture by not allowing them to be defined as singular formal entities in the first place.

The paper by *Kaarhus* echoes Ingolds concern about the disciplinary divisions between the humanities and the biological sciences and tries to set out the parameters for a possible rapprochement. Agreeing with the premise of Ingold about an overall convergence in the knowledge projects of anthropology and biology, Kaarhus observes that the two disciplines share a common intellectual history and that both disciplines have a holistic outlook. However, the holism of the two disciplines is at variance, Kaarhus argues, since the two disciplines build on the premise of 'nature' and 'culture' as distinct and mutually exclusive categories; the former being the domain of biology; the latter falling within the expertise of cultural anthropology. This has locked the disciplines into a peculiar double asymmetry where each discipline attempts to reduce the other to a subset of itself and 'tend[s] to consider the knowledge of the other as a particular instance of its own general, encompassing object of study' (p. 62).

Inspired by the early Foucault, Kaarhus analyses the rules of formation of authoritative discourse within each discipline. These rules appear to be strikingly different. Most practitioners of biology attempt to study causal mechanisms that are seen to occur as part of an overall evolutionary process. Within social anthropology, however, evolutionary theory is irrelevant at best and dangerous at worst to the generation of models of knowledge, just as causal mechanisms are seldom established or postulated. These differences give the impression that the two discourses are mutually incompatible and that a translation is therefore impossible. However, Kaarhus rejects this scenario of radical difference in which the only bridge to mutual understanding is that of translation. Translations, like discourse and rules of formation, do not encompass the persons as users and as formers of the rules of formation. A focus on scientific practice allows, however, for an understanding of 'a two way process of constitution-and-representation' that unfolds in time and is undertaken by real persons rather than being the result of blind rules. This, Kaarhus argues, allows for a shift in our conceptualisation of the disciplinary relationship between biology and anthropology from one demanding 'translation' to one offering the opportunity of 'dialogue'.

Kaarhus suggests that a common concern for diversity could constitute a basis for such dialogue. However, the double asymmetry between the disciplines requires of the participants a willingness to understand the perspective of 'the other' and to relate reflexively to their own framework. This dialogue might be facilitated, Kaarhus claims, once it is realised that dialogue, a key concept for anthropologists, and evolution, a key concept for biologists, are both creative and communicative processes and as such related types of phenomena.

The Estonian biologists and biosemioticians *Kull, Kukk and Lotman* describe how the Estonian wooded meadows, a unique type of landscape with a very high level of biodiversity, is the outcome of centuries of interaction between people and their environment. This case demonstrates that diversity, which as argued by Kaarhus is of prime concern for biologists as well as for anthropologists, is not automatically threatened by human activity as is commonly assumed within a conservationist discourse. In the case of the wooded meadows, diversity is on the contrary the outcome of a long-term stable human land use governed by aesthetic as well as functional principles. In reviewing cases of high biodiversity in combination with human use of resources, Kull et al. argue that these ecosystems, e.g., traditional lake fishery, ecological forestry, and low intensity pastures, share similar patterns of use.

There is never a total removal of particular plant or animal communities. Instead pieces of the community are used in a mosaic way that reduces the number of some dominant populations, diminishes the competition intensity of the community, and gives many species an opportunity to develop a niche. The idea of the wooded meadows, based on an interaction and intermingling between humans and their environment in a maximal spatial mosaic of nature and culture, is according to Kull et al. an important alternative to the two dominant ideational landscapes. The wilderness understood as a spatial separation and segregation of nature and culture on the one hand, and the total overlap of nature and culture in parks, gardens and an intensively managed countryside on the other. This mosaic use appears to support cultural as well as biological diversity. It requires, however, a communicative relation to the environment which is simultaneously acting as a field for production and action and as a source for experience and perception.

The presentations by Kaarhus and Ingold both analyse the classical division between the natural sciences and social/cultural anthropology in contemporary West European thinking. Across this divide both disciplinary branches attempt, as Kaarhus argued, to appropriate the knowledge of the other as a subset of itself. The Estonian semiotician, Anti *Randviir*, writes from a position where the division between nature and culture takes a somewhat different form, conceptually as well as disciplinary. Randviir is trained in the Tartu-Moscow tradition of semiotics. This loosely organised intellectual grouping and its journal *Trudy po Znakovym Sisteman* (Sign System Studies) was arguably one of the most fertile fora for the social sciences and humanities in the former Soviet Union. Apart from some works by its most prominent member, Jurij Lotman, this tradition is, however, hardly known in Western academic circles. Randviir uses the standard theoretical apparatus of the Tartu-Moscow tradition to outline how culture is a meaningfully structured domain, and nature, as we know and experience it, is part of this 'semiosphere'. Nature is therefore not the opposite of culture: once something is demarcated as 'nature', it is immediately constituted as a potentially meaningful form which is available for interpretation.

This vocabulary allows Randviir to compose a trichotomy of nature textualisations: nature as text, text in nature, and the semiotisation of culture through nature. The first instance is for Randviir the most complicated case. It is becoming increasingly popular to treat nature 'as if' it was a text. This can be found in the notion of DNA as a text composed in a language of nucleotides read by the cell to produce other structures, proteins. Randviir is, however, not convinced that nature as a text is more than a handy metaphor. The two other typologies are, however, much more clear-cut. Nature is constantly being 'read' by people, but the resulting 'texts in nature' exist only 'for us via our cultural experience' (p. 155). The third element in Randviir's typology, the semiotisation of culture through nature, is described via the example of personification.

This case parallels *Hornborg's* analysis of personhood among environmentalists and Algonquian hunter-gatherers. As a way of revealing the premises behind the efforts by leading contemporary economists to calculate the economy of the environment, Hornborg compares ecological economy to the 'animist' cosmology of North American Indian hunting communities. The two cases are similar, Hornborg observes, because in both cases 'the two groups project onto the natural world their different conceptions of the human person' (p. 106). These conceptions are obviously different: the pre-modern hunters 'have a central notion of concrete contextualised subjects' whereas the modern scientists mould their understanding of nature on 'abstract, decontextualised objects'. Nevertheless, Hornborg suggests, the parallel between the semantic universe of people and the semantic universe of non-people reveals the shamanic character of both cosmologies. It might not please authors of articles to the scientific journal *Nature* to be accused of cosmological shamanism. Hornborg argues, however, that rationalist economic theory posits the relationship between personhood and environment in a manner that is structurally related to the ways in which both pre-modern Algonquian hunter-gatherers and the postmodern 'deep ecology' movement conceptualise the relationship between man and environment. Acknowledging these parallels across the premodern-modern-postmodern divide might facilitate the development of a human ecology that approaches the relationship between humans and the environment with more circumspection.

In his contribution, *Roepstorff* describes the struggle of biologists and fishers in Greenland to come to terms with a strange stock of fish and with each other. Using a narrative framework borrowed from the Inuit myth of the Mother of the Sea, Roepstorff demonstrates how the knowledge generated by fishers and biologists respectively are inscribed in particular cosmologies. They both link an ontology of the fish and an epistemology of how to get to know it, but they do so in very different ways. One the one side, the fish is seen as a non-human person that one gets to know through interaction, on the other the fish is measured and objectified to be one exemplar of an abstract, but limited notion of the stock. Linked to the differences in epistemology and ontology are, furthermore, different conceptions of the proper use: on one side the fish is to help fulfil the needs of the fisherman, on the other the stock is a limited entity that should be used for the benefit of the modern, Greenlandic imagined community. These differences are furthermore inscribed in the linguistic translations between Danish, the language of the biological knowledge, and Greenlandic, the language of the fishermen.

Inspired by Ingold's distinction between a global perspective and a spheric perspective of the environment, Roepstorff demonstrates how the two cosmologies respectively stress and valorise either the spherical or the global phenomenological stance. His reading of the Greenlandic myth opposes, however, the facile assumption that 'global' equals modern and 'spheric' equals pre-modern. Rather, it is argued, a contemporary dialogue between fishermen and biologists requires a framework for knowledge about the fish and discussions on its proper use that allows for and encourages a shift between these perspectives.

The focus on environmental knowledge and resource use is further pursued by *Kalland*. Through a discussion of the sustainability discourse, Kalland analyses how claims to possessing environmentally sound philosophies have gained strength with many Third and Fourth World minorities in their struggle for political recognition. As a central part of a modern identity formation, these minorities depict themselves and are depicted by others as 'noble savages guided to a sustainable way of life by traditional ecological knowledge (TEK) accumulated over generations'. This understanding has for years been informed by anthropolical theory, but it is, Kalland argues, a romanticising view which actually stands in the way of incorporating 'traditional' perspectives into sustainable ways of resource management.

As an alternative, Kalland calls for a serious study of three levels of knowledge: empirical, paradigmatic and institutional knowledge. These three levels can, Kalland claims, be found in the local community of the hunters and in the scientific/legalistic discourse. Anthropologists have, Kalland claims, an important role to play in helping to mediate between these two knowledge systems. This task can, however, only be accomplished if one abandons the well-constructed but false notion of the aboriginal who lives in sustainable harmony with nature.

The chapters in this section all describe cases where nature and culture are intertwined rather than dichotomised. In each their way the contributions demonstrate how imagining nature in a contemporary context involves knowledge and representation, narratives and ethics in ways that intertwine ontology, epistemology and ethics rather than render them as distinct entities. This finding is old hat to the classical anthropological studies of 'the primitive societies' but the degree to which this finding makes sense in a contemporary context appears, as stated in the introduction, only quite recently to have been getting attention. The section therefore suggests that a detailed study of actual human practises of nature demonstrates subtle links across two epistemological distinctions: the first being the dichotomy between natural sciences and social sciences, the second being the dichotomy between science in general and cosmology. If these distinctions are shown to be difficult to uphold in their pure form, then there may be a need for other concepts to give an analytical frame. We propose that *cosmology* is a potential candidate for that, and as argued in the second section of this book, *identity* may be another such modality.

Three in one: How an ecological approach can obviate the distinctions between body, mind and culture

Tim Ingold

Introduction

Underwriting the complementarity of biology, psychology and anthropology is a tripartite division of the human being into innate biogenetic universals, acquired cultural content and – mediating between the two – the human mind. This division is supported by a powerful intellectual alliance between neo-Darwinism, cognitive science and culture theory. Yet in each of the three disciplines the dominant paradigms have come under attack, and for similar reasons: Neo-Darwinism for its inability to offer an adequate account of ontogenetic development, cognitive science for its removal of the human mind from the situations of bodily engagement in the world, and culture theory for its separation of knowledge from practical application. Combining these critiques, I propose a counter-synthesis of developmental biology, ecological psychology and the anthropological theory of practice, in which the single focus of inquiry comes to be the living organism-person in its environment.

Human beings are restless creatures. They are always moving about. One of the curiosities of twentieth century anthropology, however, is that it has proceeded as though the human body were like a statue, forever fixed in a bolt upright position, while all the activity is going on in the mind. Consequently we are still only beginning to come to terms with the realisation that much, if not all, of what we are accustomed to call cultural variation lies in the ways people move. This realisation is forcing us to think again about the orthodox distinctions between body, mind and culture that have underpinned our work up to now. I do not believe the solution lies in treating every human being as the sum of three parts, respectively bodily, mental and cultural. My argument, rather, is that this tripartite division is obsolete, as is the institutionalised separation of the disciplines of biology, psychology and anthropology that rests upon it. We need a different approach, one that does away with these traditional boundaries. I call this an obviation approach. Crucially, it entails taking a quite different view of what a human being is. We have to cease thinking of it as a kind of entity, composed of separable but mutually complementary components. Rather, I argue that every human being should be understood as a singular focus of activity and movement in the world, or in other words, as a locus of creative growth within a continually unfolding field of relationships.

The 'discovery', within anthropology, of the cultural significance and variability of human body movements is often attributed to Marcel Mauss. In a characteristically sketchy and enigmatic essay of 1934, entitled 'Techniques of the Body', Mauss declared that a complete account of the most ordinary of postures and movements, such as in walking or sitting, would require what he called a 'triple viewpoint'. That is to say, it would have to be regarded at once as a biological, sociological and psychological phenomenon (Mauss 1979: 101). Take walking for example. Bipedal locomotion, the capacity to walk on two feet, is generally supposed to be one of the hallmarks of our species, and as such to form part of an evolved human nature. Yet it is a fact that people in different societies are brought up to walk in very different ways. For the adult, as Mauss (1979: 102) observed, there is no 'natural way' of walking. One way of explaining this, which is the line Mauss actually followed, is to argue that although the body is innately predisposed to walk, it is educated by an acquired social tradition, transmitted orally or by other means, consisting of certain ideal rules and conventions that lay down standards of propriety, perhaps specific to age, sex and gender, that walkers are instructed to follow, and in terms of which their performance is evaluated and interpreted. Thus while the capacity to walk is a biological universal, particular ways of walking are expressive of social values.

Would it not be sufficient, then, to combine the biology of human nature with the sociology of cultural difference to produce a complete, 'biosocial' account of the ways people walk? Mauss's answer was that it would not. For the link between human nature and culture can only be established by way of a third term, namely what is called the 'human mind'. The discipline that exists to study the human mind is, of course, psychology. Any account of the relation between biological and sociological dimensions of human existence must leave room, said Mauss, for the 'psychological mediator' (1979: 101). Though Mauss failed to elaborate on the reasons for this, and probably lacked the conceptual tools to do so, these have been clearly spelled out in more recent contributions to the field of culture theory which have drawn much of their inspiration from developments in cognitive science. In a nutshell, the argument goes that if rules and representations for the generation of culturally appropriate behaviour are to be transmitted across generations, then certain mechanisms must already be in place that enable the novice to construct these rules and representations from the 'raw material' of sensory experience. It is, in short, a precondition for the transmission of cultural knowledge that the mind be pre-equipped with the requisite cognitive processing devices for converting the sensory input into received information (D'Andrade 1981, Sperber 1985).

We are perhaps most familiar with this idea in the case of language learning, where it is supposed that the child's acquisition of his or her mother tongue depends on the pre-existence, in the mind, of an innate language acquisition device (LAD) that is able to process the input of speech sounds so as to establish a system of grammatical and syntactical rules for the production of well-formed utterances. By the same token, there ought to exist a 'walking acquisition device' – some kind of cognitive module dedicated to the construction of a culturally specific programme for bipedal locomotion from observations of other people's movements. Such a device should, in principle, be as universal to the human mind as is the predisposition to walk on two feet to the body. It seems, therefore, that to complete our picture of the walking, talking human being we have to put together three things: (i) the human body with its built-in anatomical structures and capacities of movement; (ii) the human mind with its hard-wired, computational architecture of processing mechanisms, and (iii) the assemblage of culturally specific representations or programmes whose transmission across the generations these mechanisms make possible.

This idea of the complementarity of body, mind and culture is backed, moreover, by a formidable intellectual alliance between the theoretical paradigms of neo-Darwinism in biology, cognitive science in psychology, and culture theory in anthropology. Far from advocating this alliance, my purpose is to show that it is dangerously misconceived. Before doing so, however, I should explain how its constituent parts fit together. I start with the biology.

The complementarity thesis

1) Evolutionary biology

The central thesis of Darwinian biology, of course, is that human beings, along with creatures of every other kind, have evolved, through a process of variation under natural selection. This thesis, however, rests on a critical assumption, namely that the life-history of the individual organism – its ontogenetic development – forms no part of the evolution of the species to which it belongs. Evolution, in its Darwinian conception, is not a life process. If we ask what evolves, it is not the living organism itself, nor its manifest capabilities of action, but rather a formal design specification for the organism technically known as the genotype. By definition, the genotype is given independently of any particular environmental context of development. Its evolution takes place over numerous generations, through gradual changes brought about by natural selection in the frequency of its information-bearing elements, the genes. Ontogenetic development is then understood as the process whereby the genotypic specification is translated, within a certain environmental context, into the manifest form of the phenotype. Notice that in this orthodox account, the genotype is privileged as the locus of organic form, while the environment merely provides the material conditions for its substantive realisation. To be sure, an organism may develop different features in changed environments, but these differences are regarded as no more than alternative phenotypic 'expressions' of the same basic design. Only when the design itself changes does evolution occur.

Turning to the particular case of humankind, it follows from this account that it must be possible to specify what a human being is, independently of the manifold conditions of development under which humans grow up and live out their lives. This possibility is, in fact, entailed in the very assumption that human beings together make up a species – that is, a class of entities that may be grouped together on the grounds of their possession of certain design features transmitted along lines of descent from a common ancestral source. The sum of these features amounts to what is commonly known as 'human nature'. This notion, of course, is far older than Darwin: what Darwinian theory added was the claim that human nature is the product of an evolutionary process. So if walking, for example, is part of human nature, then we have to suppose that it has its basis in a design specification – a kind of programme for the assembly of a functioning bipedal apparatus – that has evolved alongside all the other elements of the complete genotypic endowment that each one of us receives at the point of conception. It is in this sense that human beings are said to be universally equipped with an innate capacity to walk on two feet, regardless of how they walk in practice, or of whether they walk at all – or go everywhere by car! Specific ways of walking have not themselves evolved; they are just alternative phenotypic realisations of a pre-established, genotypic trait.

2) Cognitive psychology

Now, just as neo-Darwinian biology presumes that there exists a context-independent specification for the design of the body, so cognitive psychology posits a similarly independent specification for the architecture of the mind. This architecture includes the various cognitive mechanisms or processing devices which, as I have already shown, would have to be in place before any kind of transmission of cultural representations could take place at all. When it comes to the problem of where these mechanisms come from, cognitive psychologists generally assume that this has already been solved by evolutionary biology. Since the information specifying the mechanisms cannot be transmitted culturally, it is argued that it must be transmitted genetically – that is, as one component of the human genotype. Indeed by and large, in the literature of cognitive science, the postulation of innate mental structures is taken to require no more justification than vague references to genetics and natural selection. Just as evolution has provided human beings with a body that can walk and a vocal apparatus that allows them to produce speech, so, we are told, it has also provided a mind furnished with an acquisition device that enables them to take on representations for walking in culturally particular ways, and another for speaking particular languages (Tooby and Cosmides 1992, Sperber 1996).

3) Culture theory

The final component of the trilogy, then, is a certain notion of culture, as comprising a corpus of rules and representations, or more generally of information, that is transmissible across generations independently of the contexts of its practical application in the world. This notion goes back to a celebrated definition by the anthropologist Ward Goodenough, who in 1957 pronounced that 'A society's culture consists of whatever it is one has to know or believe in order to operate in a manner acceptable to its members' (cited in D'Andrade 1984: 89). Notice how this definition effectively separates the process by which cultural knowledge is acquired from the way it is expressed in manifest behaviour. One obtains the knowledge in order to be able to operate or function in the world. This separation precisely parallels the separation of genotypic endowment and phenotypic expression in evolutionary biology. Just as the genotype contains a context-independent specification for the design of the organism, so the transmitted cultural information contains a context-independent specification for its behaviour, consisting – as Clifford Geertz once put it – of 'plans, recipes, rules and instructions' (Geertz 1973: 44). And where the genotype is said to be 'realised' in the context-specific form of a certain phenotype, through a process of development within an environment, so is culture said to be 'expressed' in the life-history of the individual by way of his or her environmentally situated behaviour.

This parallel, in turn, underwrites theories of so-called gene-culture coevolution, which start from the premise that in human populations, two mechanisms of inheritance or information transmission operate in parallel: one genetic, the other cultural (Durham 1991: 9). Each of us receives from our predecessors one set of genes, and another set of cultural instructions or 'memes', and together these pull all the strings in the development of behaviour. Thus while the human genotype contains the necessary instructions for the development of bipedal locomotion, as well as for the assembly of those innate mental acquisition devices that are prerequisite to memetic transmission, the memes contain the information that enables us to walk – to paraphrase Goodenough – in a manner acceptable to the members of our society.

Now from this summary I hope I have shown, first, how evolutionary biology, cognitive science and culture theory conspire with one another to produce a synthetic account of the living, acting human being as a creature of three components, namely of genotype, mind and culture. Secondly, all three approaches – in biology, psychology and anthropology – share one fundamental premise in common: namely that the bodily forms, intellectual capacities and behavioural dispositions of human beings are specified independently and in advance of their involvement in practical contexts of environmental activity. Yet in each of the three disciplines, the dominant paradigms have come under attack, and for similar reasons. Neo-Darwinism has been criticised for its inability to offer an adequate account of ontogenetic development, cognitive science for its removal of the mind from human beings' bodily engagement in the world, and culture theory for its separation of knowledge from situations of practical application. My contention is that by combining these three lines of criticism, coming respectively from developmental biology, ecological psychology and the anthropological theory of practice, it should be possible to produce an anti-reductionist, anti-Cartesian counter-synthesis which would be infinitely more powerful than the prevailing biopsychocultural orthodoxy. I shall now go on to spell out the elements of this synthesis.

Developmental biology

To begin, let me return to the analysis of walking. The conventional account, as we have seen, has it that walking is a capacity that is universal to human beings and that, as such, it is 'programmed' into the genotype. To this, culture is supposed to add further instructions that specify the particular ways of walking appropriate to people in society. But what, precisely, does it mean to say that I, along with all my fellow humans, possess a capacity to walk? To be sure, every human new-born, barring accident or handicap, has the potential to develop full bipedality. Most do. Presumably also, all humans can potentially be trained, as they grow up, to rest for long periods in a squatting position. For the majority of people around the world, this is a normal and seemingly natural posture to adopt while undertaking sedentary activities. Yet it is something that I – and, I would guess, you too – am quite unable to do, since I have been brought up in a society where it is usual to sit on chairs. Just because we cannot do it, and other people can, we are inclined to regard squatting as an acquired cultural technique, as opposed to one that is biologically innate.

But the fact of the matter is that human babies are no more born walking than they are born squatting: both are techniques of the body whose development presupposes an environment that includes already competent caregivers, a range of supporting objects (or rather, in the case of squatting, the absence of certain objects – namely chairs) and a certain terrain. Walking and squatting are innate in the sense that, given the requisite environmental conditions, they are more or less bound to develop; but they are also acquired in the sense that such development depends on a process of learning that is embedded in contexts of interaction with other persons and things (Ingold 1995: 191–92). A moment's reflection will show that the same must be equally true of every other bodily skill that humans have ever practised, regardless of its degree of cultural specificity, or the level of social or artefactual scaffolding entailed in its acquisition. All this points inexorably to one conclusion: that the notion of capacity is almost totally vacuous unless it refers back to the overall set of conditions that must be in place, not only in the individual's genetic constitution but also in the surrounding environment, to make the subsequent development of the characteristic or capability in question a realistic possibility. One would other-wise have to suppose that human beings were genotypically endowed, at the dawn of history, with the 'capacity' to do everything that they ever have done in the past, and ever will do in the future – not only walk and squat but also swim, do the pole-vault, ride on horseback, drive cars or fly aeroplanes.

What this means, in general terms, is that the forms and capacities of human and other organisms are attributable, in the final analysis, not to genetic inheritance but to the generative potentials of the developmental system (Oyama 1985), that is, the entire system of relations constituted by the presence of the organism in a particular environment. This is not to deny that every organism starts life with – among other things – its complement of DNA in the genome. Orthodox evolutionary theory has it that this DNA 'encodes' the formal design specification. Since, however, there is no 'reading' of the genetic code that is not itself part of the process of development, it is only within the context of the developmental system that we can say what any particular gene, or cluster of genes, is 'for'. It follows that there can be no specifica-tion of the characteristics of an organism, no design, that is independent of the con-text of development. The genotype simply does not exist. And so too, in the case of human beings, there can be no determination of what a human being is, no human nature, apart from the manifold ways in which humans become, as they live out their lives in diverse communities and native environments (Ingold 1991).

Thus in learning to walk, the infant learns to walk in the approved manner of his or her society: it is not as though the latter is somehow added on to a generalised bipedality that has miraculously appeared of its own accord, in advance of the infant's entry into the world. Hence there is no such thing as 'bipedal locomotion', as distinct from the various ways in which people actually walk. And since these ways of walking are properties of neither genes nor 'culture' (conceived as a bundle of transmissible information), but rather of developmental systems, to account for their evolution we have to understand how such systems are constituted and recon-stituted over time. The key to this understanding lies in the recognition that humans, like all other creatures, set up through their own actions the environmental conditions for their own future development and that of others to which they relate. Thus they figure not as passive 'sites' of evolutionary change but as creative agents, producers as well as products of their own evolution. We therefore seek in vain for the evolutionary 'origins' of a skill like walking. For far from having been fixed genetically, at some time in the ancestral past, such skills continue to evolve in the very course of our everyday lives. They have not originated yet, and they never will.

Clearly, neither orthodox evolutionary biology nor its complement in the field of culture theory, is able to offer a coherent account of human development. According to the complementarity thesis, every human being is in part preconstituted genetically, in part moulded through the superimposition (through 'enculturation' or 'socialisation') of ready-made structures. Real humans, however, grow in an environment furnished by the presence and activities of others. It is precisely because the dynamics of development lie at the heart of what I have called the obviation approach that it is able to dispense with the biological/social dichotomy. Walking is certainly biological, in that it is part of the modus operandi of the human organism, but it is also social – not because it is expressive of values that somehow reside in an extra-somatic domain of collective representations, but because the walker's movements, his or her step, gait and pace, are continually responsive to the movements of others in the immediate environment.

We could say that as a technique of movement, walking is 'embodied'. By this I do not mean that the human body should be understood as a kind of surface upon which social and cultural forms are inscribed. I rather use the notion of embodiment to stress that throughout life, the body undergoes processes of growth and decay, and that as it does so, particular skills, habits, capacities and strengths, as well as debilities and weaknesses, are enfolded into its very constitution – in its neurology, musculature, even its anatomy. To adopt a distinction suggested by Paul Connerton (1989: 72-73), this is a matter of incorporation rather than inscription. Walking, for example, is embodied in the sense of being developmentally incorporated through practice and training in an environment. The same goes for any other practical skill.

Ecological psychology

Let me turn, now, from biology to psychology. I have already shown that it is impossible to derive a design specification for the organism from its genetic constitution alone, independently of the conditions of its development in an environment. For cognitive psychology this problem is further compounded, for if the theory of learning as the transmission of cultural information is to work, the requisite cognitive devices must already exist, not merely in the virtual guise of a design, but in the concrete hardwiring of human brains. Somehow or other, in order to kick-start the process of cultural transmission, strands of DNA have magically to transform themselves into data processing mechanisms. This is rather like supposing that merely by replicating the design of an aircraft, on the drawing board or computer screen, one is all prepared for take-off.

Attempts in the literature to resolve this problem, insofar as it is even recognised, are confused and contradictory. To cut a rather long and tangled story short, they boil down to two distinct claims. One is that the concrete mechanisms making up what evolutionary psychologists call the mind's 'evolved architecture' (Tooby and Cosmides 1992: 28) are reliably constructed, or 'wired up', under all possible circumstances. The other is that these universal mechanisms proceed to work on variable inputs from the environment to produce the diversity of manifest capabilities that we actually observe. Consider the specific and much-vaunted example of language acquisition. Here, the alleged universal mechanism is the aforementioned 'language acquisition device' (LAD). It is assumed that all human infants, even those (hypothetically) reared in social isolation, come equipped with such a device. During a well-defined stage of development, this device is supposed to be activated, operating on the input of speech sounds from the environment so as to establish, in the infant's mind, the grammar and lexicon of the particular language spoken in his or her community. It would thus appear that language acquisition is a two-stage process: in the first, the LAD is constructed; in the second, it is furnished with specific syntactic and semantic content.

This model of cognitive development is summarised in Figure 1. Notice how the model depends on factoring out those features of the environment that are constant, or reliably present, in every conceivable developmental context, from those that represent a source of 'variable input' from one context to another. Only the former are relevant in the first stage (the construction of 'innate' mechanisms); only the latter are relevant in the second (the acquisition of culturally specific capabilities). Once again, the parallel with walking is instructive. One of the conditions for learning to walk, obviously, is that there be ground to walk on. It is reasonable to assume, without going into the wilder fantasies of science fiction, that this condition is universally fulfilled. Yet how could the infant, taking its first steps, encounter 'ground', as a concrete condition of development, not only as distinct from, but also prior to, such diverse 'walk-on-able' surfaces as sand, asphalt, meadow and heath, all of which call for different modalities of gait, balance and footwork? Bizarre as it may seem, this is precisely what is entailed if we are to hold on to the notion that specific tech-

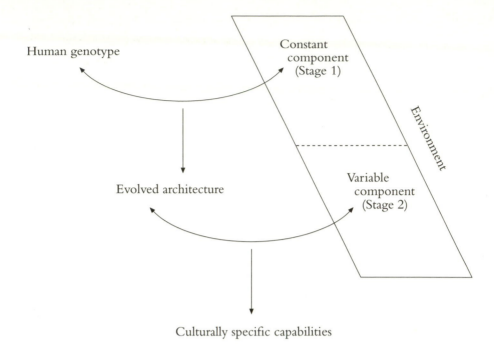

Figure 1. Two stages of cognitive development according to the complementarity model

niques of walking are superimposed upon an innate biophysical substrate in the human body. And just the same kind of partitioning in the child's experience of the environment is entailed by the notion that competence in his or her mother tongue is acquired upon the base of a preformed 'language instinct'.

Of course for comparative analytic purposes it is sometimes helpful, even essential, to sift the general from the particular, or to establish a kind of 'lowest common denominator' of development. But real environments are not partitioned in this way. Let me continue for a moment with the example of language learning. From well before birth, the infant is immersed in a world of sound in which the characteristic patterns of speech mingle with all the other sounds of everyday life, and right from birth it is surrounded by already competent speakers who provide support in the form of contextually grounded interpretations of its own vocal gestures. This environment, then, is not a source of variable input for a preconstructed 'device', but rather furnishes the variable conditions for the growth or self-assembly, in the course of early development, of the neurophysiological structures underwriting the child's capacity to speak. As the conditions vary, so these structures will take manifold forms, each differentially 'tuned' both to specific sound-patterns and to other features of local contexts of utterance. These variably attuned structures, and the competencies they establish, correspond of course to what appear to observers as the diverse languages of the world. In short, language – in the sense of the child's capacity to speak in the manner of his or her community – is not acquired. Rather, it is continually being generated and regenerated in the developmental contexts of children's involvement in worlds of speech. And if language is not acquired, there can be no such thing as an innate language learning device.

What applies specifically in the case of language and speech also applies, more generally, to other aspects of cultural competence. Learning to walk in a particular way – or to play a certain musical instrument or practise a sport like cricket or tennis – is a matter not of acquiring from an environment representations that satisfy the input conditions of preconstituted cognitive devices, but of the formation within an environment of the necessary neurological connections, along with attendant features of musculature and anatomy, that underwrite the various skills involved. This conclusion is once again concordant with an obviation approach, and it undermines one of the key ideas behind the thesis of the complementarity of body, mind and culture, namely that cultural learning is like filling a universal, genetically specified container with culturally specific content. The notion that culture is transmissible from one generation to the next as a corpus of knowledge, independently of its application in the world, is untenable for the simple reason that it rests on the impossible precondition of a ready-made cognitive architecture. In fact, I maintain, nothing is really transmitted at all. The growth of knowledge in the life history of a person is a result not of information transmission but of guided rediscovery, where what each generation contributes to the next are not rules and representations for the production of appropriate behaviour but the specific conditions of development under which successors, growing up in a social world, can build up their own aptitudes and dispositions.

The process of learning by guided rediscovery is most aptly conveyed by the notion of 'showing'. To show something to someone is to cause it to be made present for that person, so that he or she can apprehend it directly, whether by looking, listening or feeling. Here the role of the tutor is to set up situations in which the novice is afforded the possibility of such unmediated experience. Placed in a situation of this kind, the novice is instructed to attend to this or that aspect of what can be seen, touched or heard, so as to get the 'feel' of it for him – or herself. Learning in this sense is tantamount to what James Gibson (1979: 254) called an 'education of attention'. Gibson's point, in line with the principles of his ecological psychology, was that we learn to perceive by a fine-tuning or sensitisation of the entire perceptual system, comprising the brain and peripheral receptor organs along with their neural and muscular linkages, to particular features of our surroundings. Through this process, the human being emerges not as a creature whose evolved capacities are filled up with structures that represent the world, but rather as a centre of awareness and agency whose processes resonate with those of the environment. Knowledge, then, far from lying in the relations between structures in the world and structures in the mind, mediated by the person of the knower, is immanent in the life and consciousness of the knower as it unfolds within the field of practice set up through his or her presence as a being-in-the-world.

The anthropological theory of practice

We have now reached the point where we can cross the final barrier, from the psychology of perception to the anthropology of cultural difference. The key question that unites the two fields is this: Why do people perceive the world in the particular ways that they do? Mainstream cognitive psychology has long regarded perception as a two-step operation: in the first, sensory data are picked up from the environment by means of the receptor organs of the body; in the second these data are 'processed' by a range of devices in the mind, to generate images or representations, internal models of an external reality. This processing is known as cognition. By and large, psychologists have been concerned to discover universals of cognition, which are attributed to structures established in the course of human evolution. Anthropologists, by contrast, have wanted to explain why people from different cultural backgrounds perceive the world in different ways. They have done so by suggesting that human 'cognised models' are constructed on the basis of programmes or schemata that are acquired as part of a tradition, and vary from one culture to another. What people see will therefore be relative to their particular framework for viewing the world. At first glance, the universalistic claims of psychology seem incompatible with the relativistic stance adopted by social anthropology. But as we have already seen, the two perspectives are, in fact, perfectly complementary. For unless innate processing mechanisms are already in place, it would not be possible for human beings to acquire the programmes for constructing their culturally specific representations from the data of experience.

Now the approaches I have just outlined, both in psychology and anthropology, have in common that they remove the mind from the contexts of human engagement with the environment while treating the body as no more than a kind of recording instrument, converting the stimuli that impinge upon it into data to be processed. In this regard, they reproduce the classic Cartesian, mind/body dualism. By contrast, ecological psychologists reject the information-processing view, with its implied separation of the activity of the mind in the body from the reactivity of the body in the world, arguing instead that perception is an aspect of functioning of the total system of relations constituted by the presence of the organism or person in its environment. Perceivers, they argue, get to know the world directly, by moving about in the environment and discovering what it affords, rather than by representing it in the mind. Thus meaning is not the form that the mind contributes, by way of its acquired schemata, to the flux of 'raw' sensory data, but is rather continually being generated within the relational contexts of people's practical engagement with the world around them.

It follows from this approach that if people raised in different environments perceive different things, this is not because they are processing the same sensory data in terms of alternative representational schemata, but because they have been trained, through previous experience of carrying out various kinds of practical tasks, involving particular bodily movements and sensibilities, to orient themselves to the environment and to attend to its features in different ways. Modes of perception, in short, are a function of specific ways of moving around – of walking, of sitting or squatting, of tilting the head, of using implements, and so on, all of which contribute to what Pierre Bourdieu – a principal architect of the anthropological theory of practice – would call a certain 'body hexis' (Bourdieu 1977: 87). And as we have seen, these forms of motility are not added to, or inscribed in, a preformed human body, but are rather intrinsic properties of the human organism itself, developmentally incorporated into its modus operandi through practice and training in a particular environment. Hence capacities of perception, as of action, are neither innate nor acquired but undergo continuous formation within processes of ontogenetic development.

Conclusion

This result is clearly in tune with the conclusions to be drawn from an obviation approach to the relation between social, psychological and biological phenomena. In their rejection, on the one hand, of the Cartesian view of action as the bodily execution of innate or acquired programmes, and on the other, of the cognitivist view of perception as the operation of the mind upon the deliverance of the senses, the anthropological theory of practice and the ecological approach in psychology find common cause. This is why (contra Bloch 1991) I believe that an anthropology that sets out from the situated experience of the person-acting (Lave 1988: 180) has more to gain from an alliance with ecological psychology than with cognitive science. But the synthesis that could flow from such an alliance would have implications far beyond the fields of anthropology and psychology. It would call, indeed, for a complete reorientation of the human sciences around a new view of evolution, as the unfolding of a total field of relationships in which human beings, like other organisms, figure as foci of growth and emergence. In this view, the old divisions between body, mind and culture will become effectively obsolete, as will the kinds of reasoning in biology, psychology and anthropology that they have supported. Instead, the single focus of inquiry will come to be the living organism-person in its environment. Such inquiry must by nature be fundamentally ecological. Thus conceived, the ecological anthropology of the future, far from remaining a narrow sub-discipline concerned with the material conditions of cultural adaptation, will become a fulcrum around which the science of human life in the world will revolve.

In the first stage the human genotype interacts with the constant component of the environment to produce the universal mechanisms of the mind's evolved architecture. In the second, this architecture operates on variable environmental inputs to produce culturally specific capabilities.

REFERENCES

Bloch, M. 1991. Language, Anthropology and Cognitive Science. *Man* (N.S.)26: 183-98.

Bourdieu, P. 1977. *Outline of a Theory of Practice.* Cambridge: Cambridge University Press.

Connerton, P. 1989. *How Societies Remember.* Cambridge: Cambridge University Press.

D'Andrade, R.G. 1981. The Cultural Part of Cognition. *Cognitive Science* 5: 179-95.

– 1984. Cultural Meaning Systems. In *Culture Theory: Essays on Mind, Self and Emotion*, R.A. Shweder & R.A. LeVine (eds.). Cambridge: Cambridge University Press, 88-119.

Durham, W.H. 1991. *Coevolution: Genes, Culture and Human Diversity.* Stanford, CA: Stanford University Press.

Geertz, C. 1973. *The Interpretation of Cultures.* New York: Basic Books.

Gibson, J.J. 1979. *The Ecological Approach to Visual Perception.* Boston: Houghton Mifflin.

Ingold, T. 1991. Becoming Persons: Consciousness and Sociality in Human Evolution. *Cultural Dynamics* 4(3): 355-78.

– 1995. 'People Like Us': The Concept of the Anatomically Modern Human. *Cultural Dynamics* 7(2): 187-214.

Lave, J. 1988. *Cognition in Practice.* Cambridge: Cambridge University Press.

Mauss, M. 1979 Body Techniques. In *Sociology and Psychology: Essays by Marcel Mauss.* London: Routledge and Kegan Paul, 97-123.

Oyama, S. 1985. *The Ontogeny of Information: Developmental Systems and Evolution.* Cambridge: Cambridge University Press.

Sperber, D. 1985. *On Anthropological Knowledge.* Cambridge: Cambridge University Press.

Sperber, D. 1996. *Explaining Culture: A Naturalistic Approach.* Oxford: Blackwell.

Tooby, J. & L. Cosmides 1992. The Psychological Foundations of Culture. In *The Adapted Mind: Evolutionary Psychology and the Generation of Culture*, J.H. Barkow, L. Cosmides & J. Tooby (eds.). New York: Oxford University Press, 19-136.

Conceptions of diversity in biology and anthropology: Problems of translation and conditions for dialogue

Randi Kaarhus

Anthropology and biology are both disciplines concerned with *diversity,* aiming to describe observed diversity in global and holistic terms. The science of biology has basically been concerned with the enormous diversity of living species on earth, accounting for the generation of this diversity with reference to a few basic and universal mechanisms. Anthropology has aimed to describe the great variety of social and cultural forms produced by one species, our own, drawing upon a variety of concepts and models to account for the cultural diversity generated by *Homo sapiens.*

Diversity in biology and anthropology[1]

Why point to diversity as *the* issue of common concern for biologists as well as anthropologists? Why exactly use *diversity* as a bridging concept in a discussion of inter-disciplinary relationships? As an anthropologist, I will argue that the concept of diversity provides an entry point for one *possible perspective* on the fairly complex relationship between biology and anthropology as two distinct, but in a certain sense inter-related disciplinary traditions, which over the last one and a half centuries have evolved within the confines of western academia.

On the basis of what is at the present moment established knowledge in the natural science of biology, we may learn that approximately 1,700,000 species are living on our planet. That is, 1.7 million species have to date been identified and described in biological terms. Biologists' estimates of the total number of species described and yet to be described vary 'from five million to nearly 100 million' (Global Biodiversity 1992: xiii). An authoritative review of the field suggests a 'working figure of 13 million' (Global Biodiversity Assessment 1995: 5); the larger part of this highly variable – but in any case impressive – number being made up of insects and micro-organisms.

As an anthropologist I would be prone to see these numbers as *constructions.* They are, no doubt, constructed by applying existing and well-established criteria and methods of classification in the biological sub-discipline of *taxonomy.* That is, the numbers and the categories can be said to represent disciplinary constructions. But as an anthropologist I would still hesitate to say that species at the level of *living organisms* involved in processes of generation and regeneration are the constructions of biology. I would, in fact, sustain that it is possible, even when operating with a Foucaultian-inspired perspective, to conceive of a reality existing independently of our constructions of it – yet our access to this reality is mediated through conceptual constructions and narratives (Somers 1994).

There are, however, different classes of narratives. According to what anthropologists might refer to as the 'oral tradition' of biologists – and more in particular stories about animals which biologists more informally tell each other – the distinguished British biologist John Haldane was once many years ago conversing with a group of theologians: 'On being asked what one could conclude as to the nature of the Creator from a study of his creation, Haldane is said to have answered, "An inordinate fondness for beetles"' (Hutchinson 1959: 146). The message of this narrative is no doubt that *Homo sapiens* do not, in fact, even belong to the chosen order of species, neither in terms of numbers nor in terms of diversification. We are just one species among millions!

Nevertheless, as a single species we appear to have been particularly active – if not necessarily unique – in transforming both our own immediate environment and the living conditions of other species on Earth. Humans are at present actively involved in transforming the composite global whole of bio-geochemical, physical, and organic processes, e.g. through deforestation, the capture and use of nitrogen in chemical fertilisers, and through increasing emissions of carbon dioxide to the atmosphere. With the growth of the environmental movement, these human-induced transformations have tended to become conceptualised in terms of 'disturbances' of the natural environment, and as responsible social and political agents we have become accustomed to refer to an encompassing class of transformations as *environmental problems.*

One of these environmental problems, a problem which has received particular attention from the beginning of the 1990s onwards, is the *loss of biological diversity* on a global scale. The problem is commonly formulated in terms of accelerating losses of diversity at three levels: at the level of *genes,* at the level of *species,* and at the level of *ecosystems.* Part of the definition of the problem is that these are losses that result from *human* activities and human ways of relating to the world. Just to quote one authoritative source concerning this issue: Elizabeth Dowdeswell in the capacity of Executive Director of UNEP (United Nations Environment Programme) sustains that:

Biodiversity represents the very foundation of human existence. Yet by our heedless actions we are eroding the biological capital at an alarming rate. Even today, despite the destruction that we have inflicted on the environment and its natural bounty, its resilience is taken for granted. But the more we learn of the workings of the natural world, the clearer it becomes that there is a limit to the disruption that the environment can endure. (Global Biodiversity Assessment 1995: vii)

The actions of one species, our own, are in Dowdeswell's account described as a major threat to global biological diversity in its present form. But this is of course only a partial account of the relationship between *Homo sapiens* and global diversity. As creative agents 'within a total field of relations whose transformations describe a process of evolution' (Ingold 1990: 208), *Homo sapiens* is not only the product of an evolutionary process of species diversification. Humans are in fact also creators of diversity. This creativity has resulted in a diversity of what is usually called 'cultural' manifestations, as well as in the generation of diversity in biological terms, such as the 'landraces' of traditional agriculture, the 'cultivars' of modern agriculture, or the ecosystems of cultural landscapes all over the globe.[2]

Before continuing my account I shall, however, make some reflections on what we actually mean by 'diversity'. What are our basic referents when we – as anthropologists and biologists – operate with a concept that in Webster's Ninth New Collegiate Dictionary (1983) is defined as 'the condition of being different'? Being an anthropologist, I would say that the perception of differences is a fundamental aspect of *perception* as such, the creative construction of likeness and difference lying at the heart of human *communication.* And if I understand correctly the anthropologist Tim Ingold of the early 1990s, he indicated that a fundamental aspect of the *human condition* is precisely the 'capacity for generating difference' (Ingold 1994b: 22).

At the level of observed patterns and processes, this generation of differences manifests itself in an enormous variety of cultural forms – which are 'natural' as well as 'cultural'. The practitioners of the discipline of anthropology have since the latter part of the 19th century set out to describe and analyse the observable *global diversity* of these forms and processes in which humans are involved. Along with the Rumanian-American anthropologist John Murra, I will even suggest that one objective of the discipline of anthropology would be to 'celebrate this diversity' (personal communication). Within the confines of a scientific discipline there is, however, no room for unconditional celebration, and internal anthropological critics have for some years given voice to warnings against the temptations and pitfalls of exoticism, which may result from our quest for difference (e.g. Keesing 1990). I would nevertheless sustain that 20th-century anthropologists' documentation, descriptions, and analyses of diversity were basically carried out with the idea of the 'unity of mankind' as an indispensable backdrop. It is with reference to a conception of a *human universal* in the form of one-encompassing humanity that contemporary anthropologists' concern with diversity actually makes sense.

This conception of a universal humanity can, on the other hand, itself be considered a historical product. It was established – or perhaps reestablished – in the historical context of the late 19th century in an academic-intellectual milieu profoundly influenced by Darwin's theory of evolution. Below, I will return to a somewhat more detailed discussion of the common roots and parallel trajectories of contemporary biology and contemporary anthropology. At this point, I will only draw attention to the fact that the contemporary constitutions of both disciplines are rooted in 19th century frameworks and theories of evolution.

It is against this background we should consider the differential approaches of biology and anthropology in their 'common concern' with diversity. Both disciplines have set out to describe the existing diversity 'before it disappears' and seek to account for the generation – and reproduction – of diversity in time and space. The quest to describe and understand diversity does not necessarily appear so remarkable before we – as anthropologists or biologists – discover that this quest to detect and account for diversity is rather missing in the basic orientations of most other disciplines – and not only in physics or chemistry, but also in economics, political science, even sociology. But whereas mainstream neo-Darwinist biology accounts for the generation of the enormous diversity of living species on earth with reference to a few universal mechanisms within a well-established evolutionary framework, anthropologists have mostly set the theoretical framework of evolution aside in order to draw upon a much broader and continuously shifting repertoire of concepts and models in their descriptions of the social processes and cultural forms associated with *Homo Sapiens*.

The result is of course a less consistent body of knowledge than what you have in biology, and *theory* in anthropology is in this sense also less 'powerful' than that of neo-Darwinist biology. Among anthropologists there has, however, also been a whole series of attempts to construct and apply more encompassing and general theoretical frameworks. Some of the most interesting and valuable contributions in this direction are no doubt those setting out to integrate theoretical perspectives and empirical concerns of anthropology with those of biology, as found in the works of Gregory Bateson (1973), Roy Rappaport (1969), and more recently Tim Ingold (1990).

These efforts to establish unifying theoretical frameworks do, however, also bring up questions of loss and gain. The establishment of a general theory may certainly contribute to the progress of science, but even in this case there is a complex and problematic relationship between progress and diversity. Let me quote a statement of Roy Rappaport on this point. He claimed that '[n]o discourse or logic by itself is capable of comprehending all crucial aspects of the world. Any adequate grasp of the world relies, therefore, on the use of multiple discourses or logics' (Rappaport 1994: 272).

If it is true that any single perspective is partial - and most of us usually agree on this point, in principle - even a synthetic vision and an encompassing theoretical framework represent only one possible solution in a – probably – unending quest to grasp reality. At the same time, the existence – or even the promotion – of diverse disciplinary perspectives bring up questions of how we relate to this form of diversity. How do we account for the communicative relations between different science-based discourses and the differences in perspectives which these discourses represent? Is it really possible to *translate* biological knowledge into anthropological discourse and *vice versa?* And if translation is possible – an unstated premise of this article is that in some sense it is – how do we actually account for this type of translation?

Translation

Problems of translation have over the years been much discussed among anthropologists. From the 1950s and -60s onwards, 'the translation of cultures' increasingly came to be considered the distinctive task of social anthropology (Asad 1986: 141). In 1973, Edmund Leach wrote that anthropologists now:

have come to see that the essential problem is one of translation. The linguists have shown us that all translation is difficult, and that perfect translation is usually impossible. And yet we know that for practical purposes a tolerably satisfactory translation is always possible even when the original 'text' is highly abstruse. (Leach 1973: 772)

The use of the concept of 'cultural translation' implied that cultures could be analysed as 'texts' – or 'discourses'. This perspective on culture opened up new possibilities for analysis, but also created new problems. A number of problems associated with the construction of cultural phenomena as texts, and the translation of such texts into anthropological writing, were discussed among anthropologists in the 1970s and -80s (cf. Wilson 1970; Clifford & Marcus 1986).

As I see it, the particular problems of translation are not exactly the same in translation between scientific disciplines as in the translation of 'other cultures' into anthropological texts. We may say that as scientific disciplines both biology and anthropology have to a great extent constructed themselves in the form of texts or discourses. Periodically there have been inter-disciplinary transfers of problem conceptions, basic concepts, and models between the two; mostly, perhaps, from biology to anthropology. The relationship between the discourses of distinct scientific disciplines has for several decades been discussed with reference to general theories of science and more or less common-sense interpretations of Kuhn's notion of *paradigm* (Kuhn 1970). If we address the same issue in terms of 'problems of translation' this might, however, reveal some other aspects of the relationship.

An important theme that can be identified when we examine the anthropological debates on cultural translation was what I would call *asymmetrical relationships*. In these discussions, the typical asymmetrical relationship was taken to be the relationship between a North-Western social anthropologist and his local informant, normally represented by a Third-World villager. The inherent inequalities in power and access to external resources in the encounter between the anthropologist and 'his informant' were emphasised, and differences in institutionalised power were pointed out (Asad 1986: 148). The translation of 'cultural texts' into anthropological writing has traditionally been based on the assumption that the anthropological writer, as a knowledgeable scientist, would have a privileged access to the whole – to the global whole of universal knowledge. Of this whole, the particular cultural manifestation to be described would form only a part. In the debates concerning cultural translation it was pointed out that there would be an asymmetry in the relationship between the anthropologist's discourse and the informant's discourse (Clifford & Marcus 1986). In very general terms, we could call it an asymmetrical relationship of part to whole, or an asymmetrical relationship of the general to the particular, of encompassing to encompassed, or dominant to dominated. Let me, for the time being, refer to a description of this form of relationship as a description of *simple asymmetry.*

If we now turn to the relationship between biology and social anthropology, my point is not that it resembles the relationship between an anthropologist and his informant. There may be differences in institutionalised power – in favour of biology – if we are concerned with how 'a mode of description, analysis, or explanation' become 'empowered' in the sense of being able to reshape the world, and thus 'make itself true' (Rappaport 1994: 265). But my point here is rather that each of the disciplines tends to consider the knowledge of the other as a particular instance of its own general, encompassing object of study. Then the question emerges how translation is possible in such cases.

In my view, problems of translation are related to basic disciplinary conceptions of 'parts' and 'wholes', the constitution of the 'particular' in relation to the 'general', and to how disciplines classify each other in terms of parts and wholes, particular and general, encompassed and encompassing. Below I will develop somewhat further this preliminary characterisation of asymmetries in the relationship between anthropology and biology by drawing upon an analysis of how particular conceptions and models serve *as rules of formation* in the discursive constructions of the two scientific disciplines. In such a Foucaultian perspective, problems of translation can be seen as related to the use of different rules of formation in different disciplinary discourses.

It can be argued that 'translation' is not necessarily the clue if we want to understand the relationship between different disciplines such as biology and anthropology. The *real problem* – and the great challenge – has to do with the *conditions for dia-*

logue between the different disciplines. Still I believe that if one wants to discuss dialogue in ways that are meaningful in the sense of transcending a purely idealising rhetoric, a point of departure would precisely be a clarification of some of the problems inherent in 'translation'. Such a perspective opens up for questions regarding the role of different 'rules of formation' in the unfolding of intra-disciplinary, as well as inter-disciplinary communication.

Within this perspective one may ask if dialogue is possible without reference to a common repertoire of discursive 'rules of formation'? Ingold (1990) has launched a couple of such 'rules' in his formulation of a programme for an alternative biology/anthropology, a science which focuses on the *organism/person* within a field of unfolding relationships to its environment (see also this volume). The question I would like to raise in this context is to what extent the acceptance of a certain repertoire of such common rules form a necessary precondition for the unfolding of any interdisciplinary communication, and in this case for the unfolding of a dialogue between biology and anthropology. But before I continue my discussion of this particular inter-disciplinary relationship, let me make a detour of a central concept in this regard, the concept of discourse, by giving a very brief account of my own interpretation of Michel Foucault's 'archaeology', focussing on the Foucaultian concept of rules of formation.

'Rules of formation' in discursive constructions

Like many anthropologists who in the 1980s and -90s turned to French theoreticians in search of new interpretive perspectives, I found Michel Foucault's insights into the nature of discourse to be particularly illuminating. Foucault's works exhibit a continued concern with, and multiple approaches to, the relationships between knowledge representations and physical reality – the physical realities of the natural sciences, the physical reality of the body, the physical reality of the prison, of politics and policies! Drawing upon Foucault it was possible to delimit a concept of *discourse* that can serve as an analytical tool in analyses of the relationship between *knowledge,* on the one hand, and the *reality* we seek to represent in science-based discursive constructions, on the other (Kaarhus 1999).

In his works, Foucault demonstrated how the construction of knowledge discourses had real consequences in a world of physical processes; consequences which he himself tended to refer to in terms of violence: 'We must conceive discourse as a violence that we do to things, or, at all events, as a practice we impose upon them' (Foucault 1971: 22). He was concerned with the particular contexts of specific forms of knowledge, and with 'the complex and contested dynamics of knowledge production' (Rouse 1994: 111). But Foucault's work can hardly be said to constitute a neatly defined body of knowledge, neither does it contain a single and clearly defined methodological approach. According to the philosopher Gary Gutting, 'Foucault's work is at root ad hoc, fragmentary, and incomplete' (1994: 2). This incompleteness has evidently opened up for a whole stream of diverse interpretations, and the one presented here does not necessarily represent the mainstream – just now. There is, however, a general agreement that the relationships between discourse, knowledge, and power formed a recurring theme in Foucault's work, though his emphasis may have shifted over time, from discourse and knowledge towards the politics of power (Hacking 1986). Here I will, however, primarily refer to the approach to discourse associated with the 'early Foucault', his so-called *archaeology*. According to one of his many interpreters, Foucaultian archaeology was an attempt to '*isolate the level of discursive practices* and formulate the rules of production and transformation for these practices' (Davidson 1986: 227). It represented an approach to discourse which focused on the level of discursive practices, and sought to account for the 'conditions of existence' of these discursive practices.

At the same time, Foucault's 'archaeological' analyses are also concerned with the internal rules and dynamics of discourses. This focus on internal rules is, however, part of a broader vision of specific discourses being articulated in contexts constituted by other discourses. Furthermore, Foucaultian discourse analyses will seek to account for how discourses as such are related to a totality of social practices and physical objects. One could say that both (external) conditions of existence and certain identifiable *rules of formation* are important elements in a Foucaultian discourse analysis:

I would like to show that 'discourses', in the form in which they can be heard or read, are not, as one might expect, a mere intersection of things and words ... a slender surface of contact, or confrontation, between a reality and a language *(langue)* ... I would like to show with precise examples that in analysing discourses themselves, one sees ... the emergence of a group of rules proper to discursive practice. (Foucault 1972: 48-49)

The rules Foucault refers to are rules that can be shown to define a certain 'ordering' of objects at a particular point in time. This ordering is, in turn, brought about through particular discursive practices. In this sense we are dealing with 'practices that systematically form the objects of which they speak' (Foucault 1972: 49).

Now, Foucault has been criticised for using the concept of discourse to refer to rather different classes of phenomena. If one takes a pragmatic approach to his work, I believe it becomes necessary to make some choices as to the use of this concept. My choice is simply to use 'discourse' with reference to verbal discourse, that is, in the form of verbalised statements or series of statements. But it ought to be remembered that Foucault's analytic approach to discourse was not, in fact, primarily directed at everyday talk, neither at utterances such as the logician's or linguist's 'The cat is on the mat'. His analyses were directed at specific and concrete forms of discourse - but primarily what one may call authoritative discourses produced by privileged speakers in contexts which allow them 'to speak with authority beyond the range of their merely personal situation and power' (Dreyfus & Rabinow 1983: 48) – as is the case with scientific discourses.

What distinguishes one specific discourse from other discourses is, as I interpret Foucault (1972), a certain repertoire of 'rules of formation'. An archaeological analysis in Foucault's use of the term seeks to identify those specific rules which structure discursive practices in particular contexts and situations. 'Rules of formation' correspond to identifiable regularities in the ways things are talked about, represented, and discussed. They can be identified by means of singling out certain constituents that operate in the capacity of structuring authoritative statements in particular forms of discourse. Rules of formation thus refer to regularities in the discursive practices, which usually draw upon a certain repertoire of concepts and models. These regularities will also involve thematic choices, the definition of certain problems as objects of discourse and the exclusion of others (Foucault 1972: 37-38).

Within the theoretical framework that has been briefly delineated above, it is possible to identify the recurring use of certain concepts and models in the discursive practices of, say, particular scientific disciplines. Scientific concepts and models appear in a 'regulative' capacity in the sense that they are used to represent certain relationships or processes with an identifiable regularity. This regularity is, in turn, imposed upon the non-discursive reality that is being represented. 'Models' will in this context basically refer to highly simplified representations of certain aspects of processes or relationships. Drawing upon Clifford Geertz' (1973) distinction between 'models of' vs. 'models for',[3] I would in fact suggest that 'representing' and 'constituting' non-discursive realities can be seen as two aspects of the use of concepts and models in their regulative capacity within science-based discourses. Such a relationship between *representation* and *constitution* can, in fact, also be used to characterise 'rules of formation' more generally (Kaarhus 1999: 61ff).

In this way discursive *construction* can be conceived as a two-way process of *constitution-and-representation* whereby a non-discursive reality of objects, relationships, and processes are *constituted* as regular objects of discourse, and through the same process *represented* in discursive practices. The notion of practice – discursive practice – serves to add a dimension of *time* to the concept of *discourse*, which it often lacks when treated as a synonom to 'text', for example. The Foucaultian notion of 'discursive practices' opens up for a conception of *constitution-and-representation* as a process unfolding in time, thus indicating an alternative to more static interpretations of what is meant when we talk of the 'discursive construction of reality'.

Another look at biology – watching anthropology

In *The Adapted Mind* (Tooby & Cosmides 1992), a much-cited work in the 1990s, which placed itself at the interface of biology and anthropology (and psychology), the authors claimed that biology is the one really successful discipline of the three. It is one of the scientific disciplines that 'have developed a robust combination of logical coherence, causal description, explanatory power, and testability, and have become examples of how reliable and deeply satisfying human knowledge can become' (Tooby & Cosmides 1992: 19).

With regard to the social sciences in general, and social anthropology in particular, the authors, by contrast, hold that

After more than a century, the social sciences are still adrift, with an enormous mass of half-digested observations, a not inconsiderable body of empirical generalisations, and a contradictory stew of ungrounded, middle-level theories expressed in a babel of incommensurate technical lexicons (Tooby & Cosmides 1992: 23).

In the view of these authors, knowledge construction in social anthropology, is – in contrast to knowledge construction in biology – haunted by the failure of its practitioners to structure their knowledge in terms of *causality*. And if anthropologists fail, it is above all because of their reluctance to connect their knowledge-production to the networks of causality that structure the knowledge produced in the natural sciences. Anthropologists do not draw upon the causal mechanisms employed for instance in biology as rules of formation in anthropological discourses.

My intention is not really to set out and refute this view. I believe it represents one of several existing perspectives on anthropology, and it also represents a more generalised perspective on scientific knowledge production. The way the difference between the two disciplines is presented by Tooby and Cosmides (1992) is, however, even more interesting when we take into account the 'common roots' of biology and anthropology. Both disciplines were shaped during second half of the 19th century, with reference to the general theoretical framework of evolutionism. In anthropology, this framework manifested itself in a general theory of 'gradual evolutionary ascent from primitive origins to advanced civilisation' (Ingold 1994a: xiv). Within this framework, differences between societies could be explained in terms of the 'stage' a society had reached in the general progressive ascent of evolution. Now, Ingold has claimed that 'most academic disciplines and their boundaries are, in fact, the fossilised shells of burnt-out theories, and in this, anthropology is no exception' (Ingold 1994a: xiv). No doubt many would agree that evolutionary theories are 'burnt-out' in social anthropology. But it still forms a constitutive framework in modern biology. One could even say that the 'mechanisms' of evolution constitute the basic 'rules of formation' in biologic discourses. What both disciplines have inherited from 19th-century evolutionary thought – and still adhere to – is, in my view, their *holistic* ambitions; the quest to grasp and explain 'the whole' with all its encompassed diversity!

Most anthropologists still seek to describe reality in terms of socio-cultural 'wholes', while practitioners of closely related disciplines both in the social sciences and in the humanities concentrate on more specialised fields or on certain aspects of reality. This quest for the whole and the search for multi-level contexts and their interconnections no doubt provide contemporary anthropologists with a number of theoretical and methodological challenges, and even with some intellectual satisfaction (cf. Tooby & Cosmides' assertion on this point above). But I also believe that this quest for holism has some important if not self-evident implications for *inter*-disciplinary communication – for example in attempts to develop some form of dialogue between anthropology and biology.

Above, I have sustained that the two disciplines share a very particular concern with diversity. The modern varieties of both disciplines took shape within the framework of 19th-century evolutionism, and from that constitutive moment each discipline has carried on to the present its own particular breed of holism. But as Tooby and Cosmides have pointed out, anthropologists have largely 'failed' to employ causal mechanisms developed within the natural sciences as rules of formation in anthropological discourses. Can this differential position with regard to the role of *causal* mechanisms in structuring knowledge production be one clue to the problems of translation between anthropology and biology? Or is it rather the shared quest for holism which results in asymmetrical relationships in both directions?

I have argued above that translation to some extent will involve classifying others' knowledge in terms of one's own categories – and in some cases these are categories that pretend to encompass 'the other'. I have also pointed out, with reference to Foucault, that it should be possible to distinguish certain rules of formation in scientific discourses. Furthermore, I believe it ought to be possible to reach some form of consensus regarding such rules independently of one's own disciplinary position. What follows is, however, only a brief sketch of some of the basic *rules of formation* in contemporary *biological discourses* – as seen by an anthropologist!

Rules of formation in biological discourses

As I have understood it, a foundational element in the establishment of modern biology was the system of classification – the taxonomy – presented by Carl Linné in 1758 in a pathbreaking work called *Systema Naturae*. The basic method employed in Linnean taxonomy was the comparison of certain characteristics in the structure of living organisms. The method was called 'comparative anatomy' and aimed to assign to each species a position within a comprehensive hierarchical system. This was a system for classifying all living organisms, past and present.

A further and perhaps even more crucial step in the establishment of modern biology was taken one hundred years later, in 1858, when Charles Darwin and Alfred Wallace proposed to a meeting of the Linnean Society that biological evolution occurs as a result of 'natural selection' (Daly & Wilson 1983: 2). The following year, Darwin published his book *On the Origin of Species by Means of Natural Selection* (Darwin 1859). The ingenious conjuncture in the history of biology at this point was that the Linnean classificatory system lent itself to an evolutionary interpretation in terms of the mechanism presented by Darwin (Daly & Wilson 1983: 4).

What Darwin found – or constructed – was a mechanism he called 'natural selection'. This was the mechanism which, according to his theories, actually caused evolution.

What is usually called the modern synthesis of neo-Darwinism will, however, at least have to include one further component, genetics! It was Darwin's contemporary, the Austrian monk Gregor Mendel, who established its foundations through his experiments on pea plants (Daly & Wilson 1983: 7). But only when Mendel's account of his pathbreaking work with pea plants was re-discovered by the scientific community in the year 1900, genetics rapidly evolved into an extremely prolific field of knowledge production and experimental work (which today is the basis of biotechnology). But already in the 1930s, the basic rules of formation in the theoretical framework of modern mainstream biology were relatively firmly established. It is this modern synthesis that is called neo-Darwinism (Mayr 1992).

Given what I, following Foucault, call the 'rules of formation' of mainstream neo-Darwinist discourse, the question 'Why?' has one general and, one may say, ultimate answer, which is 'because of its utility... in promoting successful reproduction' (Daly & Wilson 1983: 14). This means that the mechanism of natural selection selects for so-called 'reproductive advantage'. In this perspective, adaptation basically refers to characteristics 'evolved as a consequence of natural selection' (Begon, Harper & Townsend 1990: 845). In other words, adaptations are the accumulated output of evolution by means of natural selection (Tooby & Cosmides 1992: 55). As an anthropologist, one may be struck by the formal reductionism inherent in the application of such relatively simple rules of formation in the construction of scientific discourse. To what extent, one may ask, are contemporary biologists in fact interested – or willing – to apply these rules, not only to explain the adaptations of other species, but also to explain human adaptation and the development of cultural diversity?

One – indirect – answer lies in the fact that within biology there is, in practice, a fairly high degree of specialisation. Biologists do not specialise on birds, not even on starlings. They would rather specialise on some particular aspect of starlings' nesting habits – within a taken-for-granted, general framework of 'adaptive fitness'. This specialised division of labour makes it possible for biologists to pursue their particular research interests without getting involved in highly charged social and political issues (Tooby & Cosmides 1992: 49).

Some biologists do, however, take on the task of a more ambitious holism. Their efforts may result in statements pointing out that 'human minds, human behaviour, human artefacts, and human culture are all biological phenomena' (Tooby & Cosmides 1992: 19). In sociobiology, an implication of these conceptions regarding the human species has been the claim that human minds, human behaviour, and socio-cultural phenomena – including scientific knowledge construction itself – can only be adequately explained in terms of adaptation resulting from natural selection.

The publication of Edward Wilson's book *Sociobiology: The New Synthesis* in 1975, raised fairly agitated debates precisely on this point. A number of anthropologists were also involved in these debates. At present, however, the most common attitude of anthropologists to biology seems to be that the two disciplines are basically concerned with different things, e.g. 'nature' or 'culture'. At the same time this is a contested position - as demonstrated both in the present volume and elsewhere. Let me just mention Roy Ellen's introduction to the book *Redefining Nature* (Ellen & Fukui (eds.) 1996). Ellen who, in turn, refers to Ingold, sustains that the *nature-culture* dualism in Western science presents us with a logical paradox when we try to analyse the inter-connections of nature and culture, society and environment. We may say that the objects of analysis in social anthropology, i.e. cultural phenomena, are, in biological terms, the outcomes of biological processes of evolution. But the biological theories of evolution in themselves can, in anthropological terms, be classified as cultural constructions – shaped, I would say, by specific 'rules of formation'.

On the one hand, there is 'culture' conceived as a subclass of 'nature'. Can 'nature' at the same time be classified as a subclass of 'culture'? (Ellen 1996: 31). 'Every schoolboy knows' (Bateson 1980) that for centuries this type of paradox has been discussed within western academia. Since the time of Russell and Whitehead, the paradox has often been dealt with in terms of 'logical types' (Bateson 1980: 129). It can – with some reframing of the terms of logical typing – also be said to describe a relationship of 'double asymmetry'. With regard to the interlinked relationships of 'culture' to 'nature', I would sustain that this issue of logical types or 'double asymmetries' is not, in fact, only a theoretical puzzle. Why?

Conditions for dialogue

I have already suggested that so-called 'problems of translation' can be understood in terms of relationships of 'simple asymmetry'. Within the holistic frameworks of both biology and anthropology what is defined in each of the disciplines as the object of study – nature and culture, respectively – is usually considered to be only a *subclass* within the general, encompassing framework of the other discipline. This forms a *double asymmetry,* but in my view, it does not necessarily constitute an insurmountable problem to translation. But it does, I believe, present a real problem to interdisciplinary dialogue! Why? Before I try to answer this question, let me just say a few words about 'dialogue' more in general.

Dialogue is a culturally and historically specific way of conceiving of certain verbal transactions and as such has considerable rhetorical force. (Crapanzano 1990: 270)

According to Crapanzano, the concept of dialogue – as an ideal – emphasises the integrating function of conversation (ibid.: 271). Here, then the question arises: How can such an integration be achieved if a two-way *asymmetrical* relationship is involved, such as the one described in the case of biology and anthropology?

My answer is quite simple, and not really original. In fact it has already been suggested in my discussion above of 'discursive practices', which were said to involve *representation-and-constitution* as two important aspects of *construction.* What I end up with here is a perspective that draws quite a lot upon Bateson's insights into *Mind and Nature* (1980), in particular his discussion of 'logical types' and 'classification' in relation to 'process'. The answer I come up with is in a sense a cross-disciplinary challenge, and the basic idea can be formulated as follows: *Dialogue* requires a move from 'classification' to 'process' in communication! That is, dialogue requires that we include a dynamic dimension, a dimension of time – of change, and thus of learning – into our conception and practices of communication.

In this sense dialogue is to be viewed and carried out as an unfolding process. And dialogue conceived as process – *practice* – will have to unfold both in time and space. Furthermore, dialogue in this sense probably requires that both aspects of 'construction' that have been presented above – i.e. 'representation' as well as 'constitution' – should be open to discussion. This point is also formulated by Crapanzano in his discussion of dialogue, where he sustains that 'not only is there no unchanging context, there is no single context. The dialogue has minimally two interpenetrating contexts, those of each of its participants' (Crapanzano 1990: 284). In this situation 'what unity occurs derives from the subject matter or theme' (ibid.).

If we assume that some common understanding or 'unity' can be established through the process of dialogue, can we also assume this possibility is sufficient reason for people involved in a multiplicity of other engagements to be concerned with the conditions for dialogue as such? Probably not. In order to motivate real persons to enter into the challenges of the sometimes troubling process of an interdisciplinary dialogue, there must be an overriding question, a subject matter of common concern, and a commitment to something outside the dialogue itself! With regard to biology and anthropology, the issue of 'diversity' and 'ecological relationships' – in the extended sense that encompasses both humans and our diverse environments – might in fact constitute a subject matter of common concern, and thus a starting point for dialogic processes. Still one could ask if commitment to a common problem in practice makes it possible to transcend the logical contradictions inherent in the double asymmetry of biology and social anthropology, as disciplines with distinct and mutually encompassing frameworks of understanding with holistic ambitions. As I see it, participants in a dialogue can hardly avoid getting enmeshed in double asymmetries if they are unaware of them as possible pitfalls. But there is also another condition that must be taken into account here: the willingness of participants in a dialogue to take the perspective of 'the other'. In this context, this implies an openness to continued learning, and a disposition to relate – to some extent – *reflexively* to one's own disciplinary frameworks of understanding.

Conclusion

This presentation has primarily focused on the conceptual, logical and epistemological conditions of translation and dialogue between the disciplines of biology and anthropology, with particular reference to their common concern with global diversity and a shared quest for holism. In my view, which is an anthropologist's view, the possibilities for dialogue between the two disciplines depend, in the end, on a certain form of self-reflexivity on both sides. Furthermore, I have argued that in order not to get enmeshed in latent paradoxes or locked in a relationship of 'double asymmetry', it is necessary to relate to dialogue as a process, and in this way open up a possibility for transcending the static relationships of a logical model. An important implication of a move from classification to process in this regard is that *dialogue* should not be conceived – and cannot be practised – as a zero-sum game (e.g. in Tooby & Cosmides 1992: 33). Zero-sum games can be explained logically. Dialogue must in a certain sense transcend logics, both logical contradictions and double asymmetries, in order to unfold as a creative process. And as *creative processes* dialogue and evolution probably have much more in common than we have usually been aware of – either as biologists or as anthropologists.

NOTES

1. I would like to thank the professors Norman Long, William Roseberry and Thomas Hylland Eriksen who first challenged me to take up this theme. The elaboration of the present article received financial support from the Research Council of Norway, under the Program for Research on Biological Diversity.

2. An excellent example is the wooded meadows near the Estonian coast. They represent a case of cultural-landscape diversity, remarkable not least in terms of the unusually high number of species occupying each square meter of land – but definitely dependent on human-induced 'disturbances' in the form of, for example, cattle grazing to maintain this high level of diversity (Kull et al. this volume).

3. In Geertz' words: 'The term "model" has … two senses – an "of" sense and a "for" sense – and though these are but aspects of the same basic concept they are very much worth distinguishing. In the first [model of], what is stressed is the manipulation of symbol structures so as to bring them, more or less closely, into parallel with the pre-established nonsymbolic system … In the second [model for], what is stressed is the manipulation of the nonsymbolic systems in terms of the relationships expressed in the symbolic' (Geertz 1973: 93).

REFERENCES

Asad, T. 1986. The Concept of Cultural Translation in British Social Anthropology. In *Writing Culture: The Poetics and Politics of Ethnography*, J. Clifford & G.E. Marcus (eds.). Berkeley: University of California Press, 141-64.

Bateson, G. 1973. *Steps to an Ecology of Mind*. St. Albans: Paladin.

– 1980. *Mind and Nature: A Necessary Unity*. New York: Bantam Books.

Begon, M., John L. Harper & C.R. Townsend. 1990. *Ecology: Individuals, Populations and Communities*. Boston: Blackwell.

Clifford, J. & G.E. Marcus (eds.) 1986. *Writing Culture: The Poetics and Politics of Ethnography*. Berkeley: University of California Press.

Crapanzano, V. 1990. On dialogue. In *The Interpretation of Dialogue*, T. Maranhão (ed.). Chicago: University of Chicago Press.

Daly, M. and M. Wilson 1983. *Sex, Evolution, and Behavior*. Belmont, Cal.: Wadsworth Publishing Company.

Darwin, C. 1859. *The Origin of Species*. (1st edn.) London: John Murray.

Dreyfus, H.L. and P. Rabinow 1983. *Michel Foucault: Beyond Structuralism and Hermeneutics*. Chicago: University of Chicago Press.

– 1986. What is Maturity? Habermas and Foucault on 'What is Enlightenment?' In *Foucault: A Critical Reader*, D.C. Hoy (ed.). Oxford: Basil Blackwell, 109-21.

Davidson, A. I. 1986. Archaeology, Genealogy, Ethics. In *Foucault: A Critical Reader*, D.C. Hoy (ed.). Oxford: Basil Blackwell, 221-33.

Ellen, R. 1996. Introduction. In *Redefining Nature: Ecology, Culture and Domestication*, R. Ellen & K. Fukui (eds.). Oxford: Berg, 1-36.

Ellen, R. and K. Fukui (eds.) 1996. *Redefining Nature: Ecology, Culture and Domestication*. Oxford: Berg.

Foucault, M. 1971. Orders of Discourse. *Social Science Information* 10(2), 7-30.

– 1972 *The Archaeology of Knowledge*. London: Tavistock Publications.

Geertz, C. 1973. *The Interpretation of Cultures*. New York: Basic Books.

Global Biodiversity. 1992. *Status of the Earth's Living Resources. A Report Compiled by the World Conservation Monitoring Centre*. London: Chapman & Hall.

Global Biodiversity Assessment. 1995. V.H. Heywood (ex.ed.) and R.T. Watson (chair). Published for UNEP. Cambridge: Cambridge University Press.

Gutting, G. 1994. Introduction: Michel Foucault: A User's Manual. In *The Cambridge Companion to Foucault*, G. Gutting (ed.). Cambridge: Cambridge University Press, 1-27.

Hacking, I. 1986. The Archaeology of Foucault. In *Foucault: A Critical Reader* D.C. Hoy (ed.). Oxford: Oxford University Press.

Hutchinson, G.E. 1959. Homage to Santa Rosalia or: Why are there so many kinds of Animals? *American Naturalist* 93(870), 145-59.

Ingold, T. 1990. An Anthropologist Looks at Biology. *Man* 25(2): 208-29.

– 1994a. General Introduction. In *Companion Encyclopedia of Anthropology*, T. Ingold (ed.). London: Routledge, xiii-xxii.

– 1994b. Humanity and Animality. In *Companion Encyclopedia of Anthropology*, T. Ingold (ed.). London: Routledge, 14-32.

Kaarhus, R. 1999 *Conceiving Environmental Problems: A Comparative Study of Scientific Knowledge Constructions and Policy Discourses in Ecuador and Norway*. Oslo: NIBR reprints 20/96.

Keesing, R.M. 1990. Theories of Culture Revisited. *Canberra Anthropology* 13 (2), 46-60.

Kuhn, T.S. 1970. *The Structure of Scientific Revolutions*. Chicago: University of Chicago Press.

Leach, E.R. 1973. Ourselves and Others. *Times Literary Supplement*, July 6, 1973, 771–72.

Mayr, E. 1982. *The Growth of Biological Thought: Diversity, Evolution, and Inheritance*. Cambridge, Mass.: Belknap Press.

Rappaport, R.A. 1969. *Pigs for the Ancestors: Ritual in the Ecology of a New Guinea People*. New Haven: Yale University Press.

– 1994. Disorders of Our Own: A Conclusion. In *Diagnosing America: Anthropology and Public Engagement*, F. Shepard (ed.). Ann Arbor: University of Michigan Press.

Rouse, J. 1994. Power/Knowledge. In G. Gutting (ed.) *The Cambridge Companion to Foucault*. Cambridge: Cambridge University Press, 92–114.

Somers, M.R. 1994. The Narrative Constitution of Identity. A Relational and Network Approach. *Theory and Society*, 23: 605–35.

Tooby, J. & L. Cosmides 1992. The Psychological Foundations of Culture. In *The adapted mind: Evolutionary Psychology and the Generation of Culture*, J.H. Barkow, L. Cosmides & J. Tooby (eds.). New York: Oxford University Press.

Webster's 1983. *Ninth Collegiate Dictionary*. Springfield, Mass.: Merriam-Webster Inc.

Wilson, B.R. (ed.) 1970 *Rationality*. Oxford: Basil Blackwell.

Wilson, E.O. 1975 *Sociobiology: The New Synthesis*. Cambridge, Mass.: Harvard University Press.

When culture supports biodiversity:
The case of the wooded meadow

Kalevi Kull, Toomas Kukk & Aleksei Lotman

Since most human activities decrease biodiversity, including the traditional types of nature protection which only slow down the speed of biodiversity loss, the only way to preserve biodiversity in the long run is to find ways of ecosystem management which could also increase the local species richness, without any active introduction of new species. Wooded meadows, together with several other semi-natural ecosystems, propose traditional examples of this type. This paper examines the history of wooded meadows in Estonia, gives a short review of the mechanisms of species richness preservation, and discusses current activities in the restoration and protection of wooded meadow communities. We argue for the hypothesis that the wooded meadow as a type of landscape originated in the culture of settled hunter-gatherers, and that it has in remarkable ways organised the culture-nature relationships in Estonia during eight thousand years, until the beginning of the 20th century.

Introduction

When cataloging vegetation found during our fieldwork in the semi-natural meadow communities of western Estonia, we were very surprised to find that the species diversity at some of the sites happened to exceed the highest known values of micro-scale vegetation diversity in the entire world. Neither in any other community of Western Europe, nor anywhere in the tropics, does the number of vascular plant species within a few square meters reach the numbers counted on the Estonian wooded meadows. Wooded meadows, now close to disappearing, still exist in a few places along the coasts of the Baltic Sea. They represent a common landscape which has been kept and managed by many generations of farmers probably without any thought to biodiversity in its modern sense. However, understanding the mechanisms which have created these ecosystems may be helpful in coming to grips with the much more general problem of how human activity is possible without the loss of a diverse nature.

Here we have a problem which has two quite different facets. One is a basic ecological problem; how is it possible for high biodiversity to persist in a certain management regime? The other is a challenge to cultural theory as it asks a similar question from the point of view of culture-nature relationships. Seemingly, these two problems can be integrated by an *ecosemiotic* approach, i.e, a semiotic approach to the ecosystem of culture (see Nöth 1998, Kull 1998, Hornborg 1999).

Different views on the 'ideal' of a national park represent particular nature-culture relationships and specific images of 'valuable' nature. One view is the idea of *wilderness,* based on a sharp boundary between the space of human management and that of untouched nature, and practised particularly in the United States (cf. Oelschlaeger 1991). Another view is that of *countryside,* as idealised, for example, in British or French concepts of nature protection ('landscape as a garden'). The first implies a picturesque wilderness, where human influence is kept at a minimum; the second a well-designed landscape in which most of the biocommunities are controlled and reshaped by humans. The example we will describe here does not fit well into either of these categories: Unlike the wilderness, it is managed, and unlike the countryside, it includes almost only local (i.e. non-introduced) species and it is much less controlled by human activity. Therefore, we shall call this unique type of nature the idea of *wooded meadow.*

Every species influences its environment in one way or another. This influence can lead to improved living conditions for both the actor itself and for other species, or it may be inhibiting or disastrous for both. The species may persist, whether competitive or symbiotic, if the influence is so extensive that it allows the species to use their adaptiveness to find the resources they need. We claim that some human activities throughout history have contributed to diversity and hence to our survival, whilst others have been destructive. The few examples, however, of an human influence on nature that have enhanced the species richness of communities, all deserve more detailed study, both from a point of view of ecology and of cultural history.

The importance of the biodiversity problem comes from the fact that most types of nature protection only slow down the speed of species loss, which is caused by the growth of human-induced changes on the Earth. In the long run, this could mean that the number of species in the world's ecosystems are greatly impoverished (Jablonski 1991). Therefore, the only way to preserve biodiversity is to find ways of ecosystem management, which may also increase the local species richness without the introduction of new species.

The work by Kukk & Kull (1997) reviews various available data on wooded meadows, using both literature sources and the authors' own studies. The main research undertaken previously on wooded meadows can be attributed to H. Hesselman (1904), E. Julin (1948) and H. Sjörs (1954) on Sweden; C. Cedercreutz (1927, 1931), A. Palmgren (1915-1917) and C.-A. Häggström 1983, 1987, 1990) on Finland; and H. Krall (1975, 1990) and K. Pork (Krall & Pork 1970) on Estonia. Wooded meadow research in Estonia has been concentrated in the Laelatu Biological Station in recent decades.

In this paper, we draw some conclusions from our research on wooded meadows, formulate the general conditions for high diversity in a plant community, and discuss some general aspects of ecosemiotic relationships in the context of biodiversity and species co-existence, thus on the part of biology, making an attempt towards a dialogue with anthropology (cf. Kaarhus, this volume).

Wooded meadows: a short natural history

Until the middle of the 20th century, wooded meadows were widespread traditional semi-natural ecosystems, particularly abundant in the countries around the Baltic Sea. However, they have now almost entirely disappeared due to fundamental changes in land management.

Of the many names given in various languages to wooded meadows, the best known are *Gehölzwiese (Laubwiese* in older literature) in German, *löväng* in Swedish, *lehtoniity* in Finnish, *lesolug* in Russian, and *puisniit* in Estonian.

Wooded meadows can be defined as *sparse natural stands with an annually mown herb layer*. Tree canopy cover is usually in the range 10-50%. With regard to the horizontal structure of the traditional wooded meadow, only 10-20% of its surface area is not covered by a mowable herb community. Typically, deciduous trees and several shrub species are present, which are distributed in quite small irregular patches. Regular mowing (once a year) is important, but there may be some years when mowing is interrupted. Grazing on wooded meadows can vary quite a lot, usually they are lightly grazed by sheep or cattle in late summer (after mowing), but many sites are not grazed at all. Wooded meadows look like parks, but they differ from them due to their natural (not planted) vegetation and the natural unploughed soil. However, through the selective removal of trees, their species composition and appearance are influenced by humans.

More than five hundred years ago, wooded meadows were quite common in many areas of Europe, including England. As Schama (1995: 143) describes it:

Much of the forest, even in the early Middle Ages, was already being managed as a special kind of micro-economy for its inhabitants. Hardwoods were cut at regular twelve-year intervals four to six feet from the ground, sufficiently high to prevent deer from eating the new shoots. The base 'stool' would then be left to regenerate itself rapidly into the kind of light timber that could be used to meet all manner of essential needs: fencing, wattling, tools and implements. The result was the underwood, or coppice, that was the distinctive mark of the medieval forest and which in a very few locations, like Hatfield and Hadley Chase, can still be seen in England. In contrast to the most ancient forests of Germany and Poland and to the conifer woods of the Scottish Highlands and the oak forests of the English aristocratic estates − all products of the eighteenth- and nineteenth-century crazes for picturesque and Romantic 'improvements' − these ancient woodlands seem thinner and almost patchy, with swathes of grassy meadow and wild flowers blooming between pollarded and truncated broadleaf trees. The exact opposite of what is now considered to be the ideal norm of a forest habitat − the untended wilderness − they have light and space and variety: a working room for an authentic woodland culture.

The main distribution area of wooded meadows covered (at least, during the last several centuries) the region around the Baltic Sea (many islands, western and northern Estonia, south-western Finland, central and southern Sweden), and the mountains and hillsides of central and southern Europe, but there are also cases found in North America and Asia. The wooded meadows were typically found in geographical areas that were permanently covered by snow in winter, thereby necessitating the production of hay for cattle. However, during the last 50 years, these meadows have been abandoned and have disappeared almost everywhere. The best preserved of the remaining few are situated in Estonia. Some have also been restored in Sweden and Finland.

An interesting aspect of wooded meadows is that they supposedly constitute some of the oldest human-made landscapes, formed by a continuous long-term use. Therefore, it is of interest to reconstruct a possible history of this type of nature. In the following we propose a sketch of Estonian wooded meadows as an example.

Some 13–14 thousand years ago, the area now known as Estonia was still covered by a glacier that was melting relatively quickly, and within a period of approximately two thousand years it was gone. However, as large areas were still under water, only the innermost parts of the country were inhabitable for humans and other dry land dwellers when man – the hunter – came (first signs documented are from 9,500 years ago). As a result of this glacial melting, development of the Baltic Sea and a post-glacial land-lift, the present-day Estonia was gradually shaped.

Judging from the climatic zone, the climax plant-cover of the land must have been mixed forest. Accordingly, about seven thousand years ago almost all the land should have been covered by forest, and forest-free areas would only have been expected in narrow stripes along the sea coast and along the regularly flooded riversides. However, pollen analyses indicate that there have been more open areas than predicted by this scenario. For instance, among the tree species, oak *(Quercus robur)* and hazel *(Corylus avellana)* were quite frequent. Seedlings of these species require much light and cannot survive under a dense canopy. Pollen analyses have shown that this *Ulmus-Corylus* period started 8,000 years ago in Estonia. Accordingly, there must have been some open sites.

Vera (1997, 2000) has argued for a hypothesis, which explains this phenomenon via the influence of large herbivores. If access to food was limited, large herbivores (auroch *Bos primigenius,* wild horse *Equus caballus,* European bison *Bison bonasus,* elk *Alces alces,* red deer *Cervus elaphus,* roe deer *Capreolus capreolus)* would prefer to graze in forest glades with abundant herbal vegetation. This would inhibit the trees from regenerating in these places and keep the sites open. In a primeval forest, such openings appear naturally when a large tree, due to age or storm, falls down. Also, particular deciduous species could have been severely damaged since their bark and stems were used for food by these animals (cf. Falinski 1998). According to this hypothesis, 'in prehistoric times, the natural vegetation in the lowlands of Central and Western Europe was a park-like landscape, a mosaic of grasslands, scrub and solitary trees and groves surrounded by cover and border vegetation' (Vera 1997: 421). In these conditions, oaks and hazels could regenerate. Accordingly, the history of wooded meadow-like ecosystems in Europe may go back to the beginning of the Holocene.

We would like to argue that in some cases the influence of humans on the landscape could have had a similar effect, thereby supporting the influence of large herbivores. The early humans depended very much on trees for firewood, building materials, tools etc. Different tasks required different species of trees, and furthermore, diverse herbal vegetation was likely to have been important for food and medicine. This suggests that human settlements would have been established in those places where many different species of trees and herbs grew nearby, i.e., where the local species diversity, and, accordingly, the diversity of soil conditions (particularly as related to water conditions and pH) were high. Suitable sites were to be found along river banks, also because fishing and hunting were essential. Game preferred these areas: what was good for game was also good for hunters. The sites might therefore have been prepared by animals, so that humans did not have to start from zero. Thus, the places preferred by large herbivores – and turned by them into half-open park-like sites – were almost certainly the same sites preferred by human settlers. Wooded meadows may thereby have been a traditional ecosystem for hunter-gatherers when they established themselves in one place.

If it was only the trees nearest to the settlement which were cut, the surrounding glade would permanently grow. This in turn would increase the distance between the settlement and the supply of wood, perhaps resulting in a move to another place. Conversely, if the trees were used selectively, i.e., if the nearest trees were not chopped down, a mosaic of small glades would appear, whose growth was naturally restricted. In this balanced state, the intensity of usage would equal the growth rate of new trees on the same territory. In contrast to the open meadow management, the wooded meadow can therefore be seen as a stable type of land-use already before the period when draught animals were widely used.

In Estonia, the domestication of animals first came into effect during a period of warmer climate (late Atlantic), when it was possible for the animals to find food throughout the winter. Mosaic meadows around human dwellings proposed a good place for them to graze, as well as to find twigs and the bark of trees and bushes for food. Their diet, seemingly, did not differ initially very much from that of wild herbivores, whom they replaced near the human settlements. As the climate worsened after the end of the Atlantic optimum, about 4000-5000 years ago, the winters started to become colder. The number of wild game decreased, and as a consequence domestic animals gained more attention to compensate the loss. This meant an increased communication between humans and the animals living around the settlement. Because of the deep cover of snow, these animals were dependent on human help for food. The gathering of loppings (leafy twigs from trees or shrubs) was probably the main method of obtaining fodder during two millennia, before the discovering of the scythe. Leafy twigs are more plentiful, carry more leaves, and are available closer to ground if the tree canopy is not completely closed, thus allowing more light to reach the ground. For this purpose, the wooded meadow is an ideal community – much more suitable than the forest. In Sweden, as well as in many places in Western Europe, the pollarding of trees was used for the purpose of collecting twigs (Häggström 1998, Haas et al. 1998). According to existing data, however, this method was rarely used in Estonia, which can be explained by a less intensive land use. There was a preference toward single farms and the population density was low. Thus, every farm could have its own wooded meadow (sometimes called *heinaaed,* 'hay-garden'). The tradition for collecting loppings for fodder from wooded meadows was preserved, in rare cases, until the 20th century.

Thus, wooded meadows probably started to appear considerably before mowing was invented in the Baltic area. Multifunctional use of land around settlements, which included the selective cutting of trees, the collecting of twigs for leafy fodder, and grazing, led to quite a stable wooded meadow-like ecosystem already 4000–5000 years ago. Mowing by scythe, which began about 2000 years ago, gave the meadows their typical form that is still familiar today.

Since domestic herbivores competed with humans for the plant resources available, the need for additional food plants for humans was evident. The cultivation of land started in Estonia about 3000 years ago, but the settlements mainly consisted of single farms – this has indeed been the typical type of settlement for a very long time (Lang 1996) – and the appearance of small fields hardly changed the general structure of the landscape. Later (about 1,500 years ago), the growing dependence on land cultivation and the availability of materials for tool-making, seemingly correlated with the development of a more differentiated social structure. However, the majority of man-made meadows in the Baltic area were probably wooded meadows until approximately the 19th century, when the proportion of open and cultivated meadows began to increase.

It is important to note that the introduction of agriculture did not change the traditional relationship to nature in this area. Although the inhabitants began field agriculture and ploughing, they did not change from being hunters-gatherers to being graziers (livestock farmers). There was always a piece of forest alongside the farmhouse. The fields that were established were small, and they rarely grew much. They therefore only partially fulfilled the needs of the peasants, and many plant products were still collected from the natural plant communities. The wooded meadow therefore remained a main organiser of most of their daily life.

The regular management of a wooded meadow included a series of related tasks performed in a certain order. These included: (a) the raking and picking of fallen branches (in spring), which were later burned or used as firewood; (b) mowing (in July); (c) making loppings from twigs (after hay-making), which were dried and used notably for sheep fodder in winter; (d) coppicing (not every year); (e) the cutting of trees (in winter); (f) pasturing (in August and September); (g) collecting of secondary products – birch sap in spring, berries, mushrooms, medicinal herbs, tea herbs, hazelnuts, wild apples, flowers, etc.; (h) widespread wild bee managing; (i) hunting, due to a good feeding area for large herbivores; (j) bird egg collecting (used locally); (k) maintaining of drainage systems in some wet meadows; (l) use of the place for religious rituals, and festivals.

Wooded meadows thus represented a perfect example of green management, with a very long-term and stable multifunctional use of the land. An important aspect to add is that the stability and continuation of wooded meadows was supported by their aesthetic value, a fact confirmed over and over again by old local farmers whom we questioned in our fieldwork over the last decades. This includes the colourfulness of the meadow (notably in early summer, but flowers of different colours are also present throughout the snow-free season), the presence of interesting forms of trees in different sizes and tones (which were selectively kept, and included many old ones), the hovering of insects (butterflies, dragonflies, bumblebees), the concert of birds, the even, lawn-like surface (in late summer, after mowing), and multistage views with a variable play of light and shade. These qualities have throughout thousands of years continued to impress human beings, and they are probably the reason why park-like landscapes developed independently in many parts of the world.

In most areas of Western Europe, wooded meadows disappeared already in the Middle Ages, but they persisted for a longer time in marginal regions. According to Diekmann (1994: 9), the extension of wooded meadows in Sweden culminated during the 18th century. After the introduction of more effective ploughs and artificial fertilisers, arable lands, including leys and fertilised meadows, extended their areas at the expense of wooded meadows, which suffered from a deterioration of soil and were either cut down and turned into arable land and pastures, or allowed to regrow into forest. Many of the present deciduous forests originate from former wooded meadows, often through an intervening stage of wooded pastures. The rapid decrease of the wooded meadow area can be illustrated by some figures from Gotland, where about 32,000 hectares in the year 1900 had become reduced to only 284 hectares in 1983 (Diekmann 1994: 10). Most of the wooded meadow sites that exist in Sweden today have been restored after having suffered temporal overgrowth accompanied by a reduction in the original species richness.

In the case of Estonia, the area encompassed by natural grasslands reached its maximum somewhat later, at the end of the 19th or beginning of the 20th century, when wooded meadows covered 850,000 hectares (18.8% of Estonia's surface area) (Sammul et al. 2000). According to the agricultural census of 1939, natural grasslands of various types covered altogether one-third of the surface area of Estonia, and this was considerably more than in adjacent countries. There were slightly more meadows than pastures, and more than a half of the meadows were wooded meadows. Particularly in the western part of Estonia, almost all meadows were wooded meadows. They were often quite large, covering several square kilometres, and they could include all the meadows from a whole village.

The abandonment of wooded meadows in Estonia took place in several steps: (1) a reduction of farming during World War II; (2) the cessation of mowing by hand; (3) the cessation of mowing using horses. The first meadows to disappear were wet-wooded meadows, of which no well-preserved examples exist.

A general reason for this rapid decrease was the change in agricultural management from an extensive to an intensive type. This meant that natural grasslands were replaced by cultivated grasslands, and that mowing by scythe was replaced by tractor-mowing. However, this change took place more slowly in Estonia than in Sweden and Finland due to the fact that Estonian farmers, although working on collective or state farms, kept a small number of animals for their own use. Hay was made for these animals from the old natural grasslands, often by hand or with the help of horses. It was only in the 1960s that this situation changed. After that, overgrowth in wooded meadows occurred very rapidly.

Our fieldwork from 1995-99 revealed that there are still about 500 hectares of species-rich wooded meadows preserved in quite good condition in western Estonia, plus about 200 hectares of species-poor and flooded wooded meadows in other regions of Estonia. These are mainly small, less than 5 hectares one-farm meadows. From these, about 200 hectares (in about 40 sites) of the traditional Estonian wooded meadows are mown contemporarily, i.e. these are old sites, probably never having suffered overgrowth. In addition, there are many sites where the meadow was abandoned in recent years due to the cessation of cattle raising, or due to the advanced age of those people who had worked there.

The factors of species richness

Paradoxically, there is not a single ecosystem in the world that has been completely inventoried, i.e. of which a full species list is known. In order to make such a census of species in an ecosystem, a great deal more knowledge in field biology is required than is currently available. Therefore, it is necessary for us to restrict ourselves to data about some taxonomic groups, for example, plants. Furthermore, we need to consider several methodical problems in species richness measurements.

Species richness is largely scale-dependent. By small-scale richness we mean the number of species found on plots of a size less than 10 square meters. Measurements of species richness are quite sensitive to differences in counting methods. We define the number of species in a plant community as follows:

(a) the plot is quadratic (i.e. not longitudinal), its boundaries are fixed on the ground level, and only those ramets (individual shoots) which are rooted inside the plot belong to it; (b) only ramets which possess living above-ground parts on the day of measuring are included; (c) diaspores or other unrooted parts of plants are not included. Reliable results require a good knowledge of local flora (i.e., to be able to identify vegetative shoots and seedlings), and enough time to make the descriptions.

In Estonia, the number of vascular plant species in a 1 x 1 m plot does not normally exceed 20 in forests and 30 in natural meadows; in the richest alvar meadows it can be slightly over 40; and only in wooded meadows has it been found to exceed 50. The maximum (76 species in a 1 x 1 m plot) is recorded from the Laelatu wooded meadow in Estonia. A high value (74 species in a 1 x 1 m plot, or 68 as an average of ten plots) is also recorded from the Vahenurme wooded meadow (for the list of species see Kukk & Kull 1997). The top five wooded meadows according to their local (1 m²) vascular plant species richness, on the basis of our existing data, are Laelatu (76) and Vahenurme (74) in the western part of mainland, Tagamõisa (67) and Küdema (65) in Saaremaa, and Tärkma (61) in Hiiumaa.

What are the factors determining the species richness in wooded meadows? The wooded meadows which have the highest richness in their plant communities, have been found to be similar in the following characteristics:

- They are very old, regular mowing has taken place sometimes for several centuries.
- Soil is neutral, calcium-rich.
- Grazing has not taken place and if so, not intensively.
- Their territory has been large (tens of hectares, as a minimum).
- They include some moist or wet patches.
- The tree layer is species-rich.
- The local species pool is large.

A large species pool requires a diversity of niches on a small territory – i.e. nearby sites with conditions of shade and light, moisture and dryness, rich and poor soil nutritiousness. This corresponds exactly to the conditions found in wooded meadows. The richest community patches were usually found in sites of lower productivity and with a relatively open canopy.

The density of the seed bank is quite low in wooded meadows. The number of annual species is very low; they are represented almost only by hemiparasites *(Rhinanthus, Melampyrum)*. Life cycles are extended, and vegetative reproduction dominates.

According to the measurements in Laelatu wooded meadow, the herb community's above-ground biomass reaches its maximum at the end of June. The peak of the seasonal maximum of species richness (i.e., of the number of species which have some living green organs above-ground) is wider than the biomass peak, but they generally coincide.

The number of bryophyte species in a 1 x 1 m meadow plot is usually between 4 and 10 in the Laelatu wooded meadow. In a contrast to vascular plants, less rare bryophyte species are growing on these meadows (Ingerpuu et al. 1998).

The total number of species in a terrestrial ecosystem is roughly proportional to the number of plant species. However, this correlation is not very strong. Still, according to our estimations, the diversity of bird, mammal and reptile species is higher in a wooded meadow, if compared with either a forest or an open meadow site in otherwise similar conditions. A case study about the species diversity of terrestrial molluscs and carabid beetles gave similar results (Talvi 1995; Tiina Talvi, unpublished).

In natural meadows, only about 15% of the annual biomass production is removed with the hay. Equilibrium hay-yield (i.e., productivity after long-term management) from a wooded meadow is higher than from an open meadow in otherwise similar conditions. This is due to the additional input of mineral elements from tree leaf litter, since tree roots take nutrients from deeper layers than herb roots. From the point of view of nutritional quality, the hay from wooded meadows is richer than that produced on cultivated grasslands.

The horizontal variation in small-scale species richness was very large in the investigated meadows, and the patches with extremely high richness are quite small. However, the local species richness was very stable from year to year, under regular management conditions. A great deal of the horizontal variation in the herb layer in wooded meadows is connected to the distance from trees. Closer to trees, the herb community is higher, and individual ramets are bigger, whilst the ramet density and species richness are lower than in more open sites.

Of course in stating that small-scale species richness is extremely high in west-Estonian wooded meadows, we should first ask whether plant communities with greater small-scale species diversity exist anywhere in the world? It appears that there is not much known about this, because a comparative analysis of small-scale richness in plant communities on a worldwide scale is still absent.

We do know, however, that the maximum recorded and published number of vascular plant species on a 1 x 1 m plot has been found in a meadow steppe site, located in a forest steppe region of the Central Chernozem Nature Reserve (Strelets Steppe), where Alechin (1934) described a plot with 77 vascular plant species. Later, six plots with species numbers from 61 to 87 were recorded in a regularly mown community (Afanaseva, Golubev 1962). There also exists a note about a 1 x 1 m plot of 89 species in a traditional slightly grazed mountain meadow of Argentina (Cantero et al. 1999; however, no species list has been published). These are the only sites known in the world where the small-scale species richness exceeds that of Estonian wooded meadows. However, similar communities exist in which species richness is also very high, e.g., wooded meadows in Czech mountains (L. Klimes, pers. comm.) and chalk meadows in the Netherlands. In all these sites, several features coincide:

- These are semi-natural communities with very long-term, regular and moderate management, either mowing or non-intensive grazing.
- The soil is close to neutral and calcium-rich.
- The vegetation is low.
- The local variation of conditions is high.
- The local species pool is high.
- Geographically, these sites are situated in a temperate zone.

The species richness of a community is the result of an equilibrium between immigration and extinction. Therefore, a turnover with two different pools is essential: On the one hand, the species pool (the species present in the vicinity, outside the plot), on the other hand, the dormancy pool (the species which are in a dormant state, below-ground on the plot; it includes the seed pool). The first is defined as an external turnover, the latter as an internal turnover; both are scale-dependent with a greater importance in smaller plots.

There is a clear latitudinal trend in the size of the species pool; this excludes high latitude sites from the richest ones. This also causes a good negative correlation between species richness and latitude if comparing plots of one hectar or more in size. In addition, local heterogeneity of habitat conditions increases the local species pool. On the other hand, the number of specimens on a plot is connected to the size of plants, which shows a contrariwise trend; this is one of the reasons that excludes the tropical areas from being the richest in small-scale diversity. An important factor is mowing, which diminishes the size of plants, reduces the level of competition and makes the competition more symmetrical.

The high species diversity is strongly connected to history. Although species richness may decline very quickly, it only increases again very slowly. This is the reason why the highest diversity has been found in those sites which have been in permanent use over a long period of time, perhaps for several centuries. When a wooded meadow, for example, has not been used for a while and has overgrown, the richness of the plant community is reduced, and then if the meadow is restored later, it will take considerable time to reach the previous species diversity. This is probably the main reason why most of the current wooded meadows in Sweden have much lower species diversity than the Estonia meadows. In Sweden, the wooded meadows in question have all been out of use for some period, and have only been restored later.

In global terms, the geographical region where hay-making takes place is latitudinally not very wide. The combination of relatively undisturbed nature (compared to the surrounding areas), calcareous soils, low population density, and a persistent culture possessing a long tradition for non-intensive land-management, has given these rare examples of still existing, rich and beautiful, semi-natural ecosystems.

Protection, restoration and the contemporary management of wooded meadows

The existing ways and experience in keeping and protecting wooded meadows may give some hints for understanding the possibilities of preserving biodiversity, also in more general terms. Below we describe briefly the Estonian experience on this issue.

The oldest known regulations for nature protection in Estonia were connected with restrictions for the cutting of oaks (on the islands of Naissaar in the 13th century, and Hanikatsi in the 16th century), but since oak forests were often used for hay-making, this probably also meant the protection of some wooded meadows. At the end of the 1930s, a few nature reserves were established, in which territory some wooded meadow sites existed (Puhtu), and since 1957 there have also been some nature reserves specifically for protecting wooded meadows (Tagamõisa, Laelatu, Halliste, Koiva).

During the first half of the 20th century wooded meadows represented the most common type of semi-natural ecosystems in several counties of western Estonia. In 1995-96, about 200 hectares of them were still managed, of which 60 hectares were situated within the bounds of state nature reserves.

Considering the efforts needed to preserve wooded meadows, their persistence could be achieved by an additional evaluation of the work needed (mowing, primarily). Species richness itself, as an important quality of the environment, could also be directly protected by law. Until now, there have been no regulations based on the number of species.

Biodiversity of the meadow ecosystems is connected to human use and it declines significantly if this use ceases. Since these plant communities are products of long-term interaction between man and environment, the possible man-induced threats are two-fold. Active threats include drainage, fertilisation, ploughing, etc.

However, the passive threat of stopping traditional uses like grazing or mowing is just as serious. Any conservation of these communities must therefore include active management in the form of support to traditional uses like grazing or mowing.

We can give here an example of meadow conservation in the Matsalu Nature Reserve. The area in question is situated on the western coast of Estonia, which includes Matsalu Bay, and it is surrounded by a wetland of international importance (particularly due to its value as a rich bird sanctuary) and a diverse variety of meadows, wooded meadows and forest. The Management Plan for Matsalu (MPM; for a summary see Lotman 1994) is a comprehensive document that briefly describes the wetland, evaluates its features and the threats to these, and prescribes actions to counteract these threats. Actions are assigned with budgets and with priorities that stem from the previous evaluation.

According to the MPM the meadows are among the chief values of the wetland. They are important from a botanical perspective and also as bird habitats. Activities like drainage, fertilisation, and ploughing are either banned or strongly regulated in the Nature Reserve and the passive threat caused by stopping traditional uses like grazing or mowing is recognised as being most acute at the present time.

Therefore measures to counteract abandonment of the meadows are given high priority in the MPM. These include the making of grazing or mowing contracts with farmers and paying compensation accordingly. Payments vary for grazing (either per cow or per horse day, or per sheep day) and mowing of open meadows (if mowed but not harvested, then only half of the sum is paid) and of wooded meadows (only paid if hay has been removed).

Currently all the people who participate in the meadow management in Matsalu Nature Reserve are compensated according to the MPM. The same principles apply to the management of a few other Estonian wooded meadows. Apart from mowing or grazing, bush cutting is carried out on the overgrown parts of the meadows. Some of the negative trends have fortunately been reversed, some merely slowed down. Therefore, to save the meadows in the long term, their wise use must become part of the resource use patterns once again.

In order to organise such work throughout the whole country, the Estonian Seminatural Community Conservation Association was established in 1997. In addition to the preservation of the existing old wooded meadows, the restoration of other sites has also been started. The restoration of wooded meadows could be justified for nature protection (as a habitat for many rare species, and as a very rich community), for green farming, for eco-tourism, for cultural history protection programmes, for scientific interest, for landscape design, for aesthetic reasons, etc.

The best results in wooded meadow restoration can be achieved when using abandoned wooded meadows, in which many old trees are still alive and the former structure of the meadow can be detected. Some patches of meadow vegetation may still exist in these sites, thus allowing herb species to establish more rapidly in newly opened areas.

In several cases (Viidumäe, Laelatu, Nedrema, Matsalu), volunteer camps were used to organise the work. Similar volunteer camps have been organised in a few Finnish and Swedish wooded meadows during the last decades. The main aim, however, has been to guarantee stable long-term management, which cannot be based on volunteer camps, since they cannot fulfil the basic requirement of this type of ecosystem, i.e., the sophisticated and knowledgeable communication between people who manage the ecosystem, and the local species that they use.

A well-known and much used way of organising nature protection includes the establishing of national parks. Despite using the same name – national park – the designation covers two very different types of areas. The first type consists of reserves and wilderness areas where no management is allowed and where the land is usually state- or federally-owned. This is the type of national park to be found in, for example, the United States or Australia. The other type of national park allows different land-ownership, and various levels of regulation apply within each park (as in several European countries, including Estonia; cf. Dompka 1996). With this national park model, people live and manage the areas, but there are limitations with regard to the type and intensity of management. Due to these limitations, economic growth in its contemporary meaning may be limited, however, but living conditions in terms of environmental quality may be unusually high. These areas include the protection of semi-natural communities, and only this type of protected areas can preserve wooded meadows.

Ecosemiotic remarks

Wooded meadow analogues exist also in other ecosystems where human intervention can often facilitate the preservation of biodiversity:

- Traditional non-intensive fishery in lakes, rivers or marine ecosystems with a long-term regular harvesting of fish populations (or other water organisms) focusing on the more abundant species. This reduces the competition level in the water community, and keeps the species diversity permanently high.
- So-called ecological forestry. This means forest management that does not involve clear-cutting or forest planting and where mainly the dominant species are regularly harvested.
- Low-intensity (extensive) pasturing that keeps the pastures mosaic and where many sites on the pasture are rarely visited by the animals.

In all these examples, humans use some of the natural biotic production without removing any of the selected species entirely, and without adding new species in large quantities. The soil is not turned over, and the flow of waters is not redirected. This is a management of natural communities as they are: it does not remove any plant or animal community from the area, but it uses pieces of the community in a mosaic way, and reduces the number of some of the dominant populations thereby diminishing the competition intensity of the community. Thus, many species are given a niche that may allow them to survive.

When comparing the principal ways of human-nature relationships with regard to the spatial aspects, we can distinguish between three types:

- The spatial separation of large civilised and wild areas, according to the idea of wilderness.
- The total overlapping of nature and culture, as in the countryside (in the case of intensive management), parks, or gardens.
- The maximum spatial mosaic of nature and culture, as in wooded meadows, and other semi-natural ecosystems.

In addition, the latter can, of course, also include examples other than wooded meadows, *sensu stricto,* or the examples (a) − (c) listed above. For villages and towns, this would mean a mosaic greenery consisting exclusively of a local (i.e., non-introduced) flora and fauna that is not over-cultivated. Thus, we can develop the classification proposed in the beginning of this paper (see Table 1).

We can, furthermore, see a difference in the communication aspect between these types of uses of nature. This is clearly seen if we apply the functional cycle, a

Landscape type	Ecosystem type	Spatial relationship with cultural land	Dominant human activity	Occurrence of introduced species	Meaning of indigenous species	Impact on local species richness
Wilderness	natural	separated	perception	none	positive (museal, rare)	unchanging
Country-side, park, garden	artificial	overlapping	operation	many	negative (weeds, para-sites, dodo)	decreasing
Wooded meadow	semi-natural	mosaic	balanced communi-cation	almost none	common	increasing

Table 1. Characterisation of three principal types of valued landscapes

model of the communicative act proposed by Jakob von Uexküll (1982). The functional cycle can be seen as the basic mechanism behind any subjective Umwelt. It consists of the perceptual and operational worlds, which together comprise an Umwelt, the self-world.

For humans, wilderness appears primarily via its grandiose influence on *perception*. As we are not allowed to use nature for material benefit, the perceptual side of communication (Merkwelt) dominates our relationships with wilderness.

The cultivated countryside has involved the work of people – a continuous *operation* to keep the order of things as designed by humans. Usage of nature in a well-ordered way means the dominance of motoric behaviour *(Wirkwelt)*, i.e., the operational world as a part of our communication activity. Indeed, for a well-designed area of countryside, as well as for a park or a garden, it is considered a disadvantage to leave any patch for weeds to grow. In this case, the perceptual side is subordinated to the operational, which may affect all plots of land.

With wooded meadows, neither perception nor operation can take over; they both participate as reciprocal constituents of *communication* with nature (of *Umwelt)*.

Operation is necessary, however restricted, in order to keep the semi-natural community in equilibrium.

Originally, wooded meadows were an integral part of the world of people, who lived as settled hunters and fishermen with some few domestic animals. In using the different products of the diverse ecosystem which surrounded them, they contributed to the factors which preserved the high species richness.

Now, for contemporary Western people, primeval nature and natural plant communities only exist outside of their everyday world – their *Umwelt* – despite the existence of indigenous communities in some places. For current cultures, these wilderness areas serve the function of museums. Visiting these places means that people learn how it *was,* and see examples of previous, ancient times – something rare. For most people, natural species – as small populations in wilderness areas – do not play any real functional role in their everyday cultural life, either in a utilitaristic or in an ecosystemic (recycling) sense. That nature, which surrounds the majority of contemporary people in the civilised world, consists mainly of non-indigenous cultural forms, where the local flora and fauna are represented for the most part through weeds and parasites. Even if a garden seems to be well-designed with a high concentration of developed species, the overall number of species in such an ecosystem is much lower than in a natural community, particularly due to reduced soil and insect fauna, and microbiota.

An alternative or additional possibility would be to live as a *part* of local nature, thus requiring a different type of communication with other species. This *living together* with local flora and fauna would allow us to use them to some extent, and allow them to carry on the eternal round-dance of our common nature. All this is possible if we surround ourselves with ecosystems consisting of local, indigenous biota. This is the basic idea of the wooded meadow.

REFERENCES

Afanaseva, V.A. & V.N. Golubev 1962. *Pochvenno-botanicheskij ocherk Streleckoj stepi*. Kursk: Centralno-Chernozemnyj zapovednik.

Alechin V.V. 1934. *Centralno-Chernozemnye stepi.* Voronezh: Kommuna.

Cantero, J., M. Pärtel & M. Zobel 1999. Is Species Richness Dependent on Neighbouring Stands? An Analysis of the Community Patterns in Mountain Grasslands of Central Argentina. *Oikos* 87: 346-54.

Cedercreutz, C. 1927. Studien über Laubwiesen in den Kirschpielen Kyrkslätt und Esbo in Südfinnland mit besonderer Berücksichtigung der Verbreitung und Einwanderung der Laubwiesenarten. *Acta Botanica Fennica* 3: 1-181.

– 1931. Vergleichende Studien über die Laubwiesen im westlichen und östlichen Nyland. *Acta Botanica Fennica* 10: 1-63.

Diekmann, M. 1994. Deciduous Forest Vegetation in Boreo-nemoral Scandinavia. *Acta Phytogeographica Suecica* 80: 1-112.

Dompka, V. 1996. *Human Population, Biodiversity and Protected Areas: Science and Policy Issues.* Washington: American Association for the Advancement of Science.

Falinski, J.B. 1998. Dynamics of *Salix caprea* L. Populations during Forest Regeneration after strong Herbivore Pressure. *Journal of Vegetation Science* 9(1): 57-64.

Haas, J.N., S. Karg & P. Rasmussen 1998. Beech Leaves and Twigs used as Winter Fodder: Examples from Historic and Prehistoric Times. *Environmental Archaeology* 1: 81-86.

Häggström, C.A. 1983. Vegetation and Soil of the Wooded Meadows in Nåtö, Åland. *Acta Botanica Fennica* 120: 1-66.

– 1988. Protection of Wooded Meadows in Åland – Problems, Methods and Perspectives. *Oulanka Reports* 8: 88-95.

– 1990. The Influence of Sheep and Cattle Grazing on Wooded Meadows in Åland, SW Finland. *Acta Botanica Fennica* 141: 1-28.

– 1998. Pollard Meadows: Multiple Use of Human-made Nature. In *The Ecological History of European Forests*, K.J. Kirby & C. Watkins (eds.). Wallingford: CAB International, 33-41.

Hesselman, H. 1904. Zur Kenntniss des Pflanzenlebens schwedischer Laubwiesen: Eine physiologisch-biologische und pflanzengeographische Studie. *Beihefte z. Bot. Centralbl.* 17: 311-460.

Hornborg, A. 1999. Money and the Semiotics of Ecosystem Dissolution. *Journal of Material Culture* 4(2): 143-62.

Ingerpuu, N., K. Kull & K. Vellak 1998. Bryophyte Vegetation in a Wooded Meadow: Relationships with Phanerogam Diversity and Responses to Fertilisation. *Plant Ecology* 134(2): 163-71.

Jablonski, D. 1991. Extinctions: A Paleontological Perspective. *Science* 253: 754-57.

Julin, E. 1948. Vessers Udde: Mark och vegetation i en igenväxande löväng vid Bjärka-Säby. *Acta Phytogeographica Suecica* 23: 1-186.

Krall, H. 1975. Liigirikkad puisniidud Eestis. In *Eesti loodusharulduste kaitseks*, O. Renno (ed.). Tallinn: Valgus, 114-25.

– 1990. Meadows and Wooded Meadows. In *Flora and Vegetation of Saaremaa Island*, V. Masing, E. Roosaluste, A. Koppel (eds.). Tartu: Estonian Academy of Sciences, 46-48.

Krall, H. & K. Pork 1970. Laelatu puisniit. In *Lääne-Eesti rannikualade loodus*, Kumari E. (ed.). Tallinn: Valgus, 115-28.

Kukk, T. & K. Kull 1997. Puisniidud [Wooded Meadows]. *Estonia Maritima* 2: 1-249.

Kull, K. 1998. Semiotic Ecology: Different Natures in the Semiosphere. *Sign Systems Studies* 26: 344-71.

Kull, K. & M. Zobel 1991. High Species Richness in an Estonian Wooded Meadow. *Journal of Vegetation Science* 2: 711-14.

Lang, V. 1996. *Muistne Rävala* [Prehistoric Rävala]. Tallinn: ETA Ajaloo Instituut.

Lotman, A. 1994. Management Plan for Matsalu Wetland. *WWF Baltic Bulletin* 1: 11-12.

Nöth, W. 1998. Ecosemiotics. *Sign Systems Studies* 26: 332-43.

Oelschlaeger, M. 1991. *The Idea of Wilderness: From Prehistory to the Age of Ecology*. New Haven: Yale University Press.

Palmgren, A. 1915-1917. Studier öfver löföngsområdena på Åland: Ett bidrag till kännedomen om vegetationen och floran på torr och på frisk kalkhaltig grund. *Acta Societatis pro Fauna et Flora Fennica* 42(1): 1-634.

Sammul, M., K. Kull & T. Kukk 2000. Natural Grasslands in Estonia: Evolution, Environmental, and Economic Roles. In *Conventional and Ecological Grassland Management: Comparative Research and Development*, R. Viiralt (ed.). Tartu: Estonian Agricultural University, 20-26.

Schama, S. 1995. *Landscape and Memory*. New York: Vintage Books.

Sjörs, H. 1954. Slåtterängar in Grangärde Finnmark. *Acta Phytogeographica Suecica* 34: 1-135.

Talvi, T. 1995. Carabid Beetle Assemblages (*Coleoptera*) in a Wooded Meadow and in the Adjacent Habitats on the Saaremaa Island, Estonia. *Entomologica Fennica* 6: 169-75.

Uexküll, J. v. 1982. The Theory of Meaning. *Semiotica* 42(1): 25-82.

Vera, F. W. M. 1997. *Metaphors for the Wilderness: Oak, Hazel, Cattle and Horse*. Doctoral thesis. Wageningen: Wageningen Agricultural University.

Vera, F. W. M. 2000. *Grazing Ecology and Forest History*. Oxon: CABI Publishing.

From animal masters to ecosystem services: Exchange, personhood and human ecology

Alf Hornborg

In this paper, I will try to put together some theoretical jigsaw pieces that might help us get a fuller picture of the relation between human beings and their natural environment in different cultural contexts. I will discuss some general issues of method and analysis in human ecology and then try to apply some of these thoughts to the much discussed contrast between traditional Amerindian and modern ways of approaching nature. I will suggest a correlation between varieties of personhood, ways of engaging nature and ways of engaging other human beings through exchange. Finally, I will argue that a theoretical conflation of these three aspects of human life and cosmology is facilitated by recognising their various spatial dimensions. In comparing the spatial coordinates of personhood, nature and exchange we may surmise a structural logic which permits us to juxtapose as disparate contexts as pre-modern Algonquian hunter-gatherers, modern scholars in the field of ecological economics, and the 'post-modern' deep ecology movement.

The human ecological triangle

In recent years there has been a proliferation of discourses on human-environmental relations. It seems as if each traditional discipline in the human sciences has been developing a 'green' territory of its own, e.g. environmental history, environmental sociology, environmental law, environmental ethics, ecological economics, ecological anthropology, and so on. Proponents of these discourses are faced with the perennial problem of whether to adopt the language of 'Humanists' or 'Scientists' (cf. Ingerson 1994). The former tends to imply a focus on how particular humans experience their environment, adopting the jargon of phenomenology, hermeneu-

tics or constructivism, and stylistically often verging on literature. The latter generally means assuming an objectivist stance, typically involving more exact analytical
procedures as well as quantification of various aspects of human–environmental
interaction (cf. Bates & Lees 1996: 9). I need not dwell on the mutual antagonism
that proponents of the 'two cultures' often feel vis-á-vis each other; suffice to say
that they seem to live in different intellectual universes (cf. Bernstein 1983). I sus-
pect that, in this paper, I have taken something of a middle road. I am definitely a
humanist insofar as I am concerned with the subjective dimension of human–environmental relations (and in my lack of interest in quantification), yet I share the natural scientists' predilection for conciseness and analytical precision. The result may
seem awkward and sterile to the humanist, but vague and fanciful to the scientist.
This is probably an inevitable cost of trying to deal objectively with subjectivity.

It has often been recognised that the study of human-environmental relations is
a 'triadic' research field involving what we could provisionally refer to as nature,
society and consciousness. Environmental historians such as Merchant (1989: 3),
McEvoy (1988: 229) and Worster (1993: 5) tend to use 'production' for what I have
called 'society', and 'ecology' for 'nature', but the general scheme is the same. The
greatest variation is in categories pertaining to 'consciousness'. Merchant speaks of
'forms of consciousness', McEvoy of 'cognition', and Worster of 'structures of
meaning' (cf. Worster 1988: 293 for a more elaborate explication). The geographer
Dieter Steiner (1993: 56) suggests a 'human ecological triangle' of environment,
society and person. The recurrent, triadic scheme is not arbitrary, but reflects the
complementarity of perspectives on human-environmental relations deriving,
respectively, from the natural sciences, the social sciences and the humanities. It may
seem curious to let the concept of 'person' stand for that aspect which the environmental historians call 'consciousness', 'cognition' or 'structures of meaning', but
there are good reasons for doing so. The person is the only conceivable entity which
is both a locus of consciousness, cognition and meaning and a source of tangible
agency. Although it is possible to visualise abstract patterns of 'culture', 'ideology' or
'symbolism' that transcend the individual person, it is through concrete persons that
such abstractions intervene in the world.

It is important to recognise that these three dimensions of human-environmental relations are not to be arranged into some kind of causal hierarchy reminiscent of
the Marxist model of a 'mode of production', with nature and production as 'base'
and consciousness as 'superstructure'. Steiner instead speaks of a recursivity between

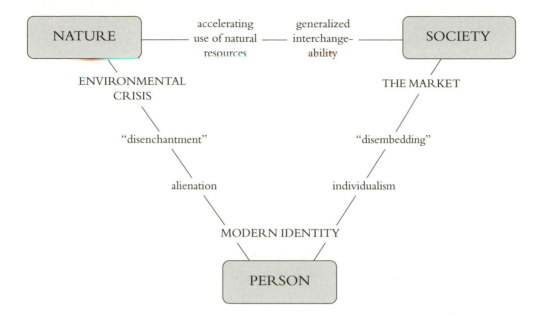

Figure 1. Modernity as "decontextualization"

the different corners of his triangle. They are three, mutually reinforcing aspects of a single, socio-ecological phenomenon. If, for instance, we want to use Steiner's model to understand a process of emergent modernisation of human-environmental relations, I believe that an adequate way of going about it would be to identify specific structures and relationships representing the three sides of the triangle, because the sides are what connect the three dimensions in mutually reinforcing (recursive) ways.

Although Steiner does not detail such a procedure himself, I have tentatively 'filled in' the corners and sides of the triangle to make it applicable to a generalised condition of modernity (Figure 1). The three corners of the triangle in modern society could perhaps be crudely characterised, respectively, in terms of environmental problems, market economy and individualism. The task is then to identify the structures and relationships that connect them. The notion of a connection between the market economy and individualism has a long history in sociology, and we might use the concept of 'disembedding' (cf. Giddens 1990) for that side of the triangle. The connection between market economy and environmental problems, on the other hand, is being explored for example in the field of ecological economics. It is not unreasonable to identify the market principle itself – i.e. the notion of generalised interchangeability – as ultimately responsible for accelerating environmental problems, since the market in effect rewards the dissipation of resources with ever more resources to dissipate (Hornborg 1998). The connection between modern, individualistic identity and environmental crisis, finally, could perhaps be summed up in the concept of 'alienation' or in Max Weber's concept of 'disenchantment'. This is the phenomenological or existential dimension of human–environmental relations: that intangible and hard-to-theorise aspect of reality that has to do with how human beings experience the world.

In closing the triangle, we are able to conclude that ecological, sociological and existential phenomena together form a whole which no single, conventional discipline can encompass. Modern environmental problems have a subjective dimension which has to do with the constitution of the modern person, as well as an objective dimension which has to do with the organisation of the market economy, but the triangle suggests that these two dimensions are ultimately aspects of a single phenomenon of modernity. Instead of arranging different aspects according to some linear, causal chain, we must visualise how a specific trajectory at one level is accompanied by structurally cognate trajectories at the other two levels. These three, specific trajectories of nature, society and personhood (which are really a single trajectory) accompany each other historically because they are mutually reinforcing. In fact, without this recursivity between them, there would be no historical movement. (In order to depict such a movement, the triangle should perhaps be drawn in three dimensions, as a series of triangles laid on top of each other.) It is by recognising their mutual interpenetration that we can see, for instance, how a society of strangers will tend to foster 'natural aliens' (cf. Evernden 1985).

Human ecology and personhood

Whether we call ourselves environmental historians, environmental sociologists or ecological anthropologists, we have probably had to struggle with some habitual dualisms of Western thought such as the dichotomies of culture/nature, society/nature, subject/object, mind/body, mental/material, etc. To replace a rigid dualism with a triadic scheme, as in Steiner's triangle, may be one way of transcending some of the problems. The dichotomy of mental and material, for instance, requires a third category – the social – in order to accommodate the kinds of mutual inter-penetration that arguably exist between the two traditional poles. It is also essential to understand human 'cognition' or 'knowledge' neither as pure representation nor as pure construction, but as a recursive relationship that constitutes both the knower (subject) and the known (object). Such a perspective is fundamental to the work of Bateson (1972), to cognitive scientists like Maturana and Varela (1987) and to environmental historians such as Bird (1987).

An implication, which this 'relationist' approach to knowledge shares with constructivism (which it subsumes), is that essentialist notions of nature will have to be more or less abandoned. If natural landscapes virtually everywhere carry traces of human activity (cf. Simmons 1993), the conclusion must be that 'nature' is imbued with human culture, and that human language intervenes in ecological processes (cf. Rappaport 1993, Ingerson 1994: 62). It can also be argued, conversely, that ecological relations have always been communicative phenomena, and that human symbolism and language are only the latest additions to the semiotics of ecosystems (Hornborg 1996).

Let us say that the challenge for a post-Cartesian theory of human-environmental relations is to recognise the significance of the human subject without itself becoming a direct expression of subjectivity (as, for instance, in poetry). The only conceivable way to achieve this, i.e. an analytical acknowledgement of the recursivity between subject and object, may be to include the person as an ubiquitous counterpart to both 'society' and 'nature'. Considerations of the 'person' as an analytical category is essential to any study of human-environmental relations which seeks to understand the cultural incentives that generate particular modes of resource management, rather than restrict itself merely to their material repercussions.

It is, in fact, symptomatic of Western thought that we should at all have to argue for the significance of personhood in human dealings with the rest of the natural world. Ingold (1996) questions the Western consignment of the notion of 'person' to an exclusively human, socio-cultural domain that is conceived as distinct from a natural, material world of 'organisms'. Such a distinction between persons and things (subjects and objects) is alien to hunter-gatherer groups like the Algonquian-speakers of northeastern North America, who tend to view all living beings as undivided centres of awareness, agency and intentionality. For the Waswanipi Cree of Quebec, non-human animals are like persons in that they act intelligently and have wills and idiosyncrasies, and understand and are understood by men' (Feit 1973: 116, quoted in Ingold 1996: 131). Much as was understood by the ethologist and semiotician Jakob von Uexküll (1982 [1940]), a crucial corollary is that even for animals 'the world exists as a meaningful place' (Ingold 1996: 135).

If we are willing to concede that humans relate to their environments as persons, not merely as organisms – or more precisely that their aspect of 'personhood' is of significance for ecology – it is only natural to consider the ecological significance of cultural variation in personhood. This has long been a subject of Western self-reflection, based on observations of culture- or class-based contrasts between different varieties of personhood in space and time (Indians versus Europeans, traditional peasants versus modern city-dwellers, etc.). Environmental historians like Martin (1978), Cronon (1983) and Merchant (1989) have interpreted the ecological transformations of northeastern North America during the past few centuries in terms which could be translated into changes in personhood. In explaining the transitions from native Indian to colonial and capitalist land use, they focus on cultural differences between Indians and Europeans, whether in the cosmology of hunting (Martin), conceptions of property (Cronon) or different 'forms of consciousness' (Merchant). All of these 'cultural' differences pertain to the phenomenological side of the human-ecological triangle.

But references to 'culture' seem unsatisfactory to the extent that the identified contrasts can be generalised for a great number of comparisons between middle-class, urban Europeans and their primitive Other. While some anthropologists caution against such dichotomous 'constructions', others try to provide analytical frameworks for validating them. Sahlins (1976: 216), for instance, sums up a complex argument by concluding that 'money is to the West what kinship is to the Rest', while Shweder and Bourne (1984) identify a contrast between Western and non-Western concepts of personhood, noting that the latter are typically based on more context-dependent and concrete modes of thinking. Rather than essentialising typically non-Western features as characteristic of specific, exotic 'cultures', such approaches ultimately imply a structural definition of 'the West' as a (geographically indeterminate) condition of modernity.

The two dichotomous characterisations of 'the West and the Rest' just referred to have bearings on two sides of the human ecological triangle. Sahlins' observation pertains to mechanisms for social exchange and thus to the link between society and person, whereas Shweder and Bourne's, in focusing on modes of thinking about (and thus of relating to) the world, is of great relevance for the interface of person and nature. Particularly interesting, of course, are perspectives which explicitly connect these two dimensions by suggesting that the modern inclination towards abstract thought, decontextualisation and objectification is structurally related to money, market institutions and the fetishisation of abstract exchange value. Such insights, formulated e.g. by Horkheimer and Adorno (1972 [1944]), Whorf (1978 [1956]), and Baudrillard (1993 [1976]), can be traced back to nineteenth century social philosophers such as Marx, Weber and Simmel.

I suggested that references merely to 'cultural' differences, taken as given, are insufficient to account for the different ecological perceptions and practices of the Indians and colonists in North America. In consequence with the tenets of our human ecological triangle, it should be incumbent on us to demonstrate structural connections between its phenomenological, social and material dimensions. In particular, we should be able to show, in specific instances as well as in general terms, how the person/nature interface is connected to the interface of person/society. A possible point of departure, discussed by Gudeman (1986), Descola (1992), Bird-David (1992) and Ingold (1996), is that the different ways in which humans engage other creatures in nature somehow correspond to different ways of engaging each other in society. Gudeman, Descola and Bird-David suggest that this occurs through the medium of social metaphors applied to human-environmental relations, for example when the land is conceptualised as ancestors, the forest as parents, crops as children, game animals as affines, etc. In transferring meanings and feelings from the world of social relations onto relations with non-human nature, such metaphors codify specific ways of relating to the latter. These authors seem to assume that social relations here conceptually precede ecological relations and serve as templates for them in a unidirectional way.

Ingold (1996), drawing on Jackson (1983), challenges this approach by suggesting that such metaphors can point to real commonalities between the two kinds of relations. Instead of merely observing that some ecological relations could be likened to specific kinds of social relations, the metaphors can draw attention to their essential unity. Such unities or equivalences would presumably pertain to the attitudes, moods and emotions – in short, what Bourdieu (1990) calls the habitus – generated in these relationships. It is of course possible to experience similar feelings and adopt similar postures with respect to phenomena which are categorically quite distinct, such as 'land' and 'ancestors'. The unity evoked in such metaphors, then, is that aspect of the person which constitutes the nexus of the conflated relations. Metaphors refer to experiential commonalities that transcend categorical disjunctions. In this sense, Ingold's objection is certainly valid. But the conflation of categorical domains is in itself the source of specific kinds of cultural logic, because the metaphors may have categorical implications which go beyond the experiential level. There are undoubtedly social metaphors which do transfer meanings from relations in the human world to relations with the non-human one, committing societies to specific trains of thought which transcend the experiential commonalities. In the next section, I will discuss two very different examples of this.

From animal masters to ecosystem services

Throughout northeastern North America, as in many other parts of the world, ethnographers have identified a pervasive inclination among pre-modern hunting peoples to project onto nature their own conceptions of society. Such cosmologies are particularly well documented among the hunting peoples of northern Asia and North America (cf. Hultkrantz 1961, Ingold 1986), but similar beliefs have been reported, for example from Amazonia (cf. Århem 1996). The various species of game animals are conceptualised as being organised into social groups similar to those of the hunters themselves, complete with leaders responsible for negotiations with human leaders. These supernatural leaders have been referred to, for example, as 'animal guardians' (Hultkrantz 1961), 'owners of the animals' (ibid.), 'lords of the animals' (Zerries 1987), 'animal masters' (Ingold 1986, ch. 10) or 'keepers of the game' (Martin 1978). They are often visualised as striking specimens of their species, by virtue of their size or (white) colour. Hunting is understood as a form of reciprocal exchange between human and animal societies, in which game animals agree to surrender to human hunters in exchange for sacrificial offerings and observances of specific rules relating to the treatment of their remains. The mutual prestations of animals and men are clearly modelled on the predominant principle of inter-group exchange in these societies. The relationship between human and animal communities could thus be said to be construed as one of 'balanced reciprocity' (cf. Sahlins 1972). The delicate pact between humans and animals is contingent on the fulfilment of mutual obligations, mediated by esoteric communication between human shamans and the animal masters.

In many pre-modern societies, we might add, the phenomenon of 'sacrifice' evokes similar ideas about balanced reciprocity between humans and non-human nature even in relation to (what Westerners perceive as) inanimate sources of livelihood, such as mountains. Thus, for instance, Taussig (1980: 224) reports how Andean peasant miners exchange gifts with the 'spirit owners' of their mines.

Before moving on to our second example, let us reiterate what the notion of animal masters is an example of. It represents a projection of a predominant principle of social exchange (here: reciprocal gift exchange) onto the realm of human-environmental relations. It is as if humans seeking guidance for behaviour in their uncertain negotiations with non-human nature have no recourse but to look to their experience of human social life. In these ecocosmologies, both the morphology (group structure) and physiology (exchange relations) of human society are extended into nature. In the process, familiar varieties of social personhood are also recognised in the behaviour of game animals. The latter are assumed to exhibit similar attitudes (resentfulness, indebtedness, etc.) as are regularly generated in the normal course of human affairs.

I will now turn to a very dissimilar social context, viz. the Institute for Ecological Economics in Solomons, Maryland, in the 1990's. Geographically we have not moved very far from the New England forests where the Passamaquoddy and other Algonquian hunters once negotiated with the masters of their game animals. But rather than the shamans of a tribe of hunter-gatherers, we are listening to the wisdom of scholars in the midst of an industrial society, published in an issue of *Nature*:

The services of ecological systems and the natural capital stocks that produce them are critical to the functioning of the Earth's life-support system. They contribute to human welfare, both directly and indirectly, and therefore represent part of the total economic value of the planet … For the entire biosphere, the value (most of which is outside the market) is estimated to be in the range of US$ 16-54 trillion (1012) per year, with an average of US$ 33 trillion per year (Costanza et al. 1997: 253).

Let us attend closely to this 'cultural text'. Clearly, like the Algonquian hunters, the authors are concerned about the sustainability of human-environmental relations. But there are several significant differences. Although non-human nature is still granted a kind of benevolent agency ('services', 'contribute'), it is no longer conceived as a personal agency. Nature has changed from a community of persons to a machine-like assemblage of things ('systems', 'produce', 'functioning'). Moreover, the perspective has shifted from the local to the global ('Earth's', 'planet'). Finally, and most intriguingly, the relations between humans and non-human nature are couched not in terms of reciprocal gift exchange but in the language of the market economy ('services', 'capital stocks', 'welfare', 'economic value', 'US$').

Perhaps none of these differences comes as a surprise to the reader, but I believe that they are worthy of reflection, for in their very differences the two groups reveal a fundamental commonality. We may observe that the Algonquian hunters and the modern scholars, in their different conceptualisations of nature, are pursuing a similar strategy. Both resort to their specific understandings of social exchange in order to construct the relation between humans and non-human nature. In their constructions of nature, furthermore, they reveal the different, basic modes of relating to the world that characterise the social contexts to which they are respectively accustomed. Where the pre-modern hunters concern themselves with concrete, contextualised subjects (cf. Shweder & Bourne 1984), the modern scholars visualise abstract, decontextualised objects. In this way, it could be argued, the two groups also project onto the natural world their different conceptions of the human person. Paradoxically, the ecological economists bring nature into the modern world of social interaction precisely by objectifying it. The experiential commonality that underlies their metaphorical conflation of nature and society is not interpersonal engagement, but detachment.

Yet, and this would no doubt surprise the ecological economists, according to the definition proposed by Descola (1992, 1996), their conceptual strategy – no less than that of the Algonquians – should be classified as an example of animism. Descola (1996: 88) defines animism as the use of 'the elementary categories structuring social life to organise, in conceptual terms, the relations between human beings and natural species'. This is precisely what the ecological economists are doing when couching the discussion of human-environmental relations in terms of 'natural capital', 'ecosystem services', 'environmental costs' and 'environmental debts'. Through a peculiar structural inversion, it seems that we should classify as 'animistic' the pricing of the world at US$ 33 trillion, or, to take another example, the 1992 Swedish estimate of its national, environmental debt at 260 billion crowns. It should be obvious that Descola's definition of animism is slightly beside the mark. Since the term refers to a 'subjectification' rather than to objectification, it only covers a particular kind of meaning transfer from society to nature.

Social metaphors applied to human-environmental relations can become problematic when used as guidance for ecological practice in times of environmental crisis. Martin (1978) has suggested that the complex of ideas about animal masters was largely responsible for the self-destructive response of the Algonquians to the encroachment of European fur traders. He posits that epidemics introduced by the Europeans, but thought to be inflicted on the Indians by the animal masters, unleashed a war of retaliation on the game animals, which merely aggravated the emaciation of these peoples by destroying their resource base. This is a highly unlikely explanation for the Indian role in depleting North American game stocks, and has been extensively criticised (cf. Krech 1981). The brunt of the responsibility must rather be borne by the European market cosmology which converted communities of animal kinsmen into abstract exchange values. The recursive ('positive feedback') structure of Martin's argument is more applicable to the market cosmology than to the (ecologically restraining) animal master complex which it displaced. Only by converting all things into abstract exchange value can the illusion be created that ecological deterioration may be alleviated by more of the same. This continues to be the alarming logic of human-environmental relations in the periphery of the world system, now as then. Money is simultaneously a measure of, and a (short-term) remedy for, the dissipation of resources.

Space, exchange and the self

In juxtaposing principles of exchange and modes of relating to non-human nature, we are advocating a renewed dialogue between economic and ecological anthropology. The relevance of fundamental economic principles such as 'reciprocity' and 'market', delineated by Karl Polanyi, obviously extends beyond the domain of human society into relations with other species. Descola (1992, 1996) and Pálsson (1996) have thus analysed different varieties of human-environmental relations in terms of different permutations of reciprocity. In this section, I would like to consider the spatial dimensions of the notion of 'nature', different principles of exchange, and personhood, as they relate to cultural constructions of human-environmental relations.

Ellen (1996: 104-5) has observed that concepts of 'nature' (or notions approximating it) are commonly defined in spatial terms, as 'some realm outside humans or their immediate living (cultural) space'. He suggests that the notion of nature as an external space is one of three 'cognitive axes or dimensions' which in various combinations generate specific models of nature. In this view, society and nature are concentrically arranged, with nature the more distant, a 'spatial other' (ibid., 120) defined in opposition to society. But Ellen also observes that 'very few languages have words which easily translate as "nature"' (ibid.), and Ingold (1996: 127-29, fig. 5.2) shows that the dichotomy of nature and society is quite alien to the worldview of hunter–gatherers.

It seems to me that the presence or absence of a concentric dualism of society versus nature would have implications for the principles of exchange that organise constructions of human-environmental relations in a particular society. My reason for speculating along these lines is that a similar, concentric arrangement organises Sahlins' (1972) analysis of generalised, balanced and negative reciprocity. The inner-most space is the realm of Malinowski's 'pure gift', for which 'an open stipulation of return would be unthinkable and unsociable' (ibid. 191). With increasing social distance, generalised reciprocity yields to balanced reciprocity, which involves a conscious reckoning with return, and finally negative reciprocity ('the unsociable extreme'), which means trying to 'get something for nothing' (ibid., 195). This continuum necessarily also has bearings on personhood. Contemplating the Maori hau, Mauss (1954 [1925]) observed that to extend a gift means extending something of one's own person (cf. also Munn 1986). Negative reciprocity, on the other hand, is 'the most impersonal sort of exchange' (Sahlins 1972: 195, italics added). The emergence of money, accordingly, most likely occurred in 'peripheral social sectors' (ibid. 229).

Towards the innermost end of the continuum, then, we have true sociability defined in terms of intimacy, gift-giving and personal trust; towards its outer end we have money, impersonality, avarice and – in societies such as the Western – an asocial 'nature'. Where non-human nature is conceptualised as external and opposed to society, as in the West, it seems unlikely that human-environmental relations should assume the sensitive and balanced form that so intrigues us in the ethnography of the Algonquians. In the Western conception, productive engagement with non-human species tends to be relegated to a marginal space where human sociability has been attenuated to the point where it is reduced to predation. (Western pets would seem an exception, but in having been incorporated into the most intimate spheres of society, they are neither the objects of productive engagement nor classified as belonging to 'nature'.) Among the Algonquians, on the other hand, humans and non-humans may apparently share the entire extent of the social continuum, without any concern for a dichotomy of society versus nature (Ingold 1996). It is thus quite feasible for these groups to experience closer kinship with local populations of beavers or moose than with neighbouring populations of humans, engaging with the former in compliance with the principle of balanced reciprocity while subjecting the latter to predation. Thus, for instance, the Recollect missionary Le Clercq (1910 [1691]: 276-77) reported that:

the [Micmac] Indians say that the Beavers have sense, and form a separate nation; and they say they would cease to make war upon these animals if these would speak, howsoever little, in order that they might learn whether the Beavers are among their friends or their enemies.

Other reports from the same period tell of seemingly unprovoked assaults on neighbouring (human) tribes (cf. Hoffman 1946: 643).

Sahlins' continuum of reciprocities suggests that, in modern society, the social space of gift-giving has contracted while the 'peripheral' domain of money transactions and negative reciprocity has imploded towards the shrinking, domestic bastions of the 'pure gift'. The readiness to give away their possessions is one of the features of the Algonquian hunting peoples that is most often commented upon by European visitors. Consider the early seventeenth century reflections of the French lawyer Lescarbot:

Our savages are praiseworthy in the exercise of this virtue [liberality], according to their poverty. For, as we have said before, when they visit one another they give mutual presents one to the other. And when some French Sagamos [leaders] cometh to them, they do the like with him, casting at his feet some bundle of beavers' or other furs, which be all their riches … This custom of the said savages proceedeth but from a liberal mind, and which hath some generosity. And, although they be very glad when the like is done unto them, yet so it falleth out that they begin the venture and put themselves in hazard to lose their merchandise. And who is he amongst us that doth more than they, that is to say which giveth but with intention to receive? … And for to show the gallantness of our said savages: they do not willingly cheapen, and do content themselves with that which is given them honestly with a willing mind, disdaining and blaming the fashions of our petty merchants, which be an hour a-cheapening for to buy a beaver-skin, as I saw being [done] at the River Saint John … that they called a young merchant of Saint Malo mercatoria, which is a word of reproach among them borrowed of the Basques, signifying, as it were, a haggling fellow. Finally, they have nothing in them but frankness and liberality in their exchanging. And, seeing the base manners of some of our men, they demanded sometimes what they came to seek for in their country, saying that they came not into ours; and, seeing that we are richer than they, we should give them liberally that which we have (Lescarbot 1928 [1609]: 262–3).

If the gift is indeed an extension of the person, this means that personhood has in a sense contracted along with it, yielding the 'atomistic' individual whom we tend to associate with modernity. In other words, and perhaps paradoxically, the more we have been implicated in global networks of market exchange, the less 'outreaching' have we become as persons. The notion of the person as something that can be more or less extended in space (and time) has an elaborate theoretical foundation in phenomenology and semiotics (cf. Relph 1976, Evernden 1985: 44–45, Singer 1984). Singer (1984: 3, 57) quotes C.S. Peirce's conclusion that 'each self has a distinctive and "outreaching identity", an "essence and a meaning subtile as may be" that is "the true and exact expression of the fact of sympathy, fellow-feeling – together with all unselfish interests, – and all that makes us feel that he has an absolute worth" '. According to Peirce, a 'man's circle of society (however widely or narrowly this phrase may be understood), is a sort of loosely compacted person, in some respects of higher rank than the person of an individual organism' (quoted in Singer 1984: 64). Singer concludes that:

Peirce's theory of personality and of personal identity has the important consequence that the self...is not identical with the individual organism. The self may be less or more than the individual organism, less when in the flow of time the inner dialogue brings a new phase of the self into life, and more when in dialogue with other organisms there emerges one loosely compacted person (ibid., 65).

Under these circumstances, personal identity is not confined to the consciousness of one's body, the 'box of flesh and blood', but extends as well to 'social consciousness', the consciousness of living others with whom one is in sympathetic communication … The boundaries of personal identity, in Peirce's theory, are somewhat indefinite and variable and depend on the social and cultural 'outreach' of a particular individual's consciousness.

Against the background of our argument so far, it is significant that the remedy for environmental problems advocated by the so-called 'deep ecology' movement should be an expansion of the human self:

Spiritual growth ... begins when we cease to understand or see ourselves as isolated and narrow competing egos and begin to identify with other humans and friends to, eventually, our species. But the deep ecology sense of self requires ... an identification which goes beyond humanity to include the non-human world (Devall & Sessions 1985: 67, quoted in Cheney 1989: 317, n. 69).

Cheney (1989) and Szerszynski (1996) express hesitation about this strategy, arguing that, like the similar ambition of the ancient Greek Stoics to identify with an abstract cosmos, it would imply an even deeper retreat into alienation. Hans Jonas writes: 'Grand and inspiring as [the Stoic] conception is, it must not be overlooked that it represented a position of retreat inasmuch as its appeal was addressed to a human subject that was no longer a part of anything except the universe ...' (quoted in Cheney 1989: 301). Cheney (1989: 300-2) posits a structural similarity between the metaphysics of Stoicism and deep ecology as reactions to the alienation resulting from, respectively, the fall of the Athenian city-state and the demise of Western modernity. In both cases, there is an attempt to retain a sense of abstract hegemony and 'containment of the other' when previous securities shatter into (Alexandrian and post-modern) 'worlds of difference'.

What needs to be recognised here is the difference between an abstract, verbal representation of embeddedness in the world, on the one hand, and the concrete phenomenology of the practice of such embeddedness, on the other. The epistemology of Spinoza, which has served as a major inspiration for deep ecology, appears to accommodate both possibilities. The former (abstraction) is evoked in Spinoza's ideal of 'seeing the universal in all the particulars of one's existence' (Cheney 1989: 321), the latter (phenomenology) in his ideal of 'direct intuitive knowledge of individual things' (Devall and Sessions 1985: 239-40, quoted in Cheney 1989: 306-7). The former is a product of intellectual reflection, whereas the latter evokes practical, bodily experience. Devall and Sessions appropriately continue by quoting Wittgenstein: 'What we cannot speak about we must pass over in silence.' The intellectual constructions of deep ecologists risk sharing with those of phenomenologists like Heidegger and Merleau-Ponty the fundamental contradiction posed by an excessive reflection over the bliss of non-reflective existence. It is one thing to posit an abstract, spiritual embeddedness in the world, another to practice embeddedness as concrete, bodily experience. The philosophy of deep ecology risks remaining a very Cartesian form of communion, an embeddedness of the mind but not of the body.

The duality of language and experience or mind and body reproduces the modern rift between abstract systems and local life-worlds. To see the specifics of our direct experience as instances of more general categories may at times be poetically inspiring but always risks detracting from the phenomenological depth of that particular experience. The pursuit of a renewed embeddedness would thus seem to have to involve something else than a cosmically expanded sense of identity. As Ingold (1993: 40) has observed, for instance, many of the global environmental problems may 'have their source in that very alienation of humanity from the world of which the notion of the global environment is a conspicuous expression'. The reestablishment of an ecologically more outreaching kind of personhood would need to be grounded not so much in abstract, Stoicist self-effacement as in the specifics of concrete, place-based practice, i.e. a reimmersion into what Ingold (ibid.) refers to as a local 'mode of apprehension' based on 'an active, perceptual engagement with components of the dwelt-in world, in the practical business of life'.

Characteristic of modernity is the movement from concrete and place-based to more abstract reference-points for identity construction. The pre-modern person is moored to specific faces, landscapes and artefacts, whereas the ideal-typically modern person is constituted in terms of abstract categories of people, spaces and commodities. The modern identification with abstract communities has tended to eclipse the identification with specific places (cf. Relph 1976), but the process may in some respects be reversible. The two structural options seem to open the person to completely different versions of the expanded Self: the anthropocentric cosmopolitan versus the ecocentric local. The deep ecology movement suggests a third possibility: the ecocentric cosmopolitan. But to identify oneself with an abstract, planetary whole, whether the human species or the biosphere, is not the same kind of self-expansion as the immersion into a local life-world. The difference between 'local' and 'global' is not a difference in scale, but in kind.

Conclusions

We have indicated how a series of transformations in human personhood may provide a theoretical link between principles of social exchange and varieties of human-environmental interaction. One conclusion might be that a reestablishment of relations of reciprocity with non-human nature is conceivable only in the practical engagement of complete persons in concrete places. The abstract concerns with global ecology, while undoubtedly justifiable in rational terms, might at another level be read as projections of human persons alienated from such embedment. The greatest challenge for environmental policy may be to find ways of transposing these concerns back into the specifics of human life-worlds without jeopardising the struggle for abstract human solidarities that is the hallmark of modernity. Social solidarity is global or it is nothing; reciprocal engagement with nature is local and personal or it is nothing. To bring these conclusions together into a single, socio-ecological equation would undoubtedly entail radical changes in the institutions that govern economic life. It would probably require some kind of institutional insulation of (more localised) subsistence practices vis-à-vis (global) communication flows, perhaps through the creation of separate markets or circulation spheres for goods and services pertaining to each sector.

The ecological economists have done us the service of estimating the price of our planet at US$ 33 trillion per year. These are the lengths to which we are prepared to go in order not to have to surrender the fetishised abstractions that rule our lives and jeopardise 'the Earth's life-support system'. But let us not despair. Beneath the jargon on underpaid 'ecosystem services' and mounting 'environmental debts', however convoluted and misleading it is as a literal understanding of environmental crisis, we may recognise an ancient concern with reciprocity, and an aspiration to bring non-human nature back into the community of humans.

REFERENCES

Århem, K. 1996. The Cosmic Food Web: Human-nature Relatedness in the Northwest Amazon. In *Nature and Society: Anthropological Perspectives*, P. Descola & G. Pálsson (eds.). London: Routledge, 185-204.

Bates, D.G. & S.H. Lees (eds.) 1996. *Case Studies in Human Ecology*. New York: Plenum.

Bateson, G. 1972. *Steps to an Ecology of Mind*. New York: Paladin.

Baudrillard, J. 1993 [1976]. *Symbolic Exchange and Death*. London: Sage.

Bernstein, R.J. 1983. *Beyond Objectivism and Relativism: Science, Hermeneutics and Praxis*. Philadelphia: University of Pennsylvania Press.

Bird, E.A.R. 1987. The Social Construction of Nature: Theoretical Approaches to the History of Environmental Problems. *Environmental Review* 11: 255-64.

Bird-David, N. 1992. Beyond 'The Original Affluent Society': A Culturalist Reformulation. *Current Anthropology* 33: 25–47.

Bourdieu, P. 1990. *The Logic of Practice*. London: Polity.

Cheney, J. 1989. The Neo-Stoicism of Radical Environmentalism. *Environmental Ethics* 11: 293–325.

Costanza, R., R. d'Arge, R. de Groot, S. Farber, M. Grasso, B. Hannon, K. Limburg, S. Naeem, R.V. O'Neill, J. Paruelo, R.G. Raskin, P. Sutton & M. van den Belt 1997. The Value of the World's Ecosystem Services and Natural Capital. *Nature* 387: 253–60.

Cronon, W. 1983. *Changes in the Land: Indians, Colonists, and the Ecology of New England*. Hill and Wang.

Descola, P. 1992. Societies of Nature and the Nature of Society. In *Conceptualizing Society*, A. Kuper (ed.). London: Routledge.

Descola, P. 1996. Constructing Natures: Symbolic Ecology and Social Practice. In *Nature and Society: Anthropological Perspectives*, P. Descola & G. Pálsson (eds.). London: Routledge, 82–102.

Devall, B. & G. Sessions 1985. *Deep Ecology: Living as if Nature Mattered*. Salt Lake City: Peregrine Smith.

Ellen, R.F. 1996. The Cognitive Geometry of Nature: A Contextual Approach. In *Nature and Society: Anthropological Perspectives*, P. Descola & G. Pálsson, (eds.). London: Routledge, 103–23.

Evernden, N. 1985. *The Natural Alien*. Toronto: University of Toronto Press.

Feit, H. 1973. The Ethno-ecology of the Waswanipi Cree: Or How Hunters Can Manage Their Resources. In *Cultural Ecology: Readings on the Canadian Indians and Eskimos*, B. Cox (ed.). Toronto: McClelland and Stewart, 115–25.

Giddens, A. 1990. *The Consequences of Modernity*. London: Polity.

Gudeman, S. 1986. *Economics as Culture: Models and Metaphors of Livelihood*. London: Routledge & Kegan Paul.

Hoffman, B.G. 1946. *The Historical Ethnography of the Micmac of the Sixteenth and Seventeenth Centuries*. Ph.D. Thesis, Department of Anthropology, University of California.

Hornborg, A. 1996. Ecology as Semiotics: Outlines of a Contextualist Paradigm for Human Ecology. In *Nature and Society: Anthropological Perspectives*, P. Descola & G. Pálsson, (eds.). London: Routledge, 45–62.

– 1998. Towards an Ecological Theory of Unequal Exchange: Articulating World System Theory and Ecological Economics. *Ecological Economics* 25(1): 127–36.

Horkheimer, M. & T. Adorno 1972 [1944]. *The Dialectic of Enlightenment*. New York: Herder & Herder.

Hultkrantz, A. (ed.) 1961. *The Supernatural Owners of Nature*. Stockholm, Goteborg and Uppsala: Almquist and Wiksell.

Ingerson, A.E. 1994. Tracking and Testing the Nature/Culture Dichotomy. In *Historical Ecology: Cultural Knowledge and Changing Landscapes*, C.L. Crumley (ed.). Santa Fe: School of American Research Press, 43-66.

Ingold, T. 1986. *The Appropriation of Nature: Essays on Human Ecology and Social Relations*. Manchester: Manchester University Press.

– 1993. Globes and Spheres: The Topology of Environmentalism. K. Milton, (ed.), *Environmentalism: The View from Anthropology*, 31-42. London: Routledge.

– 1996. Hunting and Gathering as Ways of Perceiving the Environment. R. Ellen & K. Fukui, (eds.), *Redefining Nature: Ecology, Culture and Domestication*. London: Berg, 117-55.

Jackson, M. 1983. Thinking through the Body: An Essay on Understanding Metaphor. *Social Analysis* 14: 127-48.

Krech, S., (ed.) 1981. *Indians, Animals and the Fur Trade*. Athens: University of Georgia Press.

Le Clercq, C. 1910 [1691]. *New Relation of Gaspesia with the Customs and Religion of the Gaspesian Indians*. Translated and edited by W.F. Ganong. Toronto: The Champlain Society.

Lescarbot, M. 1928 [1609]. *Nova Francia: A Description of Acadia, 1606*. Translated by P. Erondelle, 1609. London: George Routledge & Sons.

Martin, C. 1978. *Keepers of the Game: Indian-Animal Relationships and the Fur Trade*. Berkeley: University of California Press.

Maturana, H.R. & F.J. Varela 1992 [1987]. *The Tree of Knowledge: The Biological Roots of Human Understanding*. Boston: Shambhala.

Mauss, M. 1967 [1923-24]. *The Gift*. New York: Norton.

McEvoy, A.F. 1988. Toward an Interactive Theory of Nature and Culture: Ecology, Production, and Cognition in the California Fishing Industry. In *The Ends of the Earth: Perspectives on Modern Environmental History*, D. Worster (ed.). Cambridge: Cambridge University Press, 211-29.

Merchant, C. 1989. *Ecological Revolutions: Nature, Gender, and Science in New England*. Chapel Hill: University of North Carolina Press.

Munn, N. 1986. *The Fame of Gawa*. Cambridge: Cambridge University Press.

Pálsson, G. 1996. Human–environmental Relations: Orientalism, Paternalism and Communalism. In *Nature and Society: Anthropological Perspectives*, P. Descola & G. Pálsson (eds.). London: Routledge, 63-81.

Rappaport, R.A. 1993. Humanity's Evolution and Anthropology's Future. In *Assessing Cultural Anthropology*, R. Borofsky (ed.). New York: McGraw-Hill, 153-66.

Relph, E. 1976. *Place and Placelessness*. Pion.

Sahlins, M.D. 1972. *Stone Age Economics*. Chicago: Aldine.

– 1976. *Culture and Practical Reason*. Chicago: University of Chicago Press.

Shweder, R.A. & E.J. Bourne 1984. Does the Concept of the Person Vary Cross-culturally? In *Culture Theory: Essays on Mind, Self, and Emotion*, R.A. Shweder & R.A. LeVine (eds). Cambridge: Cambridge University Press.

Simmons, I.G. 1993. *Environmental History: A Concise Introduction*. London: Blackwell.

Singer, M. 1984. *Man's Glassy Essence: Explorations in Semiotic Anthropology*. Bloomington: Indiana University Press.

Steiner, D. 1993. Human Ecology as Transdisciplinary Science, and Science as Part of Human Ecology. In *Human Ecology: Fragments of Anti-Fragmentary Views of the World*, D. Steiner & M. Nauser (eds.). London: Routledge, 47-76.

Szerszynski, B. 1996. On Knowing What to Do: Environmentalism and the Modern Problematic. In *Risk, Environment and Modernity: Towards a New Ecology*, S. Lash, B. Szerszynski & B. Wynne (eds.). London: Sage, 104-37.

Taussig, M.T. 1980. *The Devil and Commodity Fetishism in South America*. Chapel Hill: The University of North Carolina Press.

von Uexküll, J. 1982 [1940]. The Theory of Meaning. *Semiotica* 42: 25-82.

Whorf, B.L. 1978 [1956]. The Relation of Habitual Thought and Behavior to Language. In *Language, Thought, and Reality*. Boston: MIT Press, 134-59.

Worster, D. 1988. Doing Environmental History. In *The Ends of the Earth: Perspectives on Modern Environmental History*, D. Worster (ed.). Cambridge: Cambridge University Press, 289-307.

Worster, D. 1993. Ecological History. In *Major Problems in American Environmental History*, C. Merchant (ed.). Lexington, MA: Health & Co., 2-9.

Zerries, O. 1987. Lord of the Animals. In *The Encyclopedia of Religion*, M. Eliade, (ed.). London: Macmillan.

Clashing cosmologies: Contrasting knowledge in the Greenlandic fishery

Andreas Roepstorff

Current worldwide discussions about management regimes for natural resources are increasingly focusing on forms of knowledge: for example on the discussion on scientific knowledge versus 'other' forms of knowledge (Inglis 1993; Scott 1996; Kalland this issue), be it 'local', 'indigenous', aboriginal, or users' knowledge. Many of these discussions have been highly politicised interactions between scientific specialists, administrators and locals. Knowledge has, in other words, become located at the 'inter-face' between the different actors ('faces') in the discourse (Roepstorff 2000). When 'knowledge' becomes more of a battleground than a field of mutual exchange, the pieces of knowledge exchanged may appear as politicised free-floating signifiers (see e.g. Agrawal 1995). This veils the fact that the pieces of knowledge discussed are normally derived from another interface: the interface between certain persons and groups and their environment, and therefore that there are important differences in what counts as knowledge and how this is constructed. I have previously suggested (Roepstorff 2000) that a study of the 'who, what and how' of knowledge may be a first step in understanding how conflicts over knowledge might conceal different conceptualisations of the very elements discussed. This chapter attempts to take this argument one step further. Based on a study of the fishery of Greenland halibut in Greenland, it demonstrates that different cosmologies are connected with the different forms of knowledge about the fish. Cosmology is here conceived as the conceptualisation of what is out there (an ontology), a method to validate and examine it (an epistemology) and a prescription for how people should ideally relate to it (an ethics).

The argument builds on case material gathered in Greenland during several fieldwork periods between 1996 and 1998, but its structure is not directly derived from the field. It is inspired by an analysis of a Greenlandic version of a common

Inuit myth. This reading is used as a tool to conceptualise a semantic topography where an epistemology of knowledge is interwoven with an ontology of nature and an ethics of the interaction with animals. This is unravelled as the hero in the narration travels back and forth between two phenomenologically different positions, a global and a spherical perspective respectively. Once this narrative space has been established, it is used to compare and contrast the phenomenological and cosmological position of the biologists and the fishers respectively in the current Greenlandic context. The choice of a 'mythical' framework is not meant to imply that in the Greenlandic reality people live out myths in their actions, or to imply that biologists or fishers subscribe to mythical explanations or rationales. Rather the choice is heuristic. The story, which is in itself interesting, establishes in an efficient way a cosmological, narrative universe: a phenomenological and semantic topography with a set of relations between people, animals and their doings and knowings. This topography is then used to discuss simplified versions of the perceptions and doings of the fishers and biologists respectively. Once they are established as permutations within a common scheme, it is easier to conceptualise the differences and understand why there are serious problems in the communication.

The Mother of the Sea

One of the best known mythological figures among Inuit is the Mother of the Sea. Known under different names such as Sedna and Nuliajuk (Central Canada, Boas 1888) Arnaqquassaaq, Sassuma Arnaa or Arnap Naalagaa (Western Greenland) or Ímap Ukûa (East Greenland), tales of this mythological being have been recorded in many versions from Alaska in the West to Greenland in the East (Boas 1901: 364) and since the first colonial encounters, the character has fascinated many missionaries, administrators and anthropologists. The story comes in many variations, and several attempts have been made to analyse versions of the myth in a comparative perspective, for example, as an expression of common Inuit ideas about the soul of man and animal (Boas 1901: 364-65), as an example of the structural elements in Inuit mythology (Savard 1970), interpreted in the light of the known ethnohistory of the Inuit (Holtved 1966/67), or as a source for early contacts between Inuit and Whites (Sonne 1990). These scholarly attempts to understand the semantics and historics of the myth seem to point in very different directions (for the most comprehensive review, see Sonne, op cit.).

Unaffected by the fact that the 'real' meaning of the myth is a disputed area among the specialists, the Mother of the Sea has been widely popularised in books, paintings, TV-shows and theatre-plays, and she is as an iconic figure probably the best known character in the Inuit mythology in Greenland today. The generalised version of the myth is a story of a girl, usually an orphan, who is expelled from the social order. She is thrown into the sea with her dog, and her fingers are cut off (Savard 1970; Sonne 1990) as she struggles to hold on to the boat. The fingers transform into various types of sea animals, whales, seals, etc. All these animals dwell with her in a house at the bottom of the sea. When the animals disappear from the visual world of the humans, it is because she retains them in her house as a punishment for different types of improper behaviour among the Inuit. The acts of impropriety conducted by humans somehow transform into dirt, which gathers in the hair of the Mother of the Sea. This infuriates her, and in order to get the animals back, a shaman or *angakkoq* has to embark on a trip to clean her hair. As a reward to the angakkoq, the Mother of the Sea releases the animals.

The version of the myth (Mathiassen 1904), which I focus on here, is found in one of Knud Rasmussen's lesser known myth collections.[1] It is one of the most detailed Greenlandic versions, and it is recorded relatively late in southwest Greenland, perhaps originating from recent immigrants from southeast Greenland (Birgitte Sonne, personal information).

A young orphan girl goes sailing in an umiak with her dog. The cox is an ill-tempered man, and he suddenly throws her overboard. As she tries to hold on to the gunwale, he cuts off her fingers with an axe in such manner that they fall into the sea. She loses her grip and sinks with the dog deeper and deeper. After an initial period of nausea the girl regains her consciousness and notices everything that happens on her way down. At the bottom of the sea she discovers four paths leading North, South, East and West respectively.[2] Heading out on the path to the West, she walks and walks until the promontories behind her are out of sight and only the inland mountains are visible. At this point, she discovers that she can take a bearing of all settlements all the way up to the North and all the way down to the South, and that nothing in the settlements can happen without her seeing it.

Here she builds a house with two rooms, one for herself and one for the animals of the sea. She places the dog on the roof. The girl and the dog grow at a fast rate. After a while the girl, who has grown up to be a woman, notices that in her sleep something nasty hits her face. It turns out to be all the waste discarded by humans in their settlements. This happened again and again and, in the end, her face swelled so much that she could not see out of her eyes, her hair was matted in refuse, a strong river gushed out of the house and the dog started barking furiously.

Finally, the angakkut (shamans) discovered that the girl who had drowned had become a powerful woman and the mistress of the sea animals: the fish, the birds and the seals. By a glance of the eyes she ruled over the animals and decided where they should swim. The shamans realised that everything that came from impure women stuck to her face and hair. This made her angry and she kept the animals of the sea away from the humans so they could not catch anything. Once, when the animals had as usual made themselves invisible, a shaman *Utarkaq* gathered his fellow villagers to tell them that he would go to clean the face of the lady of the sea …

Before we embark with *Utarkaq* on his journey to the bottom of the sea, let us analyse the semantic and physical topography of the narrative space set up by the story by following in detail the movements of the little girl. At first she sinks to the bottom of the sea. Here she finds paths leading in four directions, and she walks to the West, away from the coast, until she reaches a point from where she can see all settlements. In this Olympian position she sits as a somewhat pitiful personage, she has no fingers, and she is therefore unable to clean herself when all the waste from the settlements lands in her face and hair. She compensates, however, for her poor manual abilities with a strong gaze. This, together with her privileged position, allows her to know what is going on in all settlements. She furthermore uses her eyes to control the motions of the sea-animals living in her house, thereby deciding what the people may catch.

Topographically speaking, the world of the settlements and her dwelling are connected, she follows a continuous trajectory, and it is possible to see from one to the other. The movements of the animals of the sea – back and forth between the two places – further confirm the continuity between her dwelling and the settlements. The space is, however, not given direction by gravity since her vertical position is at the same time above and below the settlements. In terms of power and perception she overlooks them and the animals swim down the river from her house to the coast.[3] She is, however, below the sea, and in terms of the movement of pollution, she is also below as the dirt falls down on her head. Rather than moving in an orthogonal, physical space structured by gravity, our main character moves, in other words, in a curled semantic space where position is related to power and perception. The space delineates the life-world of the social, where people hunt and mate, from the home of the animals. This home is created by a person ostracised from the social world: an orphan with no one to take care of her (a classic motive in Inuit stories, e.g. (Qúpersimân 1982) or, in some versions, a girl who refuses to marry.[4]

Globes and spheres: Setting up a cosmology

How are we to understand a semantic topology as the one outlined by the story? Tim Ingold (1993) has suggested a contrast between two perceptions of the environment: the spherical and the global perspective (Figure 1), that can help to give meaning to this peculiar space. His distinction is inspired by Ann Fienup-Riordan's writings about the pre-modern cosmology of the Yu'pik eskimos (Fienup-Riordan 1990), that shares many traits with the traditional cosmology of the Greenlandic Inuits.

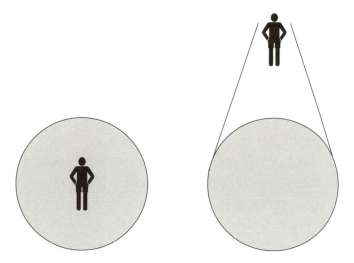

Figure 1: Two perspectives on the environment, redrawn from Ingold 1993

In a spherical perspective, Ingold suggests, the human being is set in the middle of a universe that extends outwards in a set of rings and spheres. In this perspective, the human is always embedded in the middle of a world that reveals itself through an interaction with its inborn structures, rather than through direct perception. In the global perspective, the world is constituted as an object apart from the human beings that can be studied independently. This means that the lifeworld, imagined from an experiental centre, is spherical in form, whereas a world divorced from life, that is yet complete in itself, is imagined in the form of a globe (Ingold 1993: 35).

The properties of the global perspective are very similar to the definition of reality and objectivity put forward by Thomas Nagel in his influential essay on (scientific) knowledge, *The view from Nowhere,* where 'we may think of reality as a set of concentric spheres, progressively revealed as we detach gradually from the contingencies of the self' (Nagel 1986: 5). This is an understanding of reality in which '[t]o acquire a more objective understanding of some aspect of life or the world, we step back from our initial view of it and form a new conception which has the view and its relation to the world as its object' (op.cit: 4). This conception of objectivity is, according to Nagel, inspired by standard notions in physics where '[t]he physical world as it is supposed to be in itself contains no points of view and nothing that can appear only to a particular point of view. Whatever it contains can be apprehended by a general rational consciousness that gets its information through whichever perceptual point of view it happens to view the world from' (op.cit: 14-15). This ideal of a potentially completely centreless and detached point of view as a prerequisite for objectivity underlies Nagel's suggestive title. The path to objectivity is in this conception derived from physics described metaphorically as a physical movement of detachment: a stepping out through the spheres to get a view that becomes less and less subjective, less and less bound to a particular standpoint. This understanding of objective knowledge is not only a view from nowhere, it is also an 'epistemology without a knowing subject' (Popper 1972: 106-53)

Ingold finds the spherical perspective typical of pre-modern thinking as it is exemplified by the Yup'ik Inuit cosmology outlined by Fienup-Riordan, but it can also be found in other pre-modern societies, for example in Renaissance Europe. He suggests, however, that sometime during modernity, 'something' happened that caused a change so the world came to be understood in a global perspective. This movement from spherical to global imagery is one in which 'the world' is drawn away from the matrix of our lived experiences (Ingold 1993). This marked, he claims, a change from cosmology to technology:

Cosmology provides the guiding principles for human action *within* the world; technology provides the principle for acting upon it. Thus, as cosmology gives way to technology, the relation between people and the world is turned inside out [fig. 1.b], so that what was a cosmos or lifeworld becomes a world – a solid globe – externally presented to life. In short, the movement from spherical to global imagery corresponds to the undermining of cosmological certainties and the growing belief in, and indeed dependence upon, the technological fix. It is a movement from revelation to control, and from partial knowledge to the calculated risk (op.cit: 41).

Ingold's analysis of the properties in the two perspectives, the spherical and the global, is imaginative and inspiring. It appears to suggest at least two different forms of knowing, each deriving its characteristics from a particular set of metaphors. One of them, the global, is based on detachment and visual perception. The other one, the spherical, is based on involvement and engagement, like knowing another person, his tastes, moods and idiosyncrasies (Ingold 1994: 16-17) and we shall shortly return to this fruitful distinction.[5] The analysis is, however, not convincing when Ingold historicises the phenomenology by stating a before (spherical) and an after (global). This analysis parallels one of the most powerful origin myths about modernity: Once the world was full of meaning and coherence, cosmology, but then 'something' happened, the world lost its meaning and inner coherence, and it became the way we know it today: namely technological and modern. This is a very powerful narration of decay and decadence that properly found its most powerful spokesman in Heidegger (Latour 1999: 195, 211). It is, however, not one that should just be accepted at face value (Latour 1999: 174-214). Let us therefore see how well it fits with the story just outlined.

It is tempting to identify in it the phenomenological positions outlined by Ingold. The story of the Mother of the Sea is told in the villages on the coast, and if we should follow Ingold this is at the centre of a spherical universe. Here, the angakkut have discovered the existence of a powerful entity. She is described as a person who has chosen to build a house on a particular point from where it is possible to overlook all the villages along the coast and to see/know what is going on. In other words, she is physically detached from the settlements, and she does not participate directly in the life there. On the contrary she originated as someone who did not belong properly to the social order. She is therefore a person that already from the start of the story was divorced from the life in the settlements where the story is told. She does, however, see/know this from the distance with the same gaze that gives her control over the resources that life depends on. This part of the story, therefore, appears to describe in detail how the ruler of the sea animals came to reside in a place that – relative to the settlements – fits Ingold's description of the global perspective: Phenomenologically and epistemologically she is outside in the all-perceiving distance and semantically and socially she is outside the social life understood as the actual unfolding of exchanges, hunting and procreation. This is furthermore a position that gives her a perspective reminiscent of Nagel's ideal of the objective standpoint: detached from the concrete human reality and so far away that she may oversee every village at once. With this metaphor at hand let us then follow Utarkaq on his journey.

Utarkaqs journey

As every proper hero, *Utarkaq* sets out to solve a problem. The animals have made themselves invisible, but when he travels under the sea to a place from whence his normal world may be overlooked, and in that place solves some problems, the animals can be made to reappear. On one level the myth therefore deals with the relationship between the visible animals that are available for hunting, and the invisible animals. However, in a hunting society, this is in a hunting society just one version of how to deal with life and death.

Utarkaq begins his travel with a drum-dance in a hut surrounded by his fellow villagers. From this centre in the life-world he jumps out of the window runs to the beach and jumps through the ice. As he gets to the bottom, he moves against the current of the fierce river until he comes to the house of the Mother of the sea. There he finds a large woman with a face so swollen she cannot see anything. After a fierce fight, he manages to clean her of all the dirt from impure women. When he is finished, she tells him that she will repay his friendliness:

She opened the curtain to the room beside her living room. When she opened the curtain, a young, smiling couple came tripping out, but as they went into the midpassage out of the house, Utarkaq could recognise the tail feathers of the guillemot. They were of course birds in human form that lived in her house, and as they went out, they became birds again. In this way, she released all the seabirds into the corridor. When all the birds had passed, a tiny man with a round face and dotted coat came out. He went smiling down the mid passage, and one could see a pair of seal flippers disappear into the river. He was followed by his wife and children. They were followed by another man in fine, dark clothes with tiny white patterns.

He went down the corridor and one could see the flippers of a common seal and after him came a big, heavy man in red clothes. He had a running nose and constantly wiped it as he went into the corridor. When he jumped into the river, *Utarkaq* saw that it was a walrus. In that way, the mother of the sea released all kinds of seabirds and animals.

When all the animals were released, the Mother of the Sea told *Utarkaq* that the next day, all kinds of birds and prey would appear at the settlement. That day, however, people should not go hunting. The following day the ice would disappear, and the people could go hunting, but all catch should be given to *Utarkaq*. The angak-koq then returns to his settlement and everything happens the way the Mother of the Sea foretold.

Seen from the centre of the cottage where *Utarkaq* begins his journey, he has moved out through the spheres to a very different position: a point from where his normal life world (of women and prey) appears to the Mother of the Sea as a distant object with which she can only interact through vision. Relative to his 'normal' social world, *Utarkaq* is, in other words, in a global position, at least this is the perspective that the Mother of the Sea takes on his world. In this position, however, *Utarkaq* finds another world structured just as his own: an angry, dirty woman who needs to be cleaned, living in a familiar house together with other couples. In other words, the contrast here is not only different perspectives, the global and the spherical, but also different types of knowledge. The knowledge possessed by the Mother of the Sea is bound to her vision, as is her power. *Utarkaq* has, however, to rely on a very different form of knowing, he has to rely on knowing the Mother of the Sea like a person (Ingold 1994: 16-17; Roepstorff 1999a) i.e., her mood (she is angry) her taste (she does not like to be dirty) and idiosyncrasies (she wants to fight him when he approaches). This aspect of knowing and doing, which demands engagement and attachment, is central for *Utarkaq's* success, but the myth does not mention whether *Utarkaq* gets the detached visual knowledge/power that the Mother of the Sea possesses, this does not appear to be an issue at all.

In the (life)world of the Mother of the Sea the animals appear as humans, but as they exit her world and enter *Utarkaq's* normal world, they appear as prey. In this way the story explains why prey are sometimes visible and thereby huntable, at other times invisible. Animals do not disappear, they rather withdraw to their home which, relative to the human settlement is a global, olympian point. Here the animals take on their other appearance: that of humans. An iconic similarity in figure and behaviour connects their animal existence in the domain of the villages and the human existence in the house of the Mother of the Sea.

The story appears to say that behind the plurality – both in species and abundance – which is visible in the normal human sphere, is another reality. Paralleling the apparent difference between humans and animals is a similarity, and paralleling the apparent plurality of many specimens of the same species lies a singularity, since in the world of the Mother of the Sea both distinctions are reduced to families of humans each resembling an animal. This is an ontology of nature, where nature is understood pragmatically as that which, at first glance, is not human.

In the position that appears as global relative to the world of the people, *Utarkaq* discovers that this is really just another version of the known, local world. His trip helps him to discover why the animals make themselves impossible to catch. The withdrawal is triggered by symbolic pollution imposed on the global point by ignorant people, women in particular.[6]

This ethic, dealing with pollution, and the ontology of nature, dealing with the availability of prey, are locked together in a necessary but difficult exchange. The fingerless Mother of the Sea with the powerful gaze, whose fingers gave flesh to the animals and whose gaze controls them, may be handled by the angakkoq, the only one who is able to clean her. The people, on the other hand, depend entirely on the animals, but the availability of the animals is connected to social behaviour: i.e., whether people behave properly in their interactions with matter and with each other. Phrased in 'modern' terms, the myth outlines and connects the ontology of animals with the social ethics of people. Break a rule, and the animals will make themselves invisible, behave, and there will be plenty of them.

Although the activity of people is related to availability of prey, there is no direct relationship between the hunt and the amount of animals available. Rather, the interaction is mediated via the social: the adherence to rules, norms and taboos. *Utarkaq* is of course central to the story. He travels back and forth from the spherical social life world into what appears as a global point, just to discover another version of the known, spherical world. This appears to be a very different conception of reality than the one outlined above by Nagel where 'we may think of reality as a set of concentric spheres, progressively revealed as we detach gradually from the contingencies of the self' (Nagel 1986: 5) and where proper (i.e. objective) knowledge is obtained by detachment.

Utarkaq, however, is a doing and knowing person who mediates between the global position of the distant perception and action of the Mother of the Sea (both ascribed to her vision and topographical position) and the practical knowing and doing of people in a life world that is based on action, movement and physical manipulation. It is precisely his knowing the Mother of the Sea as a person, and his ability to act accordingly — i.e., clean her after a fierce fight — that restores order, purity and abundance. In my interpretation the story therefore outlines a cosmology that relates such serious matters as the ontology of nature the phenomenology of knowledge and the social ethics. To paraphrase Bruno Latour (1993) the myth connects phenomena that are *real like nature, narrated like discourse, collective like society and existential like being;* and in the end it is — as all good narratives — about the local and the global, and about life and death.

Following Ingold's analysis, this story indeed outlines a cosmology since it provides some guiding principles for human action *within* the world. However, it does not appear to obtain this by sticking to the spherical perspective alone. On the contrary, it is the interplay between these perspectives, as they are unfolded in the movements and doings of the narrative persons, that establishes the cosmology. This could suggest that rather than being instances of two stages that follow each other in a historical development, the global and the spherical perspectives represent two types of phenomenological stances that are present and possible in the modern as well as in the pre-modern situation. Equipped with this working hypothesis, let us make a mental shift from the universe of *Utarkaq* and the Mother of the Sea in old and partly forgotten narratives to a few localities in Greenland in the late 1990s.

Biologists and the virtual stock

Since the turn of the 19th Century the Greenland halibut fishery has had its centre in the small town of Ilulissat in North Greenland where the enormous Jakobshavn Glacier, the largest in the Northern Hemisphere, creates optimal conditions for the fish in and around the deep fjord that lies between the glacier and Disko Bay. The fishery is highly sophisticated, and despite being relatively low-tech is very effective. From the middle of the 1980s onwards there was a steady increase in catches of this fish and it became — and still is — the second most important export product in the Greenlandic economy. At the same time a new area, the ice-fjord Torsukattak, further north, was opened for fishery for the Ilulissat fishermen, and new technologies, gill nets, were introduced (Roepstorff 1998; Roepstorff 2000; Simonsen & Roepstorff 2000). To some observers, however, the development was rather alarming, and the biologists at the Greenland Institute of Natural Resources were asked by the Greenland Home Rule authorities to evaluate the sustainability of the fishery. In a complicated epistemological development, these investigations created an interesting phenomenon: the 'virtual stock' of Greenland Halibut in Disko Bay. It was an attempt to define and characterise mathematically the behaviour and number of fish in Disko Bay. As described elsewhere (Roepstorff 1998) this notion was a hybrid between the mathematically describable (or narratable), biological assumptions (some of which appeared better founded than others), and political pressures (to establish firm knowledge that could be implemented). The concept slipped more or less out of the hands of the biologists, and it lived a life in a network between these biologists who created it, the politicians who used it as a rationale for the implementation of new legislation, and the fishers who disagreed with the whole concept. As such it is a knowledge phenomenon like so many others described by anthropologists of science, that at the same time is *real* like nature, *narrated* like discourse, *collective* like society and *existential* like being (Latour 1993; see Roepstorff 1999b, 2000, for a discussion).

Similar to the findings of Ian Hacking regarding certain transitory mental illnesses (Hacking 1998), the stock's mode of existence can best be understood in relation to the particular 'conceptual ecological niche' that forms and informs it and allows it to proliferate. As with real species, unless it manages to adapt, the concept goes extinct once the niche disappears, and it survives only in the works of historians, anthropologists and the like. Many things indicate that the conceptual niche in which the virtual stock of Greenland Halibut lives has already changed (Boje 1999; Simonsen & Roepstorff 2000), and the following analysis therefore describes a very young but already historical process rather than the actual state. This does not mean, however, that traces of the past cannot be found in the present.

The report that created the virtual stock of Greenland halibut in the Disko Bay (Boje 1993), contained some very serious conclusions, namely that if catches were maintained at the same level as in 1992 (6,000 tons), the total biomass of Greenland halibut would decrease from 30,000 tons in 1991 to 10,000 tons in 1998. In other words, the stock appeared to be threatened by overfishing. This is indeed a serious story which calls for heroic action in management and regulation.

The sombre predictions were based on a so-called 'Virtual Population Analysis' that attempted to put numbers on the total amount of fish in the local stock and follow their destiny through a lifetime. Of course, in order to carry out such an analysis, one has to give identity to the stock. It should – somewhat like a nation-state – consist of a community of relatively homogenous individuals, statistically describable and clearly distinct from other such entities. In other words, they should form what could be called an 'imagined community', but contrary to Anderson's (1991) imagined communities, they were not imagined in the minds of the members of the communities – the fish – but only in the minds of the describing biologists (see also General Introduction, this volume). Through a series of technical papers written in the 1980s and 1990s the hypothesis was put forward that the fish would swim into the area as young specimens from the spawning grounds, enter the fjords and grow larger and larger until they died of age or predation, in this context mainly fishery.

These papers gave the biologists a well defined community of fish, visible from a hypothetical, global viewpoint and – at least in principle – countable. The next step was to establish ways to describe the 'natural' development of the fish where natural is understood as migration, growth and mortality without human interference. Seen from a global perspective, such things do exist in theory. It is extremely difficult, however, to calculate it in praxis, but since this stock was an imagined community, in itself well-defined but comparable to other similar ones, what was more natural than to import such formula from other, similar simulations conducted elsewhere. If one 'knows' how many fish enter, how they grow, and when they die naturally, only one variable is left: death due to fishery. This variable could be obtained relatively easily from the highly reliable Greenlandic landing statistics. The system modelled was, in other words, one where fixed amounts of fish arrive in a certain area every year. They stay in that area until they die, either of natural causes – which a fixed fraction does every year – or because they are fished. The only proper variable left in the simulation is then the total fishing mortality, which is proportional to the total size of the catches. It is no wonder then, that after catch levels increased, as they did through the late 1980s, these simulations showed some extremely sombre results.

Read as a story, the report created a narrative about a *character,* the stock of fish, valuable to the society and threatened by 'overfishing'. Like the story about the Mother of the Sea it connects an ontology of nature with ethics and with a phenomenology of knowledge. Behind the single fish caught is a potentially countable meta-individual 'the stock'. This stock is in itself an entity definable as the simple sum of its parts. One fish out of the water is therefore one fish less in the stock. In the logic of the mathematical models, it is possible to calculate a hypothetical maximum with the most efficient relation between fishing efforts and catch level output. This maximum is, however, threatened by the fishers who are so busy that they 'overfish' the stock, thereby potentially diminishing the returns in a classical 'tragedy of the commons' (Feeny et al. 1990; Hardin 1968). The fate of the stock is, however, not only a matter for the biologists. Contemporary Greenland is increasingly emerging as a modern nation state (Dahl 2000: 253-60): an imagined community (Anderson 1991) that unites in one perspective all Greenlanders and all of Greenland. As a consequence of this, the stock is considered as belonging to the Greenlandic community in general and it is important to harvest it in such a way that the *output* to the society is maximised and the input minimised. The output of the fishing is therefore closely linked to social ethics, but this set of ethics is not, however, linked to any concrete individual. It does not matter to the biological models who does the fishing, the ethics concerns solely the relationship between one imagined community the 'Greenlandic community' and another imagined community 'the stock' where the members of a third imagined community 'the fishers' are caught in a complicated logic of exchange: on the one hand, it is their actions that transform the stock into actual fish that can be exchanged for money. On the other hand, it is their actions that threaten the integrity of the same stock.

The knowledge about as well the fish as the fishermen centres on concepts – the stock and overfishing – that are both 'global'. By this I mean that they are in principle determinable to an all-knowing subject, located at a point from whence one can survey the whole coast and all the villages at the same time. One may thereby count all the fish and see all the consequences of the fishery. Ideally, these concepts are therefore determinable as a view from nowhere in particular (Nagel, 1986), as knowledge without a knowing subject (Popper, 1972). In practice, however, this knowledge is not so easily acquired and the biologists need to leave the global position at the Institute of Natural Resources and enter the field to get data from both their own and the fishers' catches. These concrete, individual fish are then interpreted to be representative of the generalised stock which is behind the single fish, but only visible from the global position.

This global position is more than just a metaphor. Physically the relevant Home Rule administration and the Institute of Natural Resources are located in the capital, Nuuk, far away from the fishing grounds. Ideally, as one employee in Home

Rule administration expressed it, all information from along the coast is channelled there, so that it is possible at one and the same time to gather knowledge from the whole coast and get a broader perspective on local phenomena. In an almost ironic twist to this analysis, the newly built Greenland Institute of Natural Resources is furthermore physically built on a hill outside and partly overlooking the city of Nuuk – global not only relative to the villages along the coast but also relative to the political and administrative centre. Although the institute and the Home Rule administration may appear as 'global' – at least seen from the towns on the coast – they are of only global relative to the villages. In themselves they form local worlds of their own. The global perspective refers, in other words, to one phenomenological stance – one relationship among others to the world, rather than to an absolute, historically set condition. This was, indeed, the discovery of *Utarkaq*.

The fishers and the fish

The concepts central to a biological management of fish, namely overfishing and stock, have been notoriously difficult to communicate into Greenlandic. One of the reasons is of course the language barrier between the biologists who are mainly Danish speaking and the fishers who are mainly Greenlandic speaking. The difference is, however, not just a matter of finding the right words. It is also a question of communicating between semantic spheres that connect the 'same' words to different basic understandings. In parallel with the readings of the Mother of the Sea story and the reading of the virtual stock papers above, the concepts form yet another semantic set that integrates an ontology of nature, an epistemology of knowledge and an ethics of resource use.

I have described elsewhere in more detail (Roepstorff 2000) how the notion of the fish commonly found among the fishers is very different from the relation between the fish and the stock as a part-whole relation found in the stock estimates. Rather, the fishers usually talk about the fish – in singular and in plural – in the same way: A fish is a living and sensate being with specific habits and behaviours, an animal which, like other animals, follows its prey, avoids its enemies and has specific routes and migrational patterns. At times it may be present in large numbers, at other times it may completely disappear. In other words, behind the visible fish that is caught there is a 'general fish' whose character and behaviour one tries to understand. This ontology of the fish resembles the description of the human couple behind the prey as described in the Mother of the Sea myth, and knowledge about the fish is mainly assembled as if it were a person-like entity whose idiosyncrasies and habits one should know.

This general fish is therefore not an object, it is rather a living organism, a non-human person (Fienup-Riordan 1990: 167), and like getting to know persons, one gets to know the fish by interacting and engaging with it. One aspect of this understanding of animals as non-human persons is that they, like humans, acquire particular knowledge about their environment, knowledge that the hunter may access by engaging with the animals. If the Greenland Halibut suddenly disappears, it can, for instance, indicate that the Beluga whale, a common predator, has arrived. Similarly, fishing near major icebergs is considered relatively safe if there are seals around, but if the seals suddenly disappear it can be a sign that the iceberg is about to break up and that people ought get away as well. This emphasis on general behaviour is reflected in an impressive amount of knowledge about specific patterns in the availability of the fish. These patterns are discussed on many time scales, from different times of the day and different seasons, to decennial variations, where some draw on experiences from two generations. Similar findings on the forms of knowledge of fish common among the fishers have also been found in other studies on local environmental knowledge in Greenland (H.C. Petersen, personal information). Hitherto, these patterns have to a large extent been unknown to the biologists that only recently have become aware of the extent of spatial and temporal variability (Boje 1999; Simonsen & Roepstorff 2000; Roepstorff 2000).

Apart from the many differences in practice between the fishers and the biologists, both groups see the fish not only as a single entity or as a source of money, the fish is also interpreted as a knowledge object that points to a more general reality than the immediate visible fish. There are, however, some important differences as to what is the nature of this underlying reality.

To the biologist doing a stock analysis, the concrete fish is seen as an index of the stock, an abstract but ideally quantifiable entity. In terms of space, this abstract entity is localised within certain boundaries, but in this area it is 'smeared out' and omnipresent, so that the random samplings of the catches can create a representation of the totality. This entity is seen as changing over time in terms of abundancy and age composition, and the aim of the research is to determine changes over time on a yearly basis, rather than spatial variations.

For the fishers the generalised fish 'behind the fish' appears not to be seen as omnipresent within a confined space. Rather they see it as omnipresent in time, as something that extends back in time, has always been there, and has always been characterised by self-development and a certain unpredictability. This difference is best interpreted as related to different practical ontologies of the fish. This difference between the biologists' quantitative notion of the stock and the fishers' person-like perception of the fish, collides in the language where a common translation of Greenland halibut stock into Greenlandic is *qaleqassusseq*. Literally translated this means something like: 'the existence of Greenland halibut', a qualitative notion very different from the inherently quantitative stock (see Roepstorff 2000, for a discussion of this problématique).

The different ontologies are connected to different epistemological ideals. The fishers' most common accusation against biologists is that the latter do not engage in the constant interaction necessary to understand 'the nature of the fish'. Hence their knowledge is considered thoroughly partial, because they do not see the systematic – but unpredictable – variations in availability that underlies their samplings. The biologists are typically accused of fishing in places where 'everybody' knows there are no fish; of arriving at fishing grounds when the fish have just left; or of fishing with rotten bait, something that every fisher knows will scare the fish away. Conversely, many biologists have in interviews demonstrated a deeply grounded scepticism towards fishers' knowledge, typically for one of two reasons. Either the fishers are considered to be too personally involved in the fishery to be objective witnesses, or their knowledge is considered thoroughly partial since it is derived from one particular location only and does not take the greater perspective into account. When one moves back and forth between the fishers and the biologists, none of the criticism appears entirely fair. But the actual criticism supports the identification of two very different understandings of the fish that are coupled to very different epistemological ideals. On the one hand the fish as a living being that is best understood through constant interactions – an understanding that is compatible with a spherical phenomenology; on the other hand, the fish as an exemplar of a quantifiable stock that has to be dispassionately estimated – an understanding that favours a global phenomenology.

Turning to the other central notion in the discourse on fish management, overfishing, we see an almost parallel clash of understandings. In a very interesting article (Kristensen 1998) a prominent fisher from Ilulissat tries to explain how he understands the present state of the fish and the fishery. He describes in detail how the fish in the Torsukattak ice-fjord have become fewer and smaller, and therefore the fishers need to fish more intensively to get the same catch. This seems a perfect example of overfishing, and this is something the biologists have for years warned against in this particular fjord (Boje 1993; Riget & Boje 1987). But in Kristensen's account, the story has a semantic twist. As stated above, overfishing of a stock is a technical term that signifies that the stock could be 'harvested' more efficiently (more yield per effort), if the fishing pressure is reduced. Who exactly does the fishing is not relevant to the concept in itself. Now, according to Kristensen (and confirmed by other informants), the word used in Greenlandic for overfishing, aalisapilunneq, means something very different. It is an abstract noun related to aalisapilutoq, denoting – in a strongly reproachable manner – someone who fishes more than he needs. To be accused of aalisapilunneq is therefore to be accused of violating one of the most basic rules in the exchange with animals: namely to take more than one needs, and that is a serious insult. Even though the fishers in Torsukattak are so efficient that Kristensen describes a clear case of overfishing in the biological sense, they are not committing aalisapilunneq in the Greenlandic sense because they do not take more than they need.

Aalisapilunneq in Greenlandic is, in other words, a moral concept related directly to a person; it is not, as 'overfishing', related to a stock as an abstract entity out there. As was the case with the relation between 'the stock' and qaleqaleqassusseq, we see in the relation between 'overfishing' and aalisapilunneq a conflict between two very different phenomenological perceptions. Like 'the stock', overfishing makes sense only from a global perspective, and like qaleqaleqassusseq, aalisapilunneq is a word connected to a spherical perception where fish come and go at certain periods, but where discussions on ethical behaviour and accusations of doing the wrong thing is a constant part of life. This suggests, therefore, that the ethic which connects people to the fishing is not in itself related to the fish, it is social throughout. This understanding has elements of the ethics outlined in the Mother of the Sea story, in that there is hardly a direct ethical relation to the animal conceived as a quantifiable notion. Behind the fish is a generalised fish that is sometimes present, at other times withdrawn. In the Mother of the Sea story, the absence of animals was triggered by the wrong doings of the people, thereby connecting the actions of the people with the actions of the animals. This link is difficult to identify in the rhetoric of the fishery today. When the question of overfishing becomes phrased in terms of aalisapilunneq, the ethical dilemma becomes phrased in terms of the fulfilment of needs rather than the adherence to symbolic rules of purity. It is not, however, about the maximisation of the output to society, as with overfishing, but rather about the needs of the individual fisherman.

A similar accusation against the fishers, that they are simply modern capitalists, more concerned with the fulfilment of their own needs than with the long-term well-being of society, can be heard from other members of the community. The fishers can rightly respond, however, that their needs, in a reality of taxes and mortgages on houses and boats, are not limited and that they therefore are not guilty of *aalisapilunneq*. Within the fishing community itself, however, the issue is more complicated, and several fishers would express strong disapproval of the acts of other fishers on grounds that are compatible with *aalisapilutoq* as a central derogatory term. These discussions appear to be variations of the 'need' theme, but different from the abstract *aalisapilunneq*. This is seen, for instance, in discussions about who should be allowed to fish commercially. The standing argument among fishers is that only full-time fishers should have this prerogative since they are the ones who need the fish. There is criticism of certain types of fishing that may damage fish and render them useless for consumption. This is expressed as a strong ethical disapproval of taking something that is not used. There are also vigorous discussions about which types of fishing gear should be allowed, and where. These discussions are not phrased as an attempt to limit the total catches, as is the purpose of the imposition of quota and other 'global' regulations. It is, rather, a discussion about who should be allowed to fish and *where*, and *how*, the fishery may take place. I have, however, seldom heard this phrased in terms of 'overfishing' in the biological sense, i.e. taking more of an abstract finite resource than it can economically sustain.

Conclusion

Most of this chapter has unfolded stories and narratives, but it is an attempt to understand concrete people in concrete situations. First of all to describe how fishers and biologists in various ways make sense of the extraordinary natural phenomena, the richness of the Greenland halibut fishery in the deep ice-fjords of West Greenland. Secondly to explain the basis for the frequent misunderstandings between biologists, administrators and fishers, where one part talks of stocks and overfishing, while the other speaks of *qaleqaleqassusseq* and *aalisapilunneq*.

Hopefully, the semantic and cosmological conflicts outlined in this chapter appear quite straightforward. In the Greenlandic context, however, they are not so easy to identify. When conducting interviews mediated by excellent interpreters and in studying with bilingual newspaper articles, the translation runs smoothly back and forth between the Greenlandic and the Danish versions. Only when these are carefully compared does it become clear that although the two versions of the same text, or the same interview, both talk about fish, fishers and how they should interact, they do so in very different ways. It takes, in other words, much basic semantic work on exact wordings and metaphors before it becomes obvious that the apparently seamless interpretations connect to very different conceptual domains; two different cosmologies. This communicative situation in Greenland might be an extreme one. Greenland has developed into a highly complicated post-colonial setting, where many of the former colonial administrative and power structures have been taken over by a highly centralised administration in the capital Nuuk. An administration that relies to a large extent on young Danish-educated and Danish-speaking specialists who take a few years in Greenland as part of their career trajectory. As a consequence the ruling strata of society seem to an increasing degree to develop into a hybrid between the colonial and the local, the 'Greenlandic' and the 'Danish', the Greenlandic political and administrative elite, many of whom are educated in Denmark, and the Danish professionals. This means that differences between the centre and the periphery – to an even larger extent than in 'normal' modernised societies – are also a matter of cultural and linguistic differences.

The point of departure of this paper was a reading of a Greenlandic myth that defined a cosmology which interrelated a spherical and a global phenomenology. By separating 'nature', 'society' and 'knowledge' as different domains connected by the story, I have made a 'modern' (Latour 1993) reading, since I separate the world into different independent domains that the story claims to connect rather than separate. I then outlined how the fishers and the biologists working with Greenland halibut in Greenland perceive and interact very differently with the species. Here the same three domains re-occur in different configurations in the biological reports and practices and in the narratives and practices of local fishermen. In other words the three 'semantic universes' or 'cosmologies' all connect the social and the natural, the narrated and the knowing, but they do so in very different ways. The main differences in the actual configurations seem related to different phenomenological positions: the spherical and the global. In their writings and practice, the biologists are mainly working from an ideally 'global' position, and their concepts are linked to, and derivable from, that perspective. The biologists, of course, travel to the actual locations in the field to do their work and collect their samples, but this movement is an inversion of Utarkaq's journey since they move from the global perspective to the local place with all its difficulties, only to return again to the global position where the important work is done. The fishers, on the other hand, seem to rely on value and derive their notion from a consistently 'local' and 'spherical' perspective.

Tim Ingold suggested that the shift from the spherical to the global perspective should be seen as a historical process marking the move into modernity, a move from cosmology to technology (Ingold 1993).[7] All of the three cases do, however, appear equally non-modern (Latour 1999: 309) since none of them consistently separates the world into distinct, independent domains of the natural, the social and the narrated. In all three cases the domains are rather stabilised by the connections to the other domains and each of the cosmologies therefore create a consistent whole in itself. This could suggest that the grand narrative underlying Ingold's analysis is too simple: it is not correct that we once were pre-modern, engaged, cosmological and spherical, and then modernity came and with it disengagement, technology and the global perspective. Rather it seems, as also demonstrated by Hornborg (this volume), that cosmologies connecting the natural and the social are still very much alive, and that modernity understood as disengagement, technological, global, etc. may be seen as a grand auto-narrative about a certain epoch rather than a precise analysis of that epoch. In reality, we have, perhaps, never been modern (Latour 1993) at least not in that simplified sense as technological and disembedded, as opposed to cosmological and embedded.

Although the distinction between the global and the spherical may not be used to structure a Hegelian world history, it does identify two very different phenomenological stances taken by the fishers and the biologists respectively. The story about Utarkaq appears to relate an important point: the global perspective and the spherical perspective are related, seeing it in one way is 'to render conceivable the possibility of its logical inverse' (Ingold 1993: 41) and it further suggests that it is indeed possible and fruitful to move between the two. Rather than a given in itself, the phenomenological stance is a perspective, a relation between subject and world, and it changes when people move, physically or metaphorically. One way of getting out of the polarised discussions may therefore be to develop practices that ensure a movement, metaphorical or real, between the spherical and the global perspectives and ways of communicating and acknowledging the characteristics of the knowledge derivable from each perspective.

As discussed by Kalland (this volume), indigenous populations have often been described as ecologically noble savages, or original ecologists (Fienup-Riordan 1990: chapter 8; Voget 1994). This is a highly problematic conception, not only because it is a reproduction of a classical dichotomy between the West and the Rest as indicated by Kalland, but also because it appears to rest on a simplified conceptual analysis. A proper 'ecological analysis' that focus on the interactions between organisms and their environment as they unfold (Ingold, this volume), appears to have to switch back and forth between the spherical and the global perspective in order to see the organisms as well as the environment. This is, however, in the contemporary Greenlandic situation difficult to do since the most important actors will insist on taking only one stance.

I began this chapter with the concept of knowledge in the management of living resources, a discussion that can now be recapitulated. The knowledge form underlying most biologically based management of living resources is ideally characterised by being objectively based biological knowledge. This analysis suggests that the ideal is part of a particular cosmology that claims validity only for knowledge generated in a view from nowhere (Nagel) ideally without a knowing subject (Popper). It is cosmology that appears as exotic as the one outlined by the story of the Mother of the Sea.

In his outline of a organism/person-centred anthropology, Tim Ingold (this volume) proposes that knowledge 'far from lying in the relations between structures in the world and structures in the mind, mediated by the person of the knower, is immanent in the life and consciousness of the knower as it unfolds within the field of practice set up through his or her presence as a being-in-the-world'. This understanding of knowledge appears to describe very well why the biologists and the fishers – engaged in very different beings-in-the-world – generate almost incompatible bodies of knowledge, one talking about overfishing and stocks, the other about *aalisapilunneq* and *qaleqaleqassusseq*. This perspective does not, however, give much idea as to how one should be able to transcend these differences since forms of knowledge derived from different practices appear to be incommensurable. But perhaps there is more to knowledge than a simple unfolding through practice. Through his studies of scientific knowledge, Bruno Latour has suggested that knowledge does not reside in the face-to-face confrontation of a mind with an object, (and on this point Ingold would agree). Furthermore, knowledge is, according to Latour, able to circulate through a chain of references that transforms and changes it as it is inscribed into other networks (Latour 1999: 69-71). This understanding allows knowledge to gain an existence separated from the immediate practice that generated it. It does not, however, exist as a free-flowing entity, but it remains inscribed in particular networks and contrasted against particular references.

If Latour is correct in this understanding, then it suggests an important correction to Ingold's understanding where different knowledge – derived from particular beings-in-the-world – potentially leading to incompatible universes of knowledge. Rather, knowledge can be made to converge through being inscribed in networks that go beyond one particular life world. For this to happen, however, much work needs to be done in studying the particular set of imaginings of nature as well as of people that enter into each of the converging chains of transformations.

NOTES

1. This is a selective reproduction and not a direct translation of the myth. I have attempted to keep the wordings and metaphors close to the Danish version, which has been compared to the Greenlandic original *Arnap Nâlagâ*, found in the Knud Rasmussens Archives at the Royal Library in Copenhagen, Ny kgl. samling 2130, 2°, Eskimoiske Sagn og Fortællinger, (59-65).

2. In modern Greenlandic, a formalisation of a dialect spoken in West Greenland, as well as in the other Inuit languages, the four points of the compass are etymologically derived from orientations relative to the coast. 'North' is 'up' the coast, 'South' is 'down' the coast, 'West' 138is to the sea, and 'East' to the land. These orientations rotate compared with the absolute directions among the different Inuit groups (Fortescue 1988).

3. In an East Greenlandic version of the visit to the Mother of the Sea (Anonymous 1921) this twist of 'ups and downs' becomes even more complicated. The hero realises that the river leading to her dwelling changes direction at a certain point. It runs both into her house and onto the coast. Only after he has cleaned the woman does the river flow 'properly' to the coast so the seals can come out.

4. Rémi Savard (1970) has identified structural similarities between the Mother of the Sea and another mythological figure mainly known from the Western Inuit territory: the Man in the Moon. There appears to be interesting parallels and inversions in topography

and semantics between these two characters, see for example the myth recorded by Knud Rasmussen from Western Canada (Anonymous 1929): A woman follows her beloved that turns out to be the moon-man on a complicated journey into the sky. She finds his house full of caribou, seals and whales, and as she looks through a hole in the floor, she may view all settlements in the world.

5.   In English, these two understandings share the same verb, but it appears that in other Germanic languages, such as German or Danish, the two notions are separated onto two different verbs *kennen* and *wissen* with very different etymologies (Roepstorff 1999).

6.   If we allow 'stretching of the metaphor' this suggests that 'global pollution' is not a modern discussion only.

7.   In a later commentary on this paper, Tim Ingold has suggested that the work by Viveiros de Castro (1998) on deixis and perspectivism could provide an important analytical addition to the points pursued here.

REFERENCES

Agrawal, A. 1995. Dismantling the Divide between Indigenous and Scientific Knowledge. *Development and Change* 26: 413-39.

Anderson, B. 1991. *Imagined Communities. Reflections on the Origin and Spread of Nationalism*. London: Verso.

Anonymous. 1921. Ímap Ukûa. In *Myter og Sagn fra Grønland. I Østgrønland*, K. Rasmussen (ed.). København: Gyldendalske Boghandel, Nordisk Forlag, 95-99.

Anonymous. 1929. Kvinden der Blev Til En Edderkop. In *Festens Gave. Eskimoiske Alaska Æventyr*, K. Rasmussen (ed.). København: Gyldendalske Forlag, Nordiske Boghandel, 126-34.

Boas, F. 1888. *The Central Eskimo*. Lincoln: University of Nebraska Press.

Boas, F. 1901. The Eskimo of Baffin Land and Hudson Bay. *Bulletin of the American Museum of Natural History*, XV.

Boje, J. 1993. *Hellefisk Ved Vestgrønland, Disko Bugt*. Grønlands Fiskeriundersøgelser, København.

Boje, J. 1999. Hellefiskens Gådefulde Liv. In *Sermitsiak* 31 (August, 6), 29.

Dahl, J. 2000. *Saqqaq. An Inuit Hunting Community in the Modern World*. Toronto: University of Toronto Press.

Feeny, D., F. Berkes, B.J. McCay & J.M. Acheson 1990. The Tragedy of the Commons: Twenty-Two Years Later. *Human Ecology* 18 (1): 1-19.

Fienup-Riordan, A. 1990. *Eskimo Essays. Yu'Pik Lives and How We See Them.* New Brunswick: Rutgers University Press.

Fortescue, M. 1988. Eskimo Orientation Systems. *Meddelelser om Grønland, Man & Society* (11).

Hacking, I. 1998. *Mad Travelers. Reflections on the Reality of Transient Mental Illnesses.* Charlottesville: University Press of Virginia.

Hardin, G. 1968. The Tragedy of the Commons. *Science* 162: 1243-1248.

Holtved, E. 1966/67. The Eskimo Myth About the Sea-Woman. A Folkloristic Sketch. *Folk* 8-9: 145-53.

Inglis, J.T. (ed.) 1993. *Traditional Ecological Knowledge. Concepts and Cases.* Canadian Museum of Nature, Ottawa: Internantional Program on Traditional Ecological Knowledge.

Ingold, T. 1993. Globes and Spheres. The Topology of Environmentalism. In *Environmentalism. The View from Anthropology*, K. Milton (ed.). London: Routledge, 31-42.

Ingold, T. 1994. From Trust to Domination, an Alternative History of Human-Animal Relations. In *Animals and Human Society. Changing Perspectives*, A. Manning & J. Serpell (eds.). London: Routledge, 1-22.

Kristensen, J. 1998. Hellefisken ved Ilulissat/Ilulissat Eqqaanni Qaleralit. *Atuagagdliutit/ Grønlandsposten.* Nuuk, October 7, 21-23.

Latour, B. 1993. *We Have Never Been Modern.* New York: Harvester Wheatsheaf.

Latour, B. 1999. *Pandora's Hope: Essays on the Reality of Science Studies.* Cambridge, Mass.: Harvard University Press.

Mathiassen, A. 1904. Havets Herskerinde. In *Inuit Fortæller I. Grønlændernes Sagn og Myter. Frederikshåb, Julianehåb og Nanortalik*, K. Rasmussen (ed.). Lynge: Borgens Forlag, 142-49.

Nagel, T. 1986. *The View from Nowhere.* Oxford: Oxford University Press.

Popper, K.R. 1972. *Objective Knowledge: An Evolutionary Approach.* Oxford: Oxford University Press.

Qúpersimân, G. 1982. *Min Eskimoiske Fortid- En Østgrønlandsk Åndemaners Erindringer*, Otto Sandgren (ed.). Nuuk: Det Grønlandske Forlag.

Riget, F.F. & J. Boje. 1987. *Hellefisk ved Vestgrønland, Disko Bugt.* Grønlands Fiskeri- og Miljøundersøgelser.

Roepstorff, A. 1998. Virtual Stocks, Experts and Knowledge Traditions. In *Aboriginal Environmental Knowledge in the North*, L.J. Dorais, M. Nagy & L. Müller-Wille (eds.). Quebec: GETIC, Université Laval, 95-122.

Roepstorff, A. 1999a. Sustainability, Knowledge and Knowing What to Do. In *Dependency, Autonomy, Sustainability in the Arctic*, H. Petersen & B. Poppel, (eds.). Aldershot: Ashgate Publishing, 259-66.

Roepstorff, A. 1999b. Deconstructing Social Constructionism. *FOLK, Journal of the Danish Ethnographic Society* 41: 139-54.

Roepstorff, A. 2000. The Double Inter-Face of Environmental Knowledge: Fishing for Greenland Halibut. In *Finding Our Sea Legs: Fishery Workers, Science and Management*, B. Neis & L. Felt (eds.). St. Johns: ISER Books, 165-88.

Savard, R. 1970. La Déesse Sous-Marine des Eskimo. In *Échanges Et Communications, Mélanges Offerts á Claude Lévi-Strauss*, J. Poullion & P. Maranda (eds.). The Hague: Mouton, 1331-1355.

Scott, C. 1996. Science for the West, Myth for the Rest? The Case of James Bay Cree Knowledge Construction. In *Naked Science. Anthropological Inquiry into Boundaries, Power and Knowledge*, L. Nader, (ed.). Routledge: New York, 69-86.

Simonsen, C.S. & A. Roepstorff 2000. Udvikling og Adfærd af Fisk og Fiskere i Diskobugt-området. In *Udviklingsforskning, Udviklingspolitik og Udviklingsenterprise. Tre Faktorer i det Grønlandske Samfunds Forandring og Udvikling*, M. Holm & R.O. Rasmussen (eds.). Nuuk: Direktoratet for Kultur, Uddannelse og Forskning & Statens Institut for Folke-sundhed, 29-42.

Sonne, B. 1990. The Acculturative Role of Sea Woman. Early Contact Relations between Inuit and Whites as Revealed in the Origin Myth of Sea Woman. *Meddelelser om Grøn-land, Man & Society* 13.

Viveiros de Castro, E. 1998. Cosmological Deixis and Amerindian Perspectivism. *Journal of the Royal Anthropological Institute (New Series)* 4/3: 469-88.

Voget, F.W. 1994. Were the Crow Indians Conservationists? In *The Invention of Nature*, T. Bargatzky & R. Kuschel (eds.). Frankfurt Am Main: Peter Lang, 125-37.

Semiosis: Significative dynamics between nature and culture

Anti Randviir

Introduction

Themes connected with nature and culture involve a range of topics: from questions as to whether phenomena outside culture can be interpreted without turning them into cultural at all, to – in the field of semiotics – treatment of the somewhat problematic relationship between (cultural) semiotics and biosemiotics, specifically whether it is possible to analyse, from a semiotic perspective, phenomena of nature 'as such'. The following argument is evidently biased toward cultural semiotics, partially due to an intention to put into relation two crucial terms in contemporary semiotics: semiosis and text. The former has found application in all trends of semiotics, while 'text' has remained strongly associated with the semiotics of culture. This article will try to avoid tying these key terms to particular individuals or specific uses, but it will rather attempt to put them into the perspective of a general semiotic paradigm (if there ever is any). This implies that the relationship between cultural semiotics and biosemiotics will be considered on a general metalingual level and from a methodological angle.

It will be argued that textual semiosis – as a specific mechanism of semiotisation – conjoins the sphere of nature and culture, thus subjecting the natural phenomena inspected semiotically to pass through cultural filters. It is therefore crucial to pay attention to textualisation as a special device of semiotisation. To begin, let us consult the encyclopedically accredited knowledge to clarify the notion of semiosis.

Semiosis and communication

In pansemiotic perspective, communication is any form of semiosis
(Nöth 1990: 170).

For the sake of figurative simplicity, let us briefly and deliberately consider the possibility of seeing the relation between communication and semiosis as a transitive one. Then we see that Nöth's understanding applies well to direct communication between two individuals, but neither to textual communication nor a wide range of 'unilateral communication' (e.g. the classic example 'smoke → fire'). 'Unilateral communication' suggests rather the definition of Meyer-Eppler: communication is the 'reception and processing of physically, chemically or biologically detectable signals by a living being'. This view is quoted and commented by W. Nöth as peripheral to the analysis of communication: 'Semiosis without any activity on the side of the signal source certainly constitutes the lowest threshold of the semiotic field' (Nöth 1990: 170). This standpoint, even in its rearranged form, appears to have two misleading aspects. Firstly, it confuses the relation between communication and semiosis – a more clear differentiation would refer to semiosis as the generation of meaningful unit(s), and to communication as the exchange of it/them. Secondly, it does not seem to be productive to approach semiosic activity as taking place only between two ontologically different subjects. If we speak of the relevant realms as subjects of semiogenetic activity, there is no need for them to be different, also on the ontological plane; the emergence of meaning is made possible in the tension field between different semiotic subjects rather than ontological subjects, as suggested by the cases of 'unilateral communication', autocommunication, intracultural communication, etc.

The preference of different [semiotic] fields/spheres rather than different ontological subjects seems to be presented in Peirce's and Morris's tradition of conceiving semiosis as the 'process in which something is a sign to some organism' (Morris 1946: 366). In this line of thought, the necessary collision between something/someone and 'the Other' does not presume another physical participant in space, but rather a conceptual 'Other'. Along this line one may even hypothesise that bilateral communication, in its semiosic aspect, is on a fundamental level reducible to unilateral communication and the conceptualisation of the 'Other'. A basic device in the creation of such otherness is, in Shklovskian terms, 'estrangement'.

The concept of estrangement (sometimes referred to as defamiliarisation) was revealed by V. Shklovsky as early as in 1917 in a discussion of art where

the technique of art is to make things 'unfamiliar', to make forms difficult, to increase the difficulty and length of perception because the process of perception is an aesthetic end in itself and must be prolonged (Shklovsky 1994: 20).

This distancing from a phenomenon as part of the process of turning it into (another) *object* is in correspondence with the general prerequisites for semiosic activity. We can at this point see a possibility for a unified description of biosemiotic and culturo-semiotic perspectives, be they applied to either natural or cultural phenomena. We could namely use two conceptually related terms from the biosemiotics and cultural semiotics – *umwelt* by J. v. Uexküll, and *semiosphere* by J. M. Lotman.[1] A common principle behind these two terms would provide us with an evident concurrent ground of investigation, thereby drawing attention to the different focus they apply to objects of research, the biosemiotic trend centring on the very emergence of semiosis, and cultural semiotics dealing with further processes toward the 'text' (see Figure 2.).

The elementary common feature describing the semiotic function of the two terms of *umwelt* and semiosphere is connected with estrangement (or defamiliarisation) in the particular aspect of (self-) identification of a subject for the task of confronting 'the other' both to obtain information from the environment, locate itself, and communicate with its surroundings or surrounding subjects, etc. A comparison of *umwelt* and semiosphere can be found in a recent issue of *Semiotica* that mirrors a wide range of relevant arguments and discussions (see Sebeok 1998).

Semiotic treatment of nature and culture can be – and has often been – divided: for example as semiotics of the sign and semiotics of the code, or as semiotics of signification and semiotics of communication. In the tradition of the Tartu-Moscow semiotic school, 'nature' has often been analysed, but generally as 'non-culture' (cf. Uspenskij et al 1973: 1-28). Such a distinction is certainly most arbitrary, and – if taken literally - it indicates an important problem: No communication can be executed without signs. This entails that a semiotics of communication requires a semiotics of signification. Respectively, no signification can emerge without at least two different parties (even though both of them can be called into being by a single communicative agent); so the semiotics of the sign can hardly escape the level of code and that of communication. To demonstrate this interconnected nature of both semiotic concepts and also objects of study, let us focus on the following scheme (Figure 1).

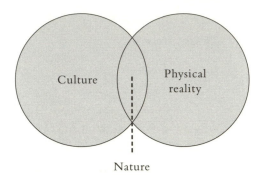

Figure 1. The triangle culture – nature – physical reality

When we talk about nature – or nature as an object of (cultural) semiotics – we usually talk about an interaction between culture and nature on the level of textual meaningfulness since we cannot intervene with semiosis in nature. Hence to deal with this we must construe it, basically on our own. We therefore have to deal with nature as an already 'semiotically accepted' or even interpreted field.

Instead of the traditional opposition of nature and culture – where the position of nature is ambiguous between, on the one hand, an independent existence and, on the other, a meaningful presence in culture – the already 'cultivated nature' hints at a triangle 'culture-nature-physical reality' (Figure 1). Even though in the common and conventional framework of cultural semiotics the component of physical reality is usually not mentioned, this does not lead to a contradiction since the object level of cultural semiotics can be described as confined to the sphere that is switched into cultural discourse and consists of cultural units. This background condition is explicitly present in the conception of the semiosphere (Lotman 1984) that claims the impossibility of dealing with 'objective reality', since physical reality, which is switched into discourse, is also included into the structure of the semiosphere. The preference for delimiting the scope of (culturo-) semiotic research to that, which is demarcated by culture and nature – thus leaving out problems concerning physical reality – may have its origins in the tradition of cultural semiotics inspired by Saussure. A Saussurean understanding of the sign entails a diadic conception: it is composed of the signifier and the signified, both of which are elements of the semiotic realm. Characteristically, physical reality cannot be dealt with within this tradition, since it can only treat natural phenomena that have already been subjected to semiotic description. Physical reality and the existence of an objective realm is, in other words, a hypothetical concept 'behind the text' of cultural semiotics.

Equally illustrative, the biosemiotic tradition cannot only approach objects that belong to the semioticised sphere of nature. This tradition – which is rooted in a triadic conception where the sign is composed of the object represented, the sign vehicle representing it, and the interpretive conception of the relationship of a semiotic representation – attempts to understand objects that inhabit a category of physical reality, which is inaccessible to cultural semiotics. In the following we will try to examine the semiotisation of nature and use of nature as a semiotisation of different (cultural) phenomena from the viewpoint centring on the semioticised categories of culture and nature.

Nature

Taking semiosis as a 'category-agent'[2] in the context of 'nature-culture', we obviously have to touch upon two major aspects. Having very briefly considered some features of 'semiosis', let us proceed to the treatment of 'nature' as an entity usable in two aspects: 'nature' as a term, and 'nature' as a phenomenon.

First, let us again try to clarify the 'official meaning' of the word by consulting a dictionary. We can learn that 'nature' has, for example, been defined as 'the material world, especially as surrounding man and existing independently of his activities', 'the natural world as it exists without man or his civilisation', 'reality, as distinguished from any effect of art: *true to nature*' (Webster's 1996: 953). This raises a question: how can we treat any phenomenon without some meaning-generating 'tools' (tools being artistic or artificial in their artifactualness) intelligible to us? In other words – how can we approach nature from a viewpoint outside culture?

Here the terms 'text' and the 'textual' turn out to be useful. Following the tradition of cultural semiotics and approaching culture as a system of texts, we can distinguish it from nature according to the principle(s) of the textual. This means that the instrumental opposition 'nature – the textual' draws a line between the 'illegible', 'unintelligible', 'hardly interpretable' etc., on the one hand, and the 'legible', 'intelligible', 'interpretable', on the other. Relations between these spheres may be characterised from two different angles. First, we may analyse them within a single domain or phenomenon. This option could have been used also in our context. For example, we could have observed the manifestation of nature in the city as a concentration spot of the 'cultural'. In a historical perspective, this would provide us not only with a picture of a materialised 'nature-culture' relationship but at the same time and – even more interesting – it would elucidate society's conception of the 'cultural' and how it has at times been sharply distinguished from anything 'natural' (e.g. city-wall in the Middle Ages as a military construction, on the one hand, and on the other, an establishment to keep out the 'savage', 'natural' and 'devilish', and to set all the latter apart from the 'cultivated'). A counter-example is embodied in the emergence of the park into urban culture. This illustrates approaching nature via the Garden of Eden, and an attempt to sense culture via nature as the substance of the divine (see for example Larsen 1994; Svirida 1994).

Instead of this option, let us use an alternative. Let us inspect how, from the aspect of textuality, the opposition 'nature-culture' is disclosed in different fields and phenomena. This makes it possible to consider the given opposition not as explanatory for a phenomenon, but to see different phenomena as explanatory for our binary opposition. This approach is also chosen to avoid the logically problematical character of the developed contrast: phenomenologically, 'nature' is a common noun for different phenomena inherent in it, whereas 'text' is a component belonging to itself, thanks to certain feature(s) in the opposite sphere, culture.

By virtue of that feature, which may be called textuality or even meaningfulness, 'text' has been turned into a metaphor applied to the explanation of miscellaneous phenomena ranging from 'nature' (e.g. a cult-tree a tree planted by an eminent person may be a 'cultural text'; an epic landscape may be seen as a 'text') to Internet pages of antique literature.

At the same time, when regarding culture as a sphere characterisable by the feature of textuality, we ought to pause at the notion of text to try to delimit the sphere of the cultural as the domain conceivable for us due to its feature of 'readability'.

Text

Within cultural semiotics the concept of text has been defined and redefined many times (for a general overview of the notion of text see Lotman 1970: 65-72). The diverse semiotic and communicative functions of text in culture and in cultural tradition – for example, as a container, a generator or a transmitter of information (see, e.g., Lotman 1981) – have made the position of the text relatively fluid on a semiotic metalevel. Indeed, even the very essence of the text as an (artifactual) object is difficult to grasp. The different conceptions of text as a cultural phenomenon are usually strongly coupled to particular conceptions of the relation between culture and its exterior. Indeed, this relation is often treated as a contingency of the text and the non-text. There is, however, still a need to review some basic features of the text.

A general culturo-semiotic viewpoint suggests 'understanding of the text as any individual message the distinction of which (from the 'non-text' or 'another text') is intuitively cognised with sufficient certainty'. This implies that 'the text possesses a beginning, an end, and a definite inner organisation' and this allows, along with other features, the creation of a typology necessary for an adequate deciphering of texts (see Lotman 1966: 83-85). In order to set the notion of text into the current framework we can describe its position through the set of semiotic stages or processes that precede it (Figure 2).

The three main features or aspects of the text, which have been described by Lotman using the terms: expressed, bordered and structured (see Lotman 1970: 67-68), come together by virtue of a general property of the different dimensions of the text: their confined or circumscribed nature. For the emergence of text into ontology, it has to be demarcated (see also Lotman 1966: 83-85; cf. Merrell 1982: 6-30). Demarcation, in turn, means the creation of a unit that is self-reliant in its relation to the environment and describable through an integral structure that makes it 'definable' from the diversity of the surroundings. Thus the text comes into being, or more correctly – is made to come into being – in the field of tension between at least two different spheres or, if you will, in the intersection between at least two systems of different semiotic structure. Indeed, it would otherwise not be semiotically intelligible: the existence of at least two different incongruent or asymmetrical realms is needed for the emergence of a semiotic structure, because – as stated in one of the most widespread elementary and commonsense understandings of the sign – 'the sign stands for something that the given sign is not itself'.[3]

Such semiotic dualism is also connected with the dynamic nature of the text that arises from the structured organisation, on the one hand, and from certain inner instability on the other. By inner instability of the text as a semiotic structure we refer to the potential of (especially artistic) texts to maintain and generate meanings that are not simply due to a diachronic change of relationship between a text and the cultural environment, but come also from the text's inner duality. This inner duality includes the text's capacity to contain different (autonomous) subtexts (see Lotman 1982: 3-4) made possible by (at least) double coding executed upon the production of a text (see also Lotman 1981).

In the following we will not dive into Bakhtinian discourse related to the theme of otherness. Instead, we will focus on nature as switched into cultural discourse; still we obviously have to do with the formation of a kind of conceptual 'Other'. Consequently, in dealing with the theme of contacts between cultural phenomena and nature, we are met with the need of brutely distinguishing between two realms: (a) the 'cultural', in the sense of it referring to a semantically or *meaningfully structured* domain, and (b) the 'natural', as an unsemioticised or *non-meaningful* sphere from the cultural insider's viewpoint.

If we prefer to exclude the dynamic problems of defining 'nature' from 'culture', we may choose to depart from this dyadic opposition. This fits into the scheme sketched above (see Figure 1) that distinguishes between culture as a meaningfully organised domain, nature as a sphere of potential meaningfulness, and physical reality that 'falls out of' cultural discourse but exists as a background hypothetical reality. It furthermore grants semiospherical constructs with the power to create contrasting differences between meaningful entities, and it guarantees the continuity of semiospheric organisations by constantly providing them with new units to be switched into discourse. Thus nature turns into a fluid zone through which new meaningful structures are constructed, and it offers the culturally meaningful sphere possibilities for self-reflection by being a convenient domain for the creation of the other. In this way we may reduce the scheme above, which contains three different spheres, to an opposition between two semiotic entitites, where one is semanticised and the other is not not semanticised (such as in the opposition between culture and physical reality), or just 'differently' semanticised (as in the contrast between culture and nature). This is depicted in Figure 2.

The contact between these different realms, or even a certain overlap of them, creates the possibility for the emergence of [new] meaning(s). Such conceptual collision, which may or may not have a physical agent in the environment, allows an outline of some of the following (culturo-)semiotically important stages of text-generation: Recognition of meaningful*ness* → interpretation (making an object meaningful) → textualisation (conceptual structuring of meaning) → texting (textualisation as formal structuring of meaning).

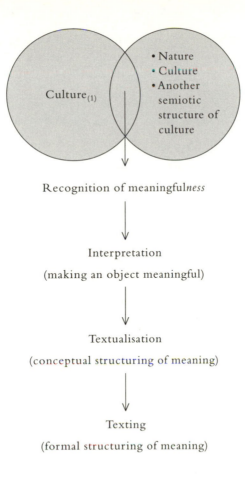

Recognition of meaningful*ness*

Interpretation

(making an object meaningful)

Textualisation

(conceptual structuring of meaning)

Texting

(formal structuring of meaning)

Figure 2. Semiotic stages involved in texting

Any meaningful phenomenon, in order to be a cultural unit proper (Schneider 1968: 2; Eco 1976: 66, 73–83), has to be demarcated and arrayed, that is, textualised and texted. It is precisely through the text that we can describe the resolution of the original collision, and it is via the 'textual' that we can semioticise the realm outside of cultural units. It is important that the conceptual range of 'text' should not be limited to written records alone. It ought to be conceived as something through which the different phenomena can be characterised and described. This conforms to the parameters of textuality (see, for instance, Leavitt 1995 for the textuality and demarcation of oral speech). The 'text' can be regarded as the object of study for cultural semiotics, whereas the preceding processual stages, until the detection of the mechanism for the emergence of meaning together with its prerequisites, are the target for the analysis.

The textual nature of cultural units and the semiotically dynamic essence of textual phenomena is, as already mentioned, connected with the fact that these entities have been constructed by applying manifold codes. The hierarchy of codes contained in texts ought to, in turn, make it possible to create a typology of texts (see Lotman 1966: 84). Therefore, the function of texts in culture, which is related to the respective codes of its construction, is to be in connection with the specific characteristics of coding, both upon the construction and interpretation of (cultural) texts. Due to the different possibilities of coding and decoding, the function of texts can be alternated. Thereby their position in a cultural context can be changed, for example a text produced in a culture for the semiotisation of nature may be turned into a cultural text of nature to semioticise culture itself, or vice versa. Such alternations are in correspondence with the emergence of meaningfulness outlined above: It is the result of a collision between two semiotically different realms which could be conceptions of culture or nature or different conceptual spheres in culture, respectively. They therefore provide a semiotic study with information about changes in the respective (semiotic) spheres themselves.

Nature as text

Considering nature as a text is by no means rare in contemporary humanitarian and scientific discourse. This is done when 'textuality' is used as an instrument to explain and describe nature from the point of view of culture, that is, when nature is observed 'as if' it was a text. We can, maybe in a slightly exaggerated manner, offer cases from biosemiotics as an example. Due to T. Sebeok's initiative (e.g. Sebeok 1990b), biosemiotics is becoming (or has already become) a subfield or 'domain' of semiotics. At least in our context it may seem to have the 'as-if-text'premise as a foundation stone.

Disputes over the justification of the use of metaphors – and the 'as if' premise belongs to this category – find substance especially at the extremes. An analysis of the semiogenesis on a microbiological level can be seen as one of these, and it appears to offer an instance of 'comfort' as an important and often elucidating criterion for the description of complex objects. This leads to a discussion about the explanatory and analytic value of metaphoric descriptions. It is, for example, 'comfortable' to view and describe DNA as if it was a text – the relevant 'text' having been composed in a 'language' which consists in how the sequence of nucleotides in the DNA chain (the primary structure of DNA) determines the sequence of amino acids in proteins. But in spite of the *comfort* fact of 'textuality' and 'text', we are far from being at ease in making conclusions about their meaning(s). We cannot examine the possible meanings of the 'language' in which, for example, DNA has been composed. Inferences used in genetic engineering do not seem to give ground to describe the field as following semiotic or meaningful rules, rather than those of trial and error and physical or chemical laws. As we are bound to humane semiosis it is very difficult and risky for us to intrude on significative processes in other spheres, let alone to ascribe meaning to these processes.

Having mentioned the accepted value of metaphors like 'language' or 'text' as heuristic extrapolation devices that helped to spread humanitarian discourse to new domains, we have to notice the danger of taking them, so to speak, as metaphor-terms that evoke new kind of conceptions, the content of which has remained para-doxically vague. Vagueness of terms, successively, shrinks the confidence in *what* we actually are analysing as our research object. This aspect leads to another, namely to compensate for vagueness of the conceptual apparatus by the help of different research equipment. Attempts to find reassurance from test gadgets are of course more welcome in fields where [natural] phenomena are beyond our perceptual reach or, more correctly, where such phenomena are left beyond our perceptual thresholds (for example, ultra-violet radiation, ultrasound, etc., etc.). We try to describe them, using certain indications or signals attained by the help of certain machinery, to get elementary or first-hand data. If we go further we can draw a parallel to analyses of natural 'texts', the 'language' of which remains only indirectly assumable for us. Therefore if we hope to examine any kind of communication based on signals (or maybe also signs) beyond the threshold of our senses, it is never guaranteed that machinery provides us with meaning or meaningfulness, and not mere physical information (see Russell 1948: ch. 3, ch. 7; Pelc 1992: 33). Thus a distinction has to be made between the existence of an entity as a sign, on the one hand, and the existence of it as being interpretable as a sign, on the other (see Pelc 1992: 26).

In spite of the problems related to rendering biological units on the level of signs and presenting them as being 'textual', it is, however, interesting to point out an opposite semiotic mechanism. This is seen in those social practices where the outcome of neuro-chemical processes is used for the creation of culturally interpretable 'texts'. An example of such a neuro-chemical intentional coding or, more exactly, of inducing a neuro-chemical coding of such 'cultural texts', can be drawn from Sebeok's analysis of conscious and unconscious semiotic behaviour. Sebeok's example dates from the inter-war period when it became a habit in Central European social life for women, wishing to draw the attention of a gentleman, to drop an essence extracted from the plant *belladonna* ('beautiful woman') into their eyes in order to cause a notable dilation of the pupils (see Sebeok 1990b: 66-71). By evoking fashionable norms of beauty in this way, a desired social behaviour was achieved (or at least made more probable).

Concerning the present topic of relations between culture, text and nature, we can find another instance that hints even more at possible connections between humane semiosis and biosemiotics. Let us once again turn to Sebeok who develops an example by H. Berg on the 'seeming intentionality' of the decisive behaviour of the ubiquitous prokaryotic bacterium *E. coli*. The 'meaningful aspect' of the bacterium's behaviour is that 'it relies on a memory lasting approximately four seconds, allowing it to compare deictically – over short times and distances – where it was, with where it is. On that basis, it "decides", with seeming intentionality, whether to tumble (stay in place) or swim and search for another indexical match somewhere else.' (Sebeok 1990a: 14). Further, Sebeok maintains that 'it may be pertinent to note that, with respect to their rhythmic movements, the *hic et nunc* that we humans perceive has a duration of three seconds. Poets and composers appear to be intuitively aware of this fact (proved by Ernst Pöppel) when they provide proper "pauses" in their texts' (Sebeok 1990a: 15).

Returning from the psychophysical background for the construction of texts to a semiotic viewpoint, we can maintain that an entity's meaningfulness, as it is conceived on the level of textual signs and their combinations, can come into being due to the unlimited possibilities of meanings that exist prior to the ascription of one concrete meaning to that entity. This is the cause of the much discussed dialogism of text. In creating new meanings, a text is in itself dialogical, it is in dialogue with the reader, and it switches into dialogue with a wider cultural context in diachrony, etc. Thus the 'universe of meaning' of the text is principally unlimited. These are characteristics that seem risky to apply to natural phenomena, since we can hardly tell anything about the origin or emergence of signs utilised in nature. It is therefore difficult to assert anything about them as demarcated units, or to say anything about their interpretive limits. Hence we have to admit that nature can be viewed as textual inasmuch as the starting point and the 'as-if' premise is remembered. In spite of these problems, 'textuality' is, however, useful as an explanatory category for attempts to a semiotisation of nature from the viewpoint of culture. The basic question is to which (elementary) level we can go, when we ascribe meanings to phenomena belonging to fields in which we lack a sufficient interpretive experience.

Text in nature

There are many typologically similar ways of looking upon nature as a text that examines how nature (in whatever above-defined meaning) has been switched into a literary or other type of work. This goes from turning it into a descriptive object and all the way to dogs and other animals dressed up to act as film stars. In addition to these possibilities, an important aspect of the current theme is texts that are uncovered in nature. Hereby we are not dealing any more with phenomena which are 'as if texts' in that they may be rendered as meaningful.

Instead, let us pay attention to those phenomena which can be 'read'; they can be read in the sense that, relying on our (cultural) experience, we are able to impose on them certain limits of interpretation and to assume with quite high predictability the semiotic origin (and therefore also the likely semiotic nature) of them. To use another widely discussed example, we may again bring forward Robinson Crusoe and the footprint in the sand. We will not use this to discuss the nature of such signs in a manner that would concern typologies of signs. We will rather try to remain at a more general level.

The trace noticed by Robinson did not only become textual due to its structure and potential meaningfulness. It also turned into a text that provided him with enough data to create a trustworthy possible world, since the footprint was (a) clearly of manlike origin, (b) it had been left by a bare foot, (c) it was of the right leg, (d) it was possible to determine the direction of the person who left it, etc.

Keeping in mind the scheme (Figure 2), we can see the depiction in Defoe's story, whether supported by an illustration or not, as an outcome of the process of secondary textualisation. Via a collision with culture and a re-textualisation, a phenomenon meaningful for Robinson, but belonging to the world of nature for an ordinary European, was 'translated' into an entity that is 'readable' both pictorially and verbally also for 'cultivated people'. Hence we can suggest that texts exist also in nature, but they do it for us via our cultural experience.

What is the difference between DNA analysed by a biologist, and a trace inspected by a hunter? How can we distinguish between phenomena in nature which are textual by virtue of recognisable meaningfulness, and natural phenomena to which semiotic nature is ascribed on the level of scholarly description? First, an idea evoked by a trace possesses a wide interpretative range – a trace may refer to a much greater amount of objects than merely to a bare-footed savage (e.g. it was left by a circus bear having wooden imitations of the human footprint under its feet). On the molecular level the limits of interpretation cannot be too wide or varying, since that would leave the very continuity of the species insecure. Regarding the relevant level of 'language', there has been long discussion about that of the dolphins or the bees. We can refer to C. Cherry for a suitable contrasting opinion. Cherry, speaking about the topic, classifies the 'language' of the bees as constant and non-changing through generations: 'It is not developable, flexible, and universal' (Cherry 1975: 18). Bringing forth another side of the topic, Cherry says that 'animal signs can relate only to the future, but never, like human language, refer to the past' (Cherry 1975: 19). Of course, the range of natural languages in nature is unlimited, just as the variability in the ability to learn and to extend the scope of tools and units of meaning-conveyance (cf. Voigt 1993).

Secondly, the connection between the three elements forming the semiotic triangle operates via the comparison of a sign with the existing 'semiotic luggage' of an individual. Only through a comparison with experience can we make inferences about a semiotic structure in – or in the meaning of – a text. Due to this the meaning*fulness* of an 'X' can be recognised. Here we can allude to H. Münsterberg who said in 1909 that the meaning of reality lies in the expectation it evokes (cited from Ogden and Richards 1972: 171). Consequently reality cannot be dealt with immediately, but only as mediated by meaningfulness or if you will, by the expectation of meaning (see Figure 2). The latter may be found in Peirce's concept of the interpretant. If this is connected with the expectation of meaning, we can see that inevitably, signs and meaning can only be treated through cultural filters.

Semiotisation of culture through nature

We have hitherto mainly focused on the semiotisation of nature through culture and on some of the obstacles that may arise on the level of a scholarly description of natural phenomena. Let us now see how elements of nature are used to make the realm of culture meaningful, and how the spheres of culture, nature, and physical reality may intermingle. This unifies that, which is both the concept of *umwelt* and of semiosphere, at an individual as well as at a cultural level.

As an example of such a collision between 'culture' and 'nature' on a general level of society, we can introduce the concept of personification, since this is a notion tightly connected with an interdependence of nature and culture as revealed in cultural discourse. It furthermore brings forth the role of *estrangement* as a device for creating the necessary presuppositions for the generation of new meanings.

Radcliffe-Brown has commented:

[Thus] personification of natural phenomena is one of the methods by which the Andaman Islander projects into the world of nature the moral forces that he experiences in society. [...] Perhaps, rather than speaking of it as a projection of moral forces into nature, we should regard it as a process of bringing within the circle of social life those aspects of nature that are of importance to the well-being of the society, making the moon and the monsoons a part of the social order and therefore a subject to the same moral forces that have sway there-in (Radcliffe-Brown 1964: 381).

We can see that behind this anthropological concept is a very significant semiotic mechanism. The personification process turns out to be making strange out of one-self (be it individual, group or society) by comparing structures in the cultural realm *(textual* entities) to physical phenomena *(non- or pretextual* entities). If we remember Shklovsky's estrangement concept mentioned above, we can see evident parallels between the 'estrangement device' in the arts and on the level of general social processes. Social reflection (e.g. *weltanschauung,* cosmology, social structure, spatial arrangement) involves estrangement as a (metalevel) technique and helps thereby to semiotisize physical reality as nature. Textualization of physical entities via estrangement of cultural structures unites the spheres of culture and nature, although understanding the unity of semiotic and natural environment may sometimes be associated with specific cultural functions that make it possible to recognise meaning transferred outside the cultural (e.g. in the case of shamanism).

However, personification, if viewed on a social scale, appears to be a very special case – this is the *auto*-estranging of oneself, that now is included into the mechanism of 'domestication' as a basic means of conceiving the personified features as the 'own'. At the level of cognition and culture-specific semiogenesis, this is a circular process that in cultivating society's own features and values, appropriates the sphere of nature. As a consequence, the semiotic constructs of a society (e.g. cosmological model of a given society) and their manifestations (e.g. the social system) begin to overlap more and more. This means that, by investigating myths, rituals and rites, social systema and their interrelations, we can get a clue to the means and habits of textualisation in a society.

Personification as an important moment in initiation rites is often completed by using names of different trees and plants. This seems to be a circular process that now serves the function of transferring the 'pre-domesticated' qualities of nature into the sociocultural domain. This conceptual textualisation of the surroundings and of the sphere of culture itself via estrangement is supported by a quote from C. Lévi-Strauss who cites what an Osage told to J. O. Dorsey: 'We do not believe that our ancestors were really animals, birds, etc., as told in traditions. These things are only *wa-wi-ku-ska'-ye* (symbols) of something higher' (Lévi-Strauss 1966: 149).

Estrangement as a device brings us to another aspect of the semiotisation of the natural into culture; this time it concerns the process of formal textualisation that is practiced in the so-called developed societies. Here one may refer to the famous conception of 'objective correlate' developed by T. S. Eliot and published in 1920 in 'Hamlet and His Problems' (Eliot 1960). This notion states that some images in [verbal] art transmit certain objects, feelings, phenomena better and *more adequately* than others. While Shklovsky dealt with the problem of estrangement in the arts as a means to depict familiar things, Eliot is concerned with how to bring 'unfamiliar' things into the cultivated sphere, suggesting that there must already be an objective connection between nature and culture. This implies that in the developed societies and their cultures that 'objective correlate' is a means to connect nature and culture, while in the myths of 'primitive' societies the structure of meaning is an intertwined complex following a 'participative logic'. At the same time the possibility and effectiveness of signification and encoding through 'objective correlate' depends on the isomorphic equivalencies for sensory contrasts. The aim of T. S. Eliot's art-constructing principle appears, in other words, to have been the same as the one governing the mythic and ritual representations! Thus, personification serves as an example of how a necessary collision between culture and nature (or another culture) is created in order to enlarge the 'semiosphere' (intertwined with *umwelt,* if you will) of the given culture by adding new textualised meaningful units to it. We see in this an example of how semiosis is triggered off, and how the level of text is reached in the symbolic use of nature as part of the construction of personal and cultural identities.

NOTES

1. In the notion of semiosphere we have to pay attention to the importance of the original terms by V.V. Vernadsky and T. de Chardin.

2. Under this notion we keep in mind both the status of 'semiosis' in the framework of the 'semiotic', and in the operative functions of it.

3. Cf. C.S. Peirce's definition: 'A sign, or representament, is something which stands to somebody for something in some respect or capacity' (CP 2.228).

REFERENCES

Cherry, C. 1975. *On Human Communication: A Review, a Survey, and a Criticism*. Cambridge, Massachusetts: The M.I.T. Press.

Eco, U. 1976. *A Theory of Semiotics*. Bloomington: Indiana University Press.

Eliot, T.S. 1960. *The Sacred Wood; Essays on Poetry and Criticism*. London, Methuen, New York: Barnes & Noble.

Larsen, S.E. 1994. *Et in Arcadia Ego:* A Spatial and Visual Analysis of the Urban Middle Space. In *Advances in Visual Semiotics: The Semiotic Web 1992-93*, T.A. Sebeok & J. Umiker-Sebeok (eds.). Berlin: Mouton de Gruyter.

Leavitt, J. 1995. The Demon of Ashes in Sanskrit Text and Himalayan Ritual. In *Beyond Textuality: Ascetism and Violence in Anthropological Interpretation*, Gilles Bibeau & Ellen Corin (eds.). Berlin, New York: Mouton de Gruyter, 79-110.

Lévi-Strauss, C. 1966. *The Savage Mind*. Chicago: University of Chicago Press.

Lotman, J.M. 1966. K probleme tipologii tekstov. In *Tezisy dokladov vo vtoroj letnej shkole po vtoritchnym modelirujushchim sistemam, 16-26 avgusta 1966,* Juri M. Lotman (ed.-in-chief). Tartu: Tartu Ülikooli Kirjastus, 83-91.

– 1970. Struktura khudozhestvennogo teksta. *Semioticheskie issledovanija po teorii iskusstva*. Moscow: Iskusstvo.

– 1981. Semiotika kultury i poniatie teksta. In *Trudy po znakovym sistemam (12): Struktura i semiotika khudozhestvennogo teksta,* J.M. Lotman (ed.-in-chief). Tartu: Tartu Ülikooli Kirjastus, 3-7.

– 1982. Ot redakcii. In: *Trudy po znakovym sistemam (15):Tipologija kultury,* J.M. Lotman (ed.-in-chief).Tartu:Tartu Ülikooli Kirjastus, 3-9.

– 1984. O semiosfere. In *Trudy po znakovym sistemam (17): Struktura dialoga kak princip raboty semioticheckogo mekhanizma,* J.M. Lotman (ed.-in-chief). Tartu: Tartu Ülikooli Kirjastus, 5-23.

Merrell, F. 1982. *Semiotic Foundations: Steps toward an Epistemology of Written Texts.* Bloomington: Indiana University Press.

Morris, C.W. 1946. *Signs, Language, and Behavior.* New York: George Braziller, Inc.

Nöth,W. 1990. *Handbook of Semiotics.* Bloomington: Indiana University Press.

Ogden, Charles K. & Ivor A. Richards, 1972. *The Meaning of Meaning: A Study in the Influence of Language upon Thought and the Science of Symbolism.* London: Routledge and Kegan Paul.

Peirce, C.S. 1931-1958. *Collected Papers.* Cambridge: Harvard University Press.

Pelc, J. 1992. The Methodological Status of Semiotics: Sign, Semiosis, Interpretation and the Limits of Semiotics. In *Signs of Humanity. Proceedings of the IVth International Congress, International Association for Semiotic Studies,* Michel Balat & Janice Deledalle-Rhodes (eds.). Berlin, New York: Mouton de Gruyter, 23-34.

Radcliffe-Brown, A.R. 1964. *The Andaman Islanders.* New York:The Free Press.

Russell, B. 1948. *An Inquiry into Meaning and Truth.* London: George Allen and Unwin Ltd.

Sebeok,T.A. 1990a. Indexiality. *American Journal of Semiotics,* 7(4): 7-28.

 – 1990b. *Essays in Zoosemiotics.* Toronto, Ontario: Humanities Publishing Services, University of Toronto.

– (ed.) 1998 *Semiotica: Journal of the International Association for Semiotic Studies.* 120(3/4).

Schneider, D.M. 1968. *American Kinship: A Cultural Account.* New York: Prentice-Hall.

Shklovsky,V. 1994. Art as Technique. In *Modern Criticism and Theory: A Reader,* David Lodge (ed.). London, New York: Longman.

Svirida, I.I. 1994. *Sady veka filosofov v Polshe: Et in Arcadia Ego.* Moscow: Nauka.

Uspenskij, B.A., et al. 1973.Theses on the Semiotic Study of Cultures (As Applied to Slavic Texts). In *Structure of Texts and Semiotics of Culture,* J. van der Eng & M. Grygar (eds.).The Hague, Paris: Mouton, 1-28.

Voigt,V. 1993. Lessons in Ape Paintings. In *Semiotics 1990 with "Symbolicity",* K. Haworth, J. Deely, T. Prewitt & J. Bernard (eds.). Lanham, New York, London: University Press of America, 191-209.

Webster's Encyclopedic Unabridged Dictionary of the English Language 1996. New York: Gramercy Books.

Anthropology and the concept 'sustainability': Some reflections

Arne Kalland

In recent decades there has been a growing concern, particularly in industrialised countries, about the present rate of degradation of the physical environment. One of the key concepts emerging from this concern is 'sustainability', made popular by the report *Our Common Future* (WCED 1987). Much has been said and written about the concept (e.g. Merchant 1992; Shiva 1992; Witoszek 1995), but anthropologists have been relatively mute on the issue. This is surprising because the concept resonates with – and thus opens doors to – several important issues that for years have been debated among anthropologists. To start with, the concept gives the impression that it is possible to live in harmony with nature; in this it resembles models developed within the functionalist and neo-functionalist schools of anthropology depicting man and nature co-existing in some kind of homoeostatic equilibrium. Not only has this contributed to uphold the notion of the ecologically noble savage – a notion both nourished and soundly criticised by anthropologists – but it has also contributed to an interest in native perceptions of nature and their knowledge in general, a knowledge that is depicted as holistic and ecocentric, in contrast to an atomistic and anthropocentric scientific knowledge allegedly prevailing in the industrialised West. This interest is more than academic. Indigenous knowledge is often seen by non-government organisations (NGOs), media and the public as an alternative to scientific knowledge, an alternative that is better fitted to addressing urgent problems of resource management.

In the environmental discourse (Milton 1993) the concept sustainability tends to be intimately interwoven with a cluster of notions: holism, ecocentrism, homoeostasis, the noble savage, subsistence, traditional knowledge, and the 'other', to name only a few of those most relevant to anthropologists. In its most extreme form the concept brings together all these notions in the image of a Garden of Eden where primitive man lives in harmony with nature and only harvests the minimum to cover nutritional and socio-cultural needs, thus living a life uncorrupted by the forces of money. This image of a noble savage guided to a sustainable way of life by traditional ecological knowledge (TEK) accumulated over generations today seems to have its main proponents among some environmental activists, eco-philosophers and operators of ethno/eco-tourism, but they have for years been informed, and are still being informed, by anthropologists.

The environmental discourse has proved a powerful critique of modern industrial society, but should itself be a target for scrutiny and deconstruction. It will be argued that it is a misconception to see sustainability in terms of the above notions, indicating along the way how anthropologists have both contributed to this misconception and to its dismissal. We should, however, be careful and not throw the baby out with the bath water. Besides being an important analytical tool in ecological sciences, 'sustainability' may have heuristic value for the social scientists. It is good to think with. Emptied for ideological content, it helps us to focus on the relationship between a group of people and the natural resources on which they depend, i.e. on the relationship between harvest levels and resource productivity. Strictly speaking, this is a research area for the biologists, but it will be argued that anthropologists can contribute in two important ways. First, they can provide a linkage between two knowledge regimes, popularly termed scientific and indigenous (or traditional, local, practical) knowledge. These often present different interpretations of the environmental situation and there are good reasons to believe that a more accurate understanding of the ecosystem and its resources can be obtained if they are brought together. Second, realising that resource management is first of all a question of social relations (and not a relationship between people and nature), anthropologists have important roles to play in designing and monitoring management institutions.

This paper, therefore, first looks into some of the notions above before it argues for the need to build robust management institutions.

The holistic approach

One of the roots for the present concern for nature in the Western world is, as stated elsewhere (Bruun and Kalland 1995: 2), a growing awareness of the inadequacies of the Cartesian worldview. A new ecological paradigm is frequently called for (e.g.

Dunlap and Catton 1980), a paradigm where 'man' and 'environment' no longer are seen as separate and opposite entities but where 'organisms and environment form part of one another' (Dickens 1992: 15). Some people (e.g. White 1967) have sought to re-interpret Western concepts and perspectives, whereas others – both scientists and laymen alike – have searched for new inspiration to correct these ills from outside Western traditions. A large body of literature offers alternative worldviews to the prevailing Western ones: usually depicting man as an integral part of nature instead of being separated from it and trying to dominate it. They portray man and environment as a harmonious unity of mutual respect, complementarity and symbiosis; their views are holistic-organic rather than atomistic-mechanistic as in the industrial West (Callicott and Ames 1989: 5). What all these writers urge is a holistic approach to the study of ecosystems.[1]

One problem with the ecosystem approach is how to demarcate system boundaries. In the days of classical functionalism, small communities were seen as self-contained isolated units, an approach also found in single-species models of the biologists. With multi-species or ecosystem models it has become much more difficult, however, to draw these boundaries.[2] These difficulties are multiplied if we are to take the recent calls for alternative worldviews seriously. How do we define the ecosystem if we have to take account of the claim that we are influenced by invisible cosmic energy flows (as in geomancy) or by the constellation of the stars (as in astrology)? And what do we do when we encounter worldviews such as the Japanese where 'nature' corresponds to the cosmic whole, i.e. the totality of existing phenomena (Kyburz 1997) or is seen as the manifestation of a 'universal principle', which is the flow of energy created by the interaction of *yin* and *yang* forces and the five elements (Ackerman 1997)? In this view nature and the universal principle *(do, tendo* in Japanese; *tao* in Chinese; 'the Way of Heaven') are inseparable and intrinsically linked. Here everything is a reflection of the other: the Universe can be understood through a stone, and the stone through the Universe or a *haiku* poem. This relationship originates in Buddhist thought in which everything is seen as connected to everything else in a web of interdependencies, both spatially and temporally, through the laws of cause and effect *(karma)*. These are natural laws in the Japanese sense of nature, and what most Westerners would classify as superstitious beliefs will for many Japanese belong to the natural sciences (Kalland and Asquith 1997). One may wonder how useful such an all-encompassing ecosystem is for management purposes. It is beyond description, and for this reason 'the holistic view paradoxically works best on the smallest scale' (Resnick 1986, quoted in Button 1988: 206). Which brings us back to the fiction of the isolated village community.

Another problem with this approach is its *determinism*. Two points should be made. The first point, which has only received scant notice, is the explanatory power of coincidence. Whereas modernism made room for coincidence – i.e., events can occur totally by chance (although still predictable through the employment of probability theory) – the notion that everything is connected with everything else denies any role to coincidence. In pre-modern societies, disease, accidents and other calamities were at least partly attributed to human agencies; a snake bite could be caused by a witch, illnesses by a loss of spirituality, and barrenness could be inter-preted as ancestral punishment. In post-modern societies, holism again reduces the role assigned to coincidence. Consequently, there is a tendency to downplay the role of natural fluctuations, and the public – and particularly the environmental move-ment – tends to attribute all changes, including global warming and ozone deple-tion, to human activities.

The other point is the often-made critique of the culture-ecological approach. Besides its ahistoricity, it confuses the effects of something as its cause (Vayda 1986). Even the most bizarre customs are seen as having an ecological function in balanc-ing human populations and activities with the natural environment (Headland 1997). Rarely did authors such as Marvin Harris and Roy Rappaport ask whether the goals could have been achieved in other, less bizarre, ways. 'Primitive' people are seen as functionally adapted to the environment through cybernetic loops and homoeostasis. In this equilibrium model, human beings behave according to pre-programmed genes or, more commonly, to a culture which is seen as the outcome of some sort of a social-Darwinian selection of behavioural traits which are ecologi-cally adaptive. Culture becomes the mechanism which balances population size with the resource base. The ecosystem controls human beings who are deprived of their free will as autonomous agents (Vayda 1986). Implicit in this view is the notion that people live in harmony with nature. Although it has been soundly criti-cised by both anthropologists and others (e.g. Broch 1977; Ellen 1986; Redford 1991; Redford and Stearman 1993), the myth of the ecologically noble savage per-sists and may even have gained in popularity as a consequence of our search for paradigms that can replace the modernist project. A similar myth exists about the ecologically noble Orientals (Lohmann 1993; Bruun and Kalland 1995). Anthropol-ogists must take their share of the blame for these myths (Edgerton 1992; Buege

1996), thus giving support to the functionalist trap of equating perceptions with practice. This is unfortunate not only for anthropology as a discipline but, more importantly, because it does not contribute constructively to the development of robust resource management regimes.

Finally, in their search for holistic-organic paradigms, new dichotomies are created. One is made between those who adhere to Cartesian dualism and those who do not. People are either one or the other; on this issue all talk about the need to contextualise seems to be forgotten. The same holds true for the even more popular dichotomy between anthropocentrism and ecocentrism (see Shaner 1989 for a discussion). Both these distinctions are made to uphold the notion of the 'other'; it is Western dualism versus non-Western monism and Western anthropocentrism versus non-Western ecocentrism, as well as Western 'modernism' versus non-Western 'traditionalism' (or 'contextualisation'), and Western commercialism versus non-Western subsistence economies.[3] Two of these dichotomies, anthropocentrism vs. ecocentrism and commercialism vs. subsistence, are of particular relevance for our discussion.

Anthropocentric versus ecocentric views

In order to construct the dichotomy between anthropocentric and ecocentric worldviews, non-Western religions – particularly native American and Asian ones – are depicted as ecocentric and as harbouring profound ecological knowledge and sound environmental ethics. Poul Pedersen (1995) has termed this approach the 'religious environmental paradigm'. Through three cases he analyses how native religious writers are reading ecological insight into Hindu, Buddhist and Islam texts. Ramachandra Guha (1998) has recently made a similar point against those who read ecological insight into the writings of Mahatma Gandhi. For Pedersen the concept of ecology is, however, intimately connected with modernity. It is the interpretation of science and has a global validity, i.e. it is universal and decontextualised. Religion, on the other hand, is contextual and embedded in local communities. This does not mean, however, that people do not have ecological insight, but this is something that must be empirically investigated – not taken for granted. However, the most profitable place to look is not necessarily religion. Neither does it mean that religious practice may not have positive ecological effects, but we should be careful not to confuse positive side effects with the cause.

Why then do people take the trouble and try to read ecological insight into their religious creeds? Pedersen suggests an answer (1995:272):

By offering to the world what they hold to be their traditional, religious values, local peoples acquire cultural significance. When they speak about nature, they speak about themselves. They demonstrate to themselves and to the world that their traditions, far from being obsolete and out of touch with modern reality, express a truth of urgent relevance for the future of the Earth. This achievement, with its foundation in appeals to imagined traditional religious values, represents a forceful cultural creativity which would not have worked by the invocation of 'pure' ecology or environmentalism.

Pedersen takes his examples from Asian religious writers; let me take an example from anthropological literature. Citing Johan Galtung (1988) who has claimed that Buddhism is closer to nature than any of the other world religions, Leslie E. Sponsel and Poranee Natadecha-Sponsel (1993) suggest that Buddhism may be used to solve the problems of loss of biodiversity. They claim that environmental ethics is an inherent part of Buddhism most clearly expressed, perhaps, through the notion of the Middle Way, the elimination of material desires, *karma,* reincarnation and a holistic perspective. I will not go into detail here but limit myself to illustrate how they juxtapose Buddhist and Western worldviews (Figure 1).

What the authors seem to compare is a Buddhist ideal and what is best termed a caricature of Western practices. It is based on a selective reading of Buddhist dogma and an equally selective reading of Western practice. In their analysis Thailand remained in a 'dynamic ecological equilibrium for millennia' (ibid.: 86) until the introduction of Western modernisation about 200 years ago. This allegedly weakened their 'adherence to traditional Buddhism and Thai culture' (ibid.: 87), causing moral collapse and environmental degradation. Typically, Western influence is blamed for all ills, and modernism is hardly given any merit whatsoever. As a contrast, the other is depicted as ecologically noble.

The same kind of analysis is used to explain environmental degradation in Japan. Influenced by Zen and Shinto, it has almost been taken axiomatically that the Japanese love – and live – in harmony with nature, or at least did so until this Garden of Eden was destroyed by modernisation (Kalland 1995). Nonetheless, Japan experienced serious deforestation about 1,200 years ago and again about 400 years ago, long before her culture was infiltrated by Western ideas (Totman 1989).

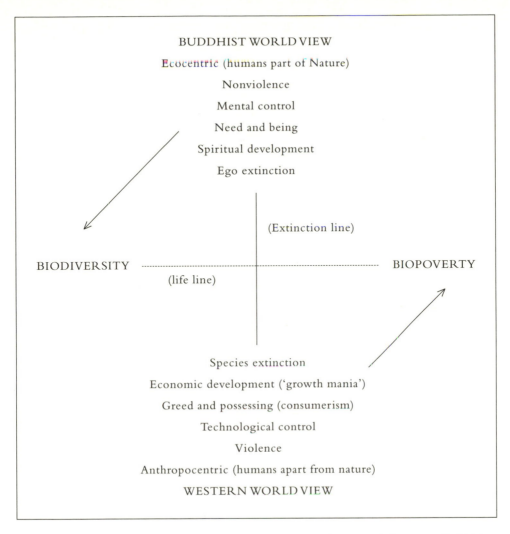

BUDDHIST WORLD VIEW
Ecocentric (humans part of Nature)
Nonviolence
Mental control
Need and being
Spiritual development
Ego extinction

(Extinction line)

BIODIVERSITY — — — — — — — — — — — — — — — BIOPOVERTY
(life line)

Species extinction
Economic development ('growth mania')
Greed and possessing (consumerism)
Technological control
Violence
Anthropocentric (humans apart from nature)
WESTERN WORLD VIEW

Figure 1. Worldview and biodiversity. Redrawn from Sponsel & Natadecha-Sponsel, 1993

Japanese perceptions of nature are complex and continuously changing. Moreover, they are contextual or situational, with no clear distinction between nature and culture or between nature and artifice (Kalland and Asquith 1997).[4] It can be argued that nature oscillates between two poles: nature in the wild (often abhorred by Japanese) and domesticated, aesthetic nature which is identical with culture (usually loved). To most Japanese then, human beings can, depending on the context, see themselves either as part of nature together with spirits, animals, plants and stones (an ecocentric view of nature) or as uniquely superior to other creatures regarding nature as a potential resource to exploit (anthropocentric view). Anthropocentrism and ecocentrism are conflated. It can be argued that the distinction between them is based on a Western categorisation with little applicability to Japan. The Japanese are either, or both, depending on the situation.[5]

The distinction between anthropocentric and ecocentric worldviews can then best be analysed as an internal Western cultural critique. As such, the ecologically noble savages and Orientals have served as powerful 'others', and it is not surprising that they have attempted to appropriate this 'global' discourse and combine it with a local repertoire for, as Pedersen (1995) states,

'to produce a tradition of a glorious ecological past, a tradition that also is depicted as the solution for the future. From being seen as conservative and backward, people emerge in this new global discourse of environmentalism as the world's teachers and saviours'.

However, as we now shall see, this has not been achieved without a cost.

Commercial versus subsistence activities

Many scholars have stressed the ambivalent position that money has in Western culture; on the one hand it is seen as a liberating force, on the other it is seen as a dangerous corrupting agent. Whereas the former dominates neo-classic economic theory, the latter is almost equally dominant within the environmental movement. In this negative view, which goes back through Marx and Aquinas to Aristotle, money is seen as corrupting social relations as well as morality (Parry and Bloch 1989). Vandana Shiva (1992) is one of the many who makes an explicit distinction between traditional, subsistence societies existing in harmony with their environment (actually there is no separation between the two; they are one and the same) and modern societies based on the market economy. To her a market economy is incompatible with sustainability. Many anthropologists hold the same opinion. Rappaport (1979: 162), for example, argues that with the loss of local self-sufficiency, there is also loss of homoeostatic capacity (cited in Hornborg 1996: 49–50). Also to him the implication is that money causes maladaptations and environmental degradation.

The same point is made again and again both by environmental activists and anthropologists. Money is seen as bad, and small-scale societies must be protected against the forces of the world market, a view also reflected in international organisations. The International Whaling Commission (IWC), to take one example, makes a distinction between commercial whaling and aboriginal subsistence whaling. There is an indefinite moratorium on the former, whereas the latter is permitted as long as the products are used locally; the condition of the whale stocks is of minor importance. This dovetails with another of the discourses at the IWC; the one on people's 'needs'. Needs are an integral part of the Brundtland Commission's definition of 'sustainable development', but it is less clear what is meant by this term. Many environmentalists, as well as leading eco-philosophers like Peter Singer (e.g. 1978), limit needs to nutritional needs, and one of the common arguments against whaling in the Faeroe Islands, Iceland, Japan and Norway is that there are no such needs to hunt marine mammals. People are affluent, they have TVs and cars and they can buy their steaks at the supermarkets. When it comes to aboriginal peoples, however, the IWC recognises that hunters have other legitimate needs, such as social and cultural needs. Thereby a dichotomy has been created between aboriginal whalers, who are recognised as having distinct cultures, and commercial whalers who are deprived of any culture of significance.[6] One may wonder whether all the needs of the commercial whalers have been commercialised and have entered the global market where, according to the metaphor of Parry and Bloch (1989), money like acid dissolves all distinctions and creates a homogenised decultured universe.

What emerges from this dichotomy between subsistent and commercial economies – a dichotomy which has been soundly criticised both on semantic (e.g. Freeman 1993) and phenomenologic (e.g. Moeran 1992) grounds – is a kind of totemic worldview with the following set of binary oppositions (Kalland 1993):[7]

whales	money
nature	man-made objects
subsistence	commercialism
tradition	modern
aboriginal peoples	industrialised peoples
good	bad
protectionists	whalers

A few examples of the rhetoric used in creating this dichotomy – which apparently also seems to fit the sealing issue (Wenzel 1991) – are in order here. The protectionists are typically depicted as good people. In a Christmas message pleading for money contributions, Brian D. Davies, the founder and executive director of the International Fund for Animal Welfare (IFAW), writes that 'we're pressing for peace ... not pain. For care and compassion ... not clubbing and killing. For kindness ... instead of cruelty' (December 1991). The commercial hunters are depicted as brutal and greedy. The war metaphor is frequently used, and eating whale meat is regarded close to cannibalism. To refrain from hunting marine mammals and eating their flesh is seen as a step towards civilisation. Commercial native hunters are creating distortions in this picture; in order to remain authentic, native hunters must be protected against the corrupting influences of money and the market. They have to remain 'uncivilised', and at the annual IWC meetings the Alaskan Eskimos have to document that they have not sold whale products on the commercial market.

This situation is not unique to whalers. Throughout the world indigenous peoples have experienced this double-edged sword. In order to obtain rights to natural resources as indigenous peoples, they are deprived of their rights of self-determination (Kalland 1992; Conklin and Graham 1995; Buege 1996). One may rhetorically ask whether we have to get rid of money and again be self-sufficient in order to attain sustainability? The world has seen one regime that has attempted to do that: Pol Pot's Khmer Rouge. I do not think that this kind of utopianism is what we should strive for. The solution to the problem of sustainability cannot lie in that direction, the costs are much too high.

A need for institutions

There must be other, less painful ways towards sustainability.[8] In environmental studies it has commonly been assumed that there exists a fundamental connection between a society's management of natural resources and its perception of nature. For instance, ecological and environmental problems in the West have been accredited to the Judaeo-Christian cosmology of man's mastery of nature (White 1967). It is the same logic which informs those who see the solutions to environmental problems in native Indian or Oriental worldviews, an assumption which is the driving force behind much of the interest devoted to 'traditional ecological knowledge' (TEK). Fikret Berkes, to take one example, claims that in order to secure sustainable use of resources, people must have (1) relevant local ecological knowledge with an appropriate technology, and (2) possess environmental ethics that inhibit their urge to over-exploitate (Berkes 1988).

I do not deny that TEK (or any worldview) may play a role in securing sustainable use of natural resources, and I have elsewhere argued that such knowledge is essential (Kalland, in press). Yet, experience from North America and Asia, and elsewhere for that matter, clearly tells us that neither profound knowledge about the environment nor sound environmental ethics, is sufficient to prevent degradation of natural resources. We therefore need to tread cautiously when inducing ecological practices from philosophical traditions. Discrepancies between theory and practice should not surprise us (cf. Holy and Stuchlik 1983). We cannot *a priori* assume that people's perceptions and norms are mirrored in their actual behaviour, and if such a connection is present this is not necessarily a result of ecological understanding and conscious conservation but might be a coincidental side-effect of something else. It is too simplistic to blame all ills on Westernisation as Sponsel and Natadecha-Sponsel do, or in terms of cultural misfits, as Callicott does (1982: 311). There exist conflicting values in all cosmologies and knowledge systems, and a religious creed which is believed to encourage people to conserve natural resources by giving moral support to certain norms, also provides people with the means to circumvent the same norms. It is tempting to suggest that any religion is likely to support values that are inhibiting over-exploitation of natural resources as well as values that are facilitating or legitimating such behaviour. Explaining behaviour from ideologies may rest on selective reading of evidence. Rather than norms determining behaviour, we find that goal-oriented behaviour is legitimised by appealing to certain norms.

Although alternative worldviews might be important sources of inspiration and make it possible to reflect on one's own understanding of the world, experience has told us that knowledge, whether 'scientific' or 'traditional', is insufficient to secure sustainable use of natural resources. The solution, therefore, does not lie in some unconscious aspects of the human mind, or in a return to a nostalgic past. The notions surrounding the concept 'sustainability' as presented within much of the environmental movement, are hopelessly inadequate to solve the problems facing us today, or will demand solutions that are unacceptable – at least in democracies.[9] But there is a way out – at least in my opinion – namely, conscious conservation; with conservation taken to mean 'the management of the human use of organisms or ecosystems to ensure such use is sustainable' (IUCN et al. 1991: 210). Brighman (1987) proposes three preconditions for conscious conservation:

1) That there are sufficient resources to allow selective exploitation.
2) That people are aware that their behaviour has an affect on the resource base (unless conservation might be an accidental side-effect of something else).
3) That there are institutionalised rights to resources.

To design a management scheme is one thing, to get people to adhere to it is a completely different matter. Enforcement has proved to be an obstacle to sustainable harvests of natural resources. Regulations are often ignored by local people, unless enforced at a considerable cost. One of the problems has been that these schemes more often than not have been imposed from above without taking the local people's interests and experience properly into account. Fortunately, there is today a growing awareness that natural resources are not only best regulated if local communities which depend on these resources for their nutritional, economic, social and cultural needs are brought into active participation but that local participation is essential to sustainable management. This principle has been incorporated into the report *Caring for the Earth: A Strategy for Sustainable Living* (IUCN et al. 1991) and 'people's participation' has been turned into one of the major issues in *Agenda 21*. In order to achieve the objective of sustainable use of natural resources, one should therefore formulate management regimes based on the premises and priorities of the local people who in many cases also have developed institutions that have had a positive effect on nature conservation although these originally might have been motivated by other considerations.

All this, perhaps in a somewhat roundabout fashion, brings us back to the question of knowledge. I have elsewhere (Kalland, 2000) called attention to three levels of knowledge: empirical, paradigmatic and institutional knowledge. The first applies to knowledge pertaining to the behaviour of animals and plants, how these can be collected and captured, and for what purpose they can be utilised. Paradigmatic knowledge deals with how empirical observations are interpreted and placed in a larger context. As paradigmatic knowledge influences people's acquisition of empirical knowledge, there is a dialectic relationship between the two. Finally, institutional knowledge refers to knowledge embedded in the social institutions. Whereas the two first levels of knowledge relate directly to Brighman's two first preconditions above, the third level addresses his third precondition, institutionalised rights to resources. In order to achieve local participation in conscious conservation – and thus develop management schemes that work at low cost – all three levels of environmental knowledge must be incorporated. And taking into account that social engineering seldom works as intended, monitoring is essential. Here anthropologists have an important role to play, not necessarily as advocates and interpreters of exotic cultures, but as mediators between two knowledge systems, the local/practical versus the scientific/legalistic. In order to do this, it is necessary to have a comprehensive understanding of all three levels of knowledge within both systems. Anthropologists have, needless to say, made important contributions when it comes to the presentation of local/practical knowledge, but we have to rid our analyses of the apologetic romanticism so often found in such studies.[10] Ideally, we should use the same critical standards when analysing other people's knowledge systems as when we analyse our own culture. This, of course, invites a number of ethical questions which, however, fall outside the scope of this paper.

NOTES

1. Holism usually implies the view that the whole is greater than the sum of its separate parts, but is also used to mean that everything is interconnected.
2. The recent *El Niño* phenomenon is a case in point. During the winter and spring of 1998, an *El Niño Bulletin* was regularly published on Internet. The editors encouraged reports on possible effects of the 1997 El Niño/Southern Oscilliation (ENSO) stating that 'we try to be inclusive and to let hindsight separate ENSO from other effects' (Report 20, 24 February 1998, http://darwin.bio.uci.edu/~sustain/ENSO.html). Not surprisingly, *El Niño* made an ideal scapegoat for everything that went wrong.
3. The list can be extended to include dichotomies such as Redfield's folk versus urban societies, Durkheim's organic versus mechanic solidarity, and Tönnies' *Gemeinschaft* versus *Gesellschaft*.
4. There might be a danger in this holistic approach, which does not make a clear distinction between nature created by gods and artifice created by human beings. In a sense, nature is everything around us, whether a mountain or a heap of garbage (Tyler 1989: 24). Hence it can even become 'natural to destroy nature' (Berque 1997:143). One may therefore ask whether contextualising nature may not constitute a threat to the environment.
5. Guha (1989) also objects to the attempts to turn Oriental religions, such as Buddhism, Hinduism and Daoism, into ecocentric religions. He looks upon this, what he calls appropriation of Oriental religions, as yet another expression of Westerners' need to

universalise their messages. This romantic view on the East is a mirror of the normally negative image of the Orient as the 'other' (Said 1978). Nevertheless, Guha argues that the myth of the ecologically noble Oriental reproduces, as its noble savage counterpart, a false dichotomy between the rational and science-oriented Occidentals and the spiritual and emotional Orientals.

6. Thus, IWC's management of 'commercial' and 'aboriginal' whaling starts at opposite poles. Whereas the former is managed according to a single species biological approach (main parameters being stock size as well as natural growth and replacement rates), the quotas allocated aboriginal whalers are based on the populations' nutritional, social and cultural needs for whale products.

7. Note that several of the terms in the left column appear in the cluster around sustainability, hence this column implies sustainability in this rhetoric.

8. If indeed sustainability is the ultimate goal. To me it is rather one of several possible means to improve people's quality of life.

9. Many activists who see themselves engaged in something like a third world war, claim that democracy is a luxury we cannot afford if we want to survive. Recently a professor emeritus in political science at the University of Oslo has expressed similar views (Wyller 1999).

10. I have to admit that I might have fallen into this trap from time to time myself.

REFERENCES

Ackerman, P. 1997. The Four Seasons: One of Japanese Culture's Most Central Concepts. In *Japanese Images of Nature. Cultural Perspectives.* P. Asquith & A. Kalland (eds.), 36-53. London: Curzon Press.

Berkes, F. 1988. Environmental Philosophy of the Chisasibi Cree People of James Bay. In *Traditional Knowledge and Renewable Resource Management in Northern Regions,* M.M.R. Freeman & L.N. Carbyn (eds.). Edmonton: Boreal Institute for Northern Studies, 7-21.

Berque, A. 1997. *Japan. Nature, Artifice and Japanese Culture.* Northamptonshire: Pilkington Press.

Brightman, R.A. 1987. Conservation and Resource Depletion. The Case of the Boreal Forest Algonquians. In *The Question of the Commons. The Culture and Ecology of Communal Resources,* B.M. McCay & J.M. Acheson (eds.). Tucson: University of Arizona Press, 121-41.

Broch, H.B. 1977. Den økologiske 'harmonimodell' sett i lyset av jegere og sankere, eller de såkalte naturfolk. *Naturen,* 3: 243-47.

Bruun, O. & A. Kalland 1995. Images of Nature. An Introduction to the Study of Man-Environment Relations in Asia. In *Asian Perception of Nature: A Critical Approach,* O. Bruun & A. Kalland (eds.). London: Curzon Press, 1-24.

Buege, D.J. 1996. The Ecologically Noble Savage Revisited. *Environmental Ethics* 18: 71-88.

Button, J. 1988. *A Dictionary of Green Ideas. Vocabulary for a Sane and Sustainable Future.* London: Routledge.

Callicott, J.B. 1982. Traditional American Indian and Western European Attitudes Toward Nature: An Overview. *Environmental Ethics* 4(4): 293-318.

Callicott, J.B. & R.T. Ames (eds.) 1989. *Nature in Asian Traditions of Thought: Essays in Environmental Philosophy.* Albany: State University of New York Press.

Conklin, B.A. & L.R. Graham 1995. The Shifting Middle Ground: Amazonian Indians and Eco-politics. *American Anthropologist* 97(4): 695-710.

Dickens, P. 1992. *Society and Nature. Towards a Green Social Theory.* London: Harvester Wheatsheaf.

Dunlap, W. & R. Catton 1980. A New Ecological Paradigm for Post-exuberant Sociology. *American Behavioral Scientists* 24(1): 15-47.

Edgerton, R.B. 1992. *Sick Societies: Challenging the Myth of Primitive Harmony.* New York: Free Press.

Ellen, R.F. 1986. What Black Elk left Unsaid: On Illusory Images of Green Primitivism. *Anthropology Today* 2(4): 8-12.

Freeman, M.M.R. 1993. The International Whaling Commission, Small-type Whaling, and Coming to Terms with Subsistence. *Human Organization* 52(3): 243-51.

Guha, R. 1989. Radical American Environmentalism and Wilderness Preservation: A Third World critique. *Environmental Ethics* 11: 71-83.

Guha, R. 1998. Mahatma Gandhi and the Environmental Movement in India. In *Environmental Movements in Asia,* A. Kalland & G. Persoon (eds.). London: Curzon Press, 65-82.

Headland, T.N. 1997. Revisionism in Ecological Anthropology. *Current Anthropology* 38(4): 605-30.

Holy, L. & M. Stuchlik 1983. *Actions, Norms and Representations.* Cambridge: Cambridge University Press.

Hornborg, A. 1996. Ecology as Semiotics. Outline of a Contextualist Paradigm for Human Ecology. In *Nature and Society. Anthropological Perspectives,* P. Descola & G. Pálsson (eds.). London: Routledge, 45-62.

IUCN/UNEP/WWF. 1991. *Caring for the Earth − A Strategy for Sustainable Living.* Gland, Switzerland.

Kalland, A. 1992. Aboriginal Subsistence Whaling: A Concept in the Service of Imperialism? In *Bigger than Whales,* G. Blichfeldt (ed.). Reine, Norway: High North Alliance.

Kalland, A. 1993. Management by Totemization: Whale Symbolism and the Anti-whaling Campaign. *Arctic* 46(2): 124-33.

Kalland, A. 1995. Culture in Japanese Nature. In *Asian Perceptions of Nature: A Critical Approach,* O. Bruun & A. Kalland (eds.). London: Curzon Press, 243-57.

Kalland, A. 2000. Indigenous Knowledge. Prospects and Limitations. In *Indigenous Environmental Knowledge and its Transformations. Critical Anthropological Approaches,* A. Bicker, R. Ellen, & P. Parkes (eds.). London: Routledge, 319-35.

Kalland, A. & P. Asquith 1997. Japanese Perceptions of Nature: Ideals and Illusions. In *Japanese Images of Nature. Cultural Perspectives,* P. Asquith & A. Kalland (eds.). London: Curzon Press, 243-57.

Kyburz, J. 1997. Magical Thought at the Interface of Nature and Culture. In *Japanese Images of Nature. Cultural Perspectives,* P. Asquith & A. Kalland (eds.). London: Curzon Press, 257-79.

Lohmann, L. 1993. Green Orientalism. *The Ecologist* 23(6): 202-4.

Merchant, C. 1992. *Radical Ecology: The Search for a Liveable World.* New York: Routledge.

Milton, K. (ed.). 1993. *Environmentalism: The View from Anthropology.* London: Routledge.

Moeran, B. 1992. The Cultural Construction of Value. 'Subsistence', 'Commercial' and Other Terms in the Debate about Whaling. *Maritime Anthropological Studies* 5(2): 1-15.

Parry, J. & M. Bloch 1989. Introduction: Money and the Morality of Exchange. In *Money and the Morality of Exchange,* M. Bloch & J. Parry (eds.). Cambridge: Cambridge University, 1-32.

Pedersen, P. 1995. Nature, Religion and Cultural Identity: The Religious Environmentalist Paradigm. In *Asian Perception of Nature: A Critical Approach,* O. Bruun & A. Kalland (eds.). London: Curzon Press, 258-76.

Rappaport, R. 1979. *Ecology, Meaning, and Religion.* Berkeley: North Atlantic Books.

Redford, K. 1991. The Ecologically Noble Savage. *Cultural Survival Quarterly* 15: 46-48.

Redford, K.H. & A.M. Stearman. 1993. Forest-dwelling Native Amazonians and the Conservation of Biodiversity. *Conservation Biology* 7(2): 248-55.

Said, E. 1978. *Orientalism.* New York: Vintage Books.

Shaner, D.E. 1989. The Japanese Experience of Nature. In *Nature in Asian Traditions of Thought: Essays in Environmental Philosophy,* J.B. Callicott & R.T. Ames (eds.). Albany: State University of New York Press, 163-82.

Shiva, V. 1992. Recovering the Real Meaning of Sustainability. In *The Environment in*

Question. Ethics and Global Issues, D.E. Cooper & J.A. Palmer (eds.). London: Routledge, 187-93.

Singer, P. 1978. Why the Whale should Live. *Habitat* 6(3): 8-9.

Sponsel, L.E. & P. Natadecha-Sponsel 1993. The Potential Contribution of Buddhism in Developing a Environmental Ethic for the Conservation of Biodiversity. In *Ethics, Religion and Biodiversity. Relations between Conservation and Cultural Values,* L.S. Hamilton (ed.). Cambridge: The White Horse Press, 75-97.

Totman, C. 1989. *The Green Archipelago: Forestry in Pre-industrial Japan.* Berkeley: University of California Press.

Tyler, R. 1989. Fra hellige fjell til elektrisk fuglesang – om japanernes kjærlighet til naturen. *Dyade* 21(1): 20-27.

Vayda, A. 1986. Holism and Individualism in Ecological Anthropology. *Reviews in Anthropology,* Fall: 295-313.

WCED (World Commission on Environment and Development). (1987). *Our Common Future.* Oxford: Oxford University Press.

Wenzel, George. 1991. *Animal Rights, Human Rights – Ecology, Economy and Ideology in the Canadian Arctic.* Toronto: University Press of Toronto.

White, L. 1967. The Historical Roots of our Ecological Crisis. *Science* 155 (3767): 1203-1207.

Witoszek, N. 1995. Er vi alle protestanter nå – paradokser ved bærekraftig kultur. In *Bærekraftig utvikling. Om utviklingens mål og bærekraftens betingelser,* W. Lafferty & O. Langhelle (eds.). Oslo: Ad Notam Gyldendal, 279-92.

Wyller, T.C. 1999. *Demokratiet og miljøkrisen.* Oslo: Universitetsforlaget.

Section II

Identities

Introduction

The chapters in this section demonstrate an intimate relationship between the understanding of social and cultural identity on the one hand, and imaginings and practices of nature on the other. They show how 'nature' and 'identity' seem to evolve and interact in interchanging loops, and this suggests that particular conceptions of and relationships with 'nature' are more than just a classificatory order. Rather, a particular sense of self is established as people orient themselves meaningfully in the world, and in this process of identity formation nature appears to be much more than a blank blackboard upon which a particular social and cultural identity is inscribed. Although engagement with and conception of 'nature' is therefore intrinsically bound up with political and historical processes of identity formation, these practices of nature appear to form a non-discursive background for the maintenance and meaningful coherence of particular identities.

Witoszek advances this argument forcefully in her comparative study of the place of 'nature' in Scandinavian and German national mythology respectively. She demonstrates how, at the turn of the 19th century, the German and Scandinavian elites resorted to different conceptions of nature to define national identity. Despite the fact that 'nature' occupied functionally equivalent places in the constructions of national identity in both Germany and Scandinavia, the semantic contours of 'nature' were, and are, very different. Whereas the German politico-cultural elite dichotomised 'nature' and 'culture' in a way that made the dichotomy into an external equivalent of the psychological opposition between emotion and reason, the Scandinavian elites fused and reconciled the opposites. Using Jurij Lotman's notion of semiosphere, also employed by Randviir (this volume), Witoszek argues that the current Scandinavian conception of nature can be traced back to a historically constituted set of values. This value system, which is continuously re-enacted, gives a pragmatic and distinctly anti-Romanticist tone to contemporary intellectual discussions like Nordic eco-humanism and environmental practices such as whale hunting.

In their paper on the Fulani people in northern Burkina Faso, *Paarup-Laursen and Krogh* demonstrate how the relationship between environmental knowledge/practice and identity is both complex and heterogeneously structured. Much environmental knowledge about soil, landscape and the weather is shared and valued in the same terms by FulBe and RimayBe, the two status groups in Fulani society. In one particular context, however, no such consensus reigns, namely where perceptions of the landscape touches upon a sense of authentic identity. This is demonstrated in the perception of the *ladde,* the bush. The aristocratic FulBe, who were traditionally cattle herders, see the bush not only as a potential pasture but also as a symbolic space where *'pulaaku',* the qualities proper to the Fulani man, may be cultivated and enacted. This perception still prevails among the FulBe, although the traditional cattle herding practices have been increasingly abandoned in recent years. The low-status RimayBe, who used to be slaves of the FulBe and were prevented from owning cattle, do not share the FulBe evaluation of the bush. Among the RimayBe the realm of *ladde* is not positively marked, since the bush was not a domain of male economic activity in which a gendered version of ethnic identity could be cultivated. The divergence in the perceptions of nature among the FulBe and RimayBe spring, in other words, from differences in the interplay of environmental practices and priorities, which are intimately bound up with processes of ethnic differentiation. Importantly, the difference in the nature-identity complexes is, as Paarup-Laursen and Krogh show, one of the reasons why the two Fulani groups have reacted very differently to contemporary development schemes.

A strikingly similar link between practice, identity, and uses of nature is highlighted in Bjerkli's analysis of the coastal Saami community in Manndalen, Norway. *Bjerkli* argues that distinct practices of nature in Manndalen, which are manifested in very competitive ways of organising the exploitation of natural resources, have established a particular ethos in the Manndalen people and have become an important arena in which links with their Saami past are maintained. The competitive slant to the Manndalen practices of nature, as compared to the neighbouring communities, meant that Manndalen developed into a leading community when Saami ethnopolitics erupted in earnest during the 1970s. In his historical analysis Bjerkli argues that the unbroken continuity in the management of the commons has served as an important vehicle for self-consciously acting and enacting Saaminess in Manndalen. As a consequence of the ethos instilled by their distinctly competitive practices of nature, the tone of engagement with the Norwegian state has from the outset been confrontational, although the actual form which the confrontation has taken, has changed historically. From being merely a matter of control over access to natural resources, the Manndalen confrontational policy of engagement is today also evident in their struggle for symbolic, ethnic recognition.

Bjerkli's paper suggests that a practice, which appears at first glance to be restricted to issues related to the environment, can be intrinsically related to other domains as well. This same argument is meticulously unfolded in *Pedersen's* account of the Tsaatang nomads of the Mongolian plains. Taking spatio-environmental practices as his point of departure, Pedersen argues that the nomads perceive their landscape as a relational network of various actors, humans as well as non-humans. The non-human actors range from being mountains and other sacred localities to being the winds and incorporeal deities. The spatial layout of this non-modern, 'latourian' actor-network is clearly distinct from a modern agricultural landscape characterised by distinct spatial boundaries with an inside and an outside. Through a careful ethnographic analysis of his experiences with the Tsataang trekking nomads, Pedersen demonstrates how their movements in space – evinced in both everyday practice and ritual – establishes a conception of 'floating' social space. As Pedersen argues their practices of space constructs in profound ways the Tsataang's phenomenology of environmental perception as well as the very notion of being Tsaatang.

In the analysis of both Pedersen and Ingold, this volume, the concrete movement of persons in space and time is the starting point for explicating a particular phenomenology that connects environment and person. *Brauckmann,* who is trained as a philosopher of science, extends this perspective. Brauckmann outlines how the Kantian theory of space presupposes the construction of an abstract *a priori* ideal of the *homo scientificus* who possesses the know-how of an experienced mathematician. To counter the problems of these assumptions Brauckmann uses the German-Estonian biologist Jakob von Uexküll's ecological analysis of *Umwelts,* subjective spheres of significance that encompass and surround every living being, to reinterpret the Kantian notion of space. This shift from Kantian spatial *a priori* to phenomenological lifeworlds entails a move from an abstractly constructed space to concretely experienced *places* through which people perceive and act upon their surroundings. In their cultivation of an abstract nature, people thus convert the surroundings of space into an environmental place. Building houses is one way people construct places, and in an analysis of the neoclassic houses, Villa Savoye by Le Corbusier and Fallingwater by Frank Lloyd Wright, Brauckmann demonstrates how buildings as instances of places may be set either as counterpoints against or as integrated components of their natural surroundings.

The contributions suggest a complex interaction between political processes of identification and the historical sedimentation of particular ways of engaging the surrounding world. Imaginings of nature are therefore not only statements *about* this world that can be taken apart with various deconstructive tools, they are also particular instantiations of a practical engagement with the world and are thus reflections *of* this world. As shown by several contributions, this relationship between identity and nature evidences a remarkable historical continuity which appears bound to hexic aspects of practice that may outlive more explicit political discourses. 'Nature' is thus not only a source for metaphors of identity but also an arena for activities and practices that are at once both practical and symbolic, political and cultural.

The chapters in the cosmology section demonstrated that even scientific imaginings of nature, supposedly highlighting only an epistemic aspect, interrelate with imaginings of culture and personhood and understandings of ethics and moral. This called for an alternative to a dichotomisation of nature and culture where one act as a background for the other. We suggested in the introduction that cosmology could be a useful organising modality through which one may analytically grasp the interplay and development of nature and culture and their derivatives such as science and humanities. The common message conveyed by the contributions to this section is that *identity* may be thought of as a similar modality. It appears ontologically to be a meta-level organiser of social, semantic and physical practices and epistemologically to constitute an analytical prism through which one may undertake a comparative study of interplaying imaginings of nature and culture.

Nature and ideology:
The case of Germany and Scandinavia

Nina Witoszek

From Charlemagne, who in AD 722 had the Irminsul (the sacred ash and holy axis of Germanic religion) cut down, to the Reichskulturkammer's call for the primordial Heimat, Northern nature has been an active – if puzzling – constituent of various ideological agendas (Lovejoy 1948; Jordanova 1986; Short 1991). In Scandinavia, just as in Germany, the process of nation building involved an often tricky readaptation of nature-rooted identity to modern needs. Especially intriguing in the light of twentieth century history are the very different moral communities that emerged from a common, nature-imbued mythology and from a similar story of origins. Put bluntly – and stereotypically – Scandinavia has been taken to represent the benign, inspiring face of modernity, while Germany has stood for all that was malign and destructive. These readings derive most immediately from the divergent paths of Germany and Scandinavia before and during World War II and from what Eric Hobsbawm oddly – and inaccurately – called 'the Golden Age' of modern European history (Hobsbawm 1995).

To put the matter in narrative terms: during the Great Crisis of the 1930s, two ancient nature stories which had unifying and mobilising power circulated in both communities. The German one drew on Tacitus's account of an ancient warrior race that commemorated its birth from the woodlands by offering human sacrifice and displaying corpses on tree trunks. Simon Schama, who has pursued the gradual accretions and embellishments of the Tacitian story of the Great Patriotic German Forest argues that 'it is these morbid associations ... between blood sacrifice, prostrate servitude, primitive woodland freedom, and a myth of ethnic origins that [will] cast the longest and darkest shadow over the fate of German nationality'(Schama 1995: 85). Seduced in part by Tacitus's account (replete with such apposite section headings as: 'The Germans are a unique race, unpolluted by intermarriages'), Hitler,

Himmler and Rosenberg demanded a 'return to the natural homeland' and staged a savage Darwinist spectacle to restore the original purity of the race.

Interestingly, at the time when the Germans were busily appropriating the elemental mythology of the North – from solar symbols to flying Valkyrias and ferocious Vikings – the Scandinavians themselves remained relatively unmoved both by *Blut und Boden* and by their own heroic past. Even the 'Aryan Renaissance' launched by native Nazi intellectuals in Norway and Sweden did not fully germinate the ancient seeds. It is as if the violent sagas left no progeny, the virile force died down, the horned terminators were without sequel.

Both the Scandinavians and the Germans profusely employed the common mantras of modernity: Heimat, Gemeinschaft, Bildung, freedom, socialism. But while the German Heimat opposed modernity (unreflectively identified with city culture, exile, decadence and Jewish domination) to an original home, where blood, race and soil remained forever pure and devoid of politics, the Social Democratic idea of the folkhem (people's home) attempted to reconcile modernity with community, the progressive with the conservative, the past with the future, nature with culture. While the Germans dichotomised and contrasted, the Scandinavians fused and reconciled. While the Germans marched, the Scandinavians reasoned.

Numerous questions present themselves. Why, at a time of crisis, did the German nature mythology become intertwined with an anti-individualist, coral-reef mentality and a story of Teutonic superiority, while in Scandinavia it remained affiliated with an egalitarian ethos? Why have the semiotic referents of Scandinavian identity – all of them based on salient emblems of nature – never upset the balance of primordial and civic ingredients? Why, in this case, were blood-and-soil allegiances so elegantly tempered by doctrines of liberalism and individual rights? Is it just the respective socio-political structures and economic predicaments which account for these different trajectories? Or perhaps there is something in the indigenous nature tradition which made the Scandinavians both sceptical about the barbarous holism of the Germans and indifferent to the myth of Nordic Herrenvolk?

In the argument below I shall attempt to illuminate some of these questions by drawing attention to the differences between the German and the Scandinavian 'semiosphere'. The term, launched by Juri Lotman, designates a space analogous with biosphere, within which all the multifarious aspects of a culture are interconnected. Lotman writes:

… imagine a museum hall where exhibits from different periods are on display, along with inscriptions in known and unknown languages, and the instructions for decoding them; besides there are the explanations composed by the museum staff, plans for tours and rules for the behaviour of the visitors. Imagine also in this hall tour-leaders and visitors and imagine all this as a single mechanism (which in a certain sense it is). This is an image of the semiosphere. Then we have to remember that all elements of the semiosphere are in dynamic, not static, correlations whose terms are constantly changing (Lotman 1990: 127).

There are, to be sure, immense economic and political changes which have taken place in the vast span of time between the old Nordic perception of humans as violent players in the theatre of honour and revenge, and the modern Næssian insistence on the cosmic humility of mankind. How have the ancient nature images – and values attached to them – mutated over time and interacted with socio-political transformations?

Nature as ancestor

If we were to follow Lotman and assemble together the main exhibits of the Viking semiosphere – Skaldic poetry, runic alphabet, Viking ships, mythological gods and heroes, various artefacts and their ornamentations along with cult objects – one feature would assert itself above all others: a nature which colonises everything. The actions of gods and heroes imitate elemental forces. The Ringerike serpents, plants and people are joined in an eternal embrace. Trees, snakes and dragons bind the world together and therefore are objects of cultic attention. Animals are ensouled, their spirits outlined by dots, their movements rhythmic and cyclic as in ritual.

This is a world ruled by a universal *imitatio natura;* it remembers its foundation myths as recorded in the Eddas, where everything is made from the body of the god Imir and where gods and heroes are as unpredictable, violent, and uncontrollable as Nature itself.

What is most interesting from the point of view of an imaginal history of Nordic cultures is that, while nature remains an extraordinarily strong marker of personal, tribal and, finally, national identity, nature mythologies and iconography 'forget' violence over time. From the thirteenth century onward, the brutal–heroic narratives characteristic of the sagas are deleted and replaced by largely chaste, prosaic–pastoral images and stories. How can this be accounted for, considering that Christianity was slow to penetrate the Northern wilderness?

One contributing social factor, at least in Norway, might well have been the very disappearance of the aristocracy as a social group cultivating and perpetuating codes of violence. In Denmark and Sweden, where the nobility remained robust over the centuries, myths of supremacy and imperial ambitions lingered on well into the nineteenth century. Yet even here the grand recitals of 'wolf times' never recovered their energising force.

Perhaps by bracketing the sagas, and looking elsewhere for clues, a more legitimate cultural explanation of the short-lived efficacy of the Viking semiosphere might be offered? Presumably, like all epic literature, the savage tales did not encode a 'storied residence' of people at large but recreated a highly selective, grandiloquent, inflated, version of society as a 'community of heroes'. As was the case with nineteenth century travel writers who were more addicted to tales of cannibalism than African tribes ever were to eating their neighbours – the Scalds privileged slaughter not because it was the order of the day but because peaceful life was not considered a proper subject matter for story-telling (Steblin-Kamenskij 1956: 101).

If we look closer at the ancient texts we see that they register not only the individualist deeds of a warrior race but also a much milder, much more symbiotic, even opportunistic, communal ethos. A world of aristocratic feuds exists side by side with a world of pragmatic fishermen and farmers struggling with the elements. What I want to suggest is that there are in fact two opposed moral narratives in Norse literature which spring from two contrasting views of Nature. One, heroic, stresses the beauty of violence and destruction and the sublimity of passion. The other, 'ecological', emphasises survival, balance and self-preservation. The finest example of the second, pragmatic code is to be found in 'Sayings of the High One' ('Håvamål') in the poetic Edda.

Sometimes spurned as a catechism of truisms, didactic proverbs and anecdotes about Odin's amorous misadventures, 'Håvåmal' points, in fact, to a normative ideal which not only has been remarkably durable in Scandinavian life and literature, but which also shows close affiliation with an 'environmentally sound' system of values:

… Have thy eyes about thee when thou enterest
be wary always be watchful always…(1)

… To be bright of brain let no man boast
but take good heed of his tongue (6)

... No mock make thou of any man,
though thou comest among kinsmen.(30)

... Not great things needs give to a man:
bringeth thanks oft a little thing;... (52)

... Middling wise every man should be:
beware of being too wise....(54)

... A wise man will not overweening be,
and stake too much on his strength...(64)[1]

This is not a moral philosophy as such but rather a wisdom, an overall system of knowledge, a set of codes to live by and rules worth following. ('Wisdom' in the Batesonian sense, we might say, as a recognition of, and guidance by, knowledge of a systemic nature). Though it imparts the teachings of the High One, 'Håvamål' contains no reference to a transcendent which would function as a moral absolute or moral authority. It talks of no sanctions and no punishments for wrong conduct; the ultimate punishment is death, the ultimate reward, survival.

Better alive than lifeless be
to the quick fall ay the cattle;
the hearth fire burned for the happy heir–
outdoors a dead man lay. (70)

All 'sustainable values' are included in Odin's ethical advice: carefulness, acceptance of one's own place in the scheme of things, modesty, humility, sympathy for one's fellows. But above all: restraint. Be wise but not too wise, be indulgent but not too indulgent, generous but not too generous, be presentable but not overdressed. Keep measure.

It has been argued that in its elision of such values as honour, excellence and the imperative of revenge, 'Håvamål' stems from and embodies a moral folk tradition and its assorted wisdom (Wax 1969: 95). This seems to be only partially the case, for its impact is to be felt not merely in the ethics of small farmers and fishermen. Again, if we look closer, all the key stories of the Northern gods and heroes are tales of punished incontinence. Odin who craves too much knowledge has to pay for it with his eye. Balder, who is too beautiful, too good and too popular suffers a premature death. Kvasir, who is too wise, is killed by the gods so that his wisdom can be diluted in mead and thus become more equally distributed among his peers. In many respects these are prototypal, divine *Jante lov* (a Danish concept) stories where the main principle is: 'Thou shall not think thou are better than us' (and 'Thou shall not mock us'). Nothing survives when pushed to its limits: neither goodness nor badness. The Christian ideal of the saint who incarnates absolute piety and perfection ('Be ye perfect as your Father in Heaven is perfect'), and the counter-ideal of the devil who is infinitely evil, have been refused entry into this indigenous, 'ecological' code. It has been argued that 'Håvamål' is an ethical wisdom, which had its sources in classical pre-Christian morality. *Disticha Catonis,* the famous schoolbook from late antiquity and gnomic poetry such as the *Irish Book of Proverbs* are mentioned as prototypal texts (Von See 1972; Kålsrud 1958). The provenance of 'Håvamål' does not in any way lessen the vital role of values it registered and transmitted. The values in question were those of a peasant society combating the elements. The sheer struggle for survival turned men, women and animals into a community of interest and strong interdependence. The rampant individualism of the Vikings needed as its counterbalance the spirit of organic solidarity, of being part of a social body, a self-helping, self-sufficient community whose interests must lie beyond personal attachments and animosities (Turville Petre 1974; Holmsen 1976). In such a community pragmatic calculation was more precious than intellectual or imaginative extravagance, while hierarchy was a fragile construct prone to collapse in the face of 'forest democracy'.

There are many indications that the 'ecological' strain in Norse literature established a durable pragmatic nature myth: an enduring existential-ethical narrative which evolved over time and which competed successfully against the romantic fever.

Nordic Light against Germanic Götterdämmerung

Much of the confusion in modern discussions of Scandinavian Romanticism springs from two related misunderstandings: The first one has to do with the omnipresence of Nature (not necessarily Romantic – just Nature in any 'style') as a semiotic referent of Scandinavian identity in the nineteenth century and later. The second confusion stems from the fact that notions of the North as the quintessence of 'Romantic Nature' were largely a creation of more southerly latitudes.

The end of the eighteenth and the beginning of the nineteenth century signalled a breakthrough in geographical fashions and passions. Suddenly the existing moral geography was turned on its head: what once was regarded as a realm of 'ice tongues, foul air and miasmas'(Burton 1927) was now elevated into a region of the sublime: of freedom, vastness, infinity and magnificence. The seven hills of Rome were replaced by soaring peaks and bottomless fjords. The depth of the Northman's soul was set against the shallowness of the Mediterranean character. Anthropology of exclusion became an anthropology of emulation.

Already for Voltaire and Montesquieu the North was synonymous with the original home of freedom *(officina nationum* and *vagina gentium),* while the Nordic man was not only the healthy opposite of Southern decadence; wonderfully free from tyranny and slavery he embodied the Enlightenment ideals of liberty and equality (Castren 1910). Madame de Staël, who is today increasingly burdened with the 'invention of Romanticism', established a durable image of the North as the quintessence of Romantic landscape: *sombre et nébuleuse,* inhabited by ghosts and by passionate, angst-ridden rebels (Staël 1968; Isbell 1994). For Herder and Heine – and later Baudelaire – the religion of nature concealed in runic hieroglyphs was to be found only north of the Baltic Sea (Herder n.d; Baudelaire 1962). For Maurycy Mochnacki, the leading Polish romantic historian and philosopher, the superior Nature of the North was *natura naturans* (i.e. active, creative force) while that of the South, *natura naturata* (i.e. passive nature) (Janion & Zmigrodzka, 1978). Carlyle was virtually obsessed by the 'broad simplicity' and 'superior sincerity of the Scandinavians' as opposed to the 'light gracefulness of the old Greek paganism'. The whole Norse way of looking at the Universe, and adjusting oneself there, has an incredible merit for us', he exulted. 'A rude childlike way of recognising the divinity of Man; most rude, yet heartfelt, robust, giant-like; betaking what a giant of a man this child would grow to' (Carlyle 1911: 26, 40). Mary Wolfestonecraft, in the best tradition of religious pilgrimage, undertook a journey to the Northern mecca of freedom to check for herself. Her travel diary is an interesting document of sober demystification. It speaks of a 'manly race; for not being obliged to submit to any debasing tenure ... they act with an independent spirit'. The independent spirit, however, she finds a bit puzzling, for they 'sing republican songs but are attached to a (Danish) prince royal'. Nature is a spiritual anti-climax: The forests are 'full of philosophers rather than nymphs'. Equality is a diluter of excellence, since a 'mistaken modera-tion which borders on timidity, favours the least respectable of the people'. In a self-revealing passage, Mary Wolfstonecraft concludes: 'I am, therefore half-convinced that I could not live very comfortably exiled from the countries where mankind are so much further advanced in knowledge …' Wolfstonecraft 1796: 76, 79, 110, 117).

How did the nature perceptions of the native elite measure up to these outside representations?

What is clear is that by the mid-nineteenth century Nature and nature-related imagery were recognised as a 'totemic' possession of the Swedes, the Norwegians and the Finns. What is much less clear is the romantic provenance of these represen-tations. For while it is true that Nature is the orbit around which everything else moves in nineteenth century Norwegian writing, the movement itself follows a curiously unromantic trajectory.

In most European cultures Romanticism in literature and the arts was a replica of a revolutionary experiment in the social realm: breaking boundaries, defying taboos, assaulting received canons. Camus, who argued that Romanticism was not so much a cult of individuality but a celebration of the theatrical persona, captures the essence of Romantic anthropology (Camus 1991: 63). The archetypal Romantic rebels – those Giaurs, Corsairs and poets 'wandering lonely as a cloud' – were all actors in a spectacle which was about testing the limits of the natural and the super-natural.

In Scandinavia such actors and such testing were a rarity. The Romantic cult of a superhuman individual staging miracles and defying gods is significantly absent from all Nordic literatures. So is the narcissistic omnipotence of the poet. The Christian ethos accepted by the 'Romantics' in Norway, Sweden and Denmark, was permeated by a deep awareness of human weakness and a consequent subordination to God. As such it went against Hölderlin's ideal of infinite aspiration: 'Das is die Herlichkeit des Menschen, dass ihm ewig nichts genüg'. (Hölderlin 1924: 204). Tegnér's Fridtjof and Rydberg's Faust were created less as versions of Nordic Über-mensch and more as egalitarian idealists struggling against spiritual and worldly serf-dom. Oehlenschläger's Romantic heroes were Danish bourgeois in disguise, taking pleasure in middle-class comfort and eschewing both violent rhetorics and spectac-ular feats. And Grundtvig insisted: 'We were not born to grandeur and magnifi-cence, to stick to the earth will serve us best' (Danstrup 1949: 116). Even his much quoted 'First Man then Christian' advocated not the Romantic challenge to

Christian ideals but what might be called a 'procedural republic', under which all beliefs were to be equally tolerated and protected.

Romanticism as a spectacular theatre of transcendence − of moving beyond personal limitations, social norms and conventions, beyond urban decadence or the horrors of national oppression, beyond humanity itself − could not but be an extraneous implant in countries which lacked cities, aristocracy and professional philosophers. Victor Hugo's *tous les systemes sont faux; les gents seules sont vraix* made little sense in latitudes where lies were as rare as pineapples.

Contrary to received interpretations, Romanticism was banished from, rather than admitted into, the Scandinavian semiosphere (Witoszek 1998). The majority of the cultural elite of the day received it as an anomaly, a violation of native cultural codes of perception and expression, an ethics and aesthetics of excess which very few were prepared to stomach. With very few exceptions (the poetic experiments of Wergeland and the myths of the Swedish Götiska Forbundet come especially to mind), neither romantic formal experiments in literature nor an iconoclastic Faustian-Promethean mythology found real followers in the first half of the nineteenth century. The proliferation of such myths was curbed both by Christian ontology and anthropology and by the native, largely peasant, pragmatic tradition which, for all its 'radicalism', offered a conservative resistance to untried novelty and large scale social revolution.[2]

In Scandinavia the Enlightenment semiosphere remained remarkably unscathed. The 'sound' and 'simple' Nature of Montesquieu and Fenelon − the birthplace of reason, equality and tolerance − was never really challenged by the amoral realm of lust, will and passion. A fascinating, if overlooked, aspect of the Scandinavian narrative creation of the 'peasant mystique' is, precisely, its flight from Romantic stereotypes. In Norway, it was not the 'atavistic', spiritual peasant at one with Nature, but the rationalist *bonde* (farmer) who was elevated into a cultural hero. The 'national' peasant, as celebrated by Moe, Brun and Vinje, was more the bearer of Enlightenment and old classical virtues than of a *pensée sauvage*. Indeed he was something of a village encyclopaedist. Jacob Aall gives an account of the *bønder* (farmers) in Telemark who, with 'their knowledge of the sagas prepared the ground for rationalist theology'. Henrik Steffens exulted over the 'the power of rationalism' in the Opplands' countryside (Paasche 1970; Østerud 1978). Even Wergeland praised the peasants of the sagas, not because they were bearers of a wild spirit, but because they embodied the 'classical virtue of freedom' (Sannes 1959: 122). Similarly

Geijer's *Odalbonden* depicts not so much a primitive peasant in touch with the mystical realm but an individual who was 'his own man' on 'his own ground'. The poem establishes the peasant's credentials as a citizen and producer of national welfare, an important and useful participant in the national community. Very much like the Danish and Norwegian representations of the peasantry, Geijer's peasant may be idealised, but he is hardly the manifestation of a romantic return to a Golden Age of primeval unity with nature. He is a representative, not of a *via antiqua* but of *via moderna*.

The curious 'ventriloquist Romanticism' and the largely utilitarian aspect of Scandinavian representations of Nature is corroborated by the worldview of nascent science and philosophy. Although it is difficult to generalise from a vast body of texts and *bons mots,* it is especially Norwegian thought in the period 1814-1850 which dissociated itself from a romantic *nature mystique*. Niels Treschow, the most influential philosopher of the 'Romantic' period, attempted to restrain and counteract both and the temptations of an emergent positivism and the sinister implications of holism. Treschow's nature was 'a complete, organic whole consisting of independent parts'. Only the revolutionary fanatic will sacrifice an individual for the well being of the whole. 'The particular or the individual is not a means or a tool through which to reach the universal but the goal itself' (Treschow 1963).

The singularity of Norwegian thinking about nature and humanity in the period 1800-1850 becomes especially striking in the comparative context of the dominant German *Naturphilosophie*. The crux of the German Romantic mythology, the kernel around which everything else was elaborated, was the idea of separation and strife. All evil and wickedness were due to an alienation of men (and men they were) from nature, their setting themselves in opposition to the outside world. 'So long as I myself am identical with nature', argued Schelling, 'I understand what a living nature is as well as I understand my own life ... As soon, however, as I separate myself ... from nature, nothing more is left for me but a dead object' (Schelling 1956-61: 57-58). This two dimensional fission between man and external nature, and between the human mind and natural instincts and desires, had an ambivalent ring to it. However negative, the man–nature split was the *sine qua non* condition of German speculative philosophy whose aim was to reconcile oppositions and restore unity (op. cit. 77). However painful, the ever-evolving process of oppositions, reconciliations and renewed oppositions was a constructive movement in humanity's *Bildungsgeschichte*. For Schiller, the separation from nature was ultimately a fortunate division: for it is culture *(eine höhere Kunst)* which will lead us back to nature again (Schiller 1967: 49-53). In Schlegel's attempts to revive the communion with nature – *jebes alldurchdringende tiefe Naturgefhühl, an die geistige Naturverehrung der Edda* – Nature dissolved into genius, and vice versa. Such Nature – alienated and projected into the superhuman – was a narcissistic process which coincided with the Romantic aesthetic ideal (Schlegel 1975: 225-41). In the extreme, ominous vision of Hölderlin, all the suffering and evil ensuing from the separation from Nature was necessary in order to achieve a new, higher synthesis: 'Men fall from thee, O Nature, like rotten fruits; oh let them perish, for thus they return to thy root; so may I too, O tree of life, that I may grow green again with thee' (Hölderlin 1946-1962: 159).

These matters are worth rehearsing if only to see that the main ideational premise for romantic philosophising about Nature (or rather the divorce of humanity from nature) was largely absent from the experience of nineteenth century Scandinavians. Certainly in Norway the paucity of metropolitan culture deprived discursive forays into nature of their necessary antithesis and compelling *raison d'être*. There was simply no negative foil against which to construe a truly romantic narrative of return to an 'authentic, rooted existence' or indeed to inspire mystical raptures over a living tree. In their conflation of Nature, History and Nation, none of the Norwegian 'romantics' envisioned, with Schiller, an aesthetic state beyond and apart from Christian-ethic ideals. As Wolfgang Weber has argued, in Scandinavian discourse Nature by and large preserved its more 'prosaic' status as people's primary environment. Its beauty was less terrible or awesome, and more intimate and familiar (Weber 1996).

The Norwegian reception of German romantic philosophy reveals further interesting discrepancies. It is striking that, from the very beginning, the point of heightened sensitivity in Norwegian responses to German Romanticism was, paradoxically, the very 'unnaturalness' of the latter. Nature that submitted so readily to the terrorism of language, to the passion for unintelligible truths and pompous verbiage, was not celebrated but deleted. Already in the eighteenth century a Norwegian poet sneered: 'Germany, oh Germany, in Hermans awash / how deep you are sunk in nonsense and tosh' (Caspari 1917: 2). Irritated and repelled by German philosophical baroque, Norwegians studying philosophy and theology in Copenhagen felt a redoubled nostalgia for the sweet simplicity of their native idiom and cast themselves ever more zealously into the other extreme: the salty rationalism of the dwellers by the fjords.

The native assault on German romantic philosophy intensified in the 1830s. For the leading national poet Welhaven, Hegelianism was but a 'play with auxiliary verbs' (Aall 1911: 398). Norwegian writers sided with the classical persona of Goethe, a staunch opponent of Romanticism, which he defined as a sickness (Goethe 1969: 328). Anton Martin Schweigaard declared German nature philosophy remote from reality and therefore un-Norwegian ('unorsk') in the extreme. In particular, he scoffed at the *a priori* school, which proceeded 'without entering into any relation to the outer world, without deriving from it, without enriching itself with facts and experience' (Schweigaard 1883: 137; 1904: 243).[3] And Treschow, that empiricist *par excellence,* criticised German philosophy from a Christian position:

Even according to the latest tenets of Nature philosophy, the struggle for individuation is common throughout the natural world. But what does it mean without the assumption of the ultimate and unchanging form? It seems that Schelling confuses this struggle with the desire for separation, isolation and independence from the Absolute. This confusion leads inevitably to abandoning the world of Ideas for the world of the senses and thus to degeneration and moral decay (Treschow 1927: 192-23).

The message was clear: The Norwegians embraced nature, God and reality, the Germans, for all their *Naturphilosophie,* betrayed them all. The Norwegians cultivated healthy common sense, the Germans went for 'pie in the sky'. So unequivocal and comprehensive was the native rejection of Germanic *romantische Schwarmerei* that, for some Danish literati, Norwegian steadfast common sense became a hallmark of 'true healthy nordicity' which in Denmark was in imminent danger of Germanisation (Dietrichson 1866: 151).

There are many indications that, in spite of the later impact of Hegelianism, the Scandinavian elite's early self-image of themselves as guardians of Enlightenment values against the dark energies of the German romantics proved to be a durable component of the national self-perceptions (Bruun 1898: 111, 117).

There were of course exceptions – the Norwegian Romantic painters were, after all, the graduates of German art academies. Yet even here the canvases which became the icons of the nation were not so much celebrations of an inscrutable, esoteric or erotic Nature as Tideman and Gude's *landschafts* with festive peasants posed against predictable, measurable, four dimensional Nature. It is the convex clarity and intelligibility of Dahl's green-blue skies, light-suffused birches, dreaming sunrays on the red trunks of pines rather than the mystic, suffering forests of Hertervig or Cappelen which represent the 'soul' of Norway. The collective memory has preferred – and preserved – landscapes of the mind rather than the romantic scenery of the tormented soul.

A confidence in the unsullied authority of Reason as an agent of benevolent forces within Nature, remained dominant in the Scandinavian intellectual tradition for the greater part of the nineteenth century. It may well be that, 'prosaic' but tenacious as it was, it effectively withstood the hypnotic power of Reason's natural competitors: will, instinct and race. Not until the *fin de siècle* generation of alienated vitalist writers *(vide* Hamsun), did Nature usurp the role of Reason and force it to bow to the deeper wisdom of community and tradition, to blood, soil and the subterranean forces of the psyche.

'Ecohumanism'

It is, then, one of the meta-ironies of Romanticism that, while nineteenth century Europe was romancing the North as an incarnation of romantic rebellion, the North itself embraced a 'middle course' in which brains were certainly more precious than blood. It evoked nostalgia for a comprehensible, rational, ecologically 'simple and natural' world. It embodied the Romantic ideal without being quite Romantic, like a Pre-Raphaelite beauty with the soul of a milkmaid.

To speak of 'Nordic classicism' is to impute a derivative character to what was basically a native tradition going back to the folk wisdom of the Eddas. I wish to suggest that what gives the period of nation-building its ideological and poetic coherence and integrity is a tradition which might be tentatively described as 'eco-humanist.'[4] Eco-humanism in this case refers to a cosmology based on humanist ideals, but one in which the symbolic referents of identity derive from nature imagery and from a particular allegiance to place. The basic premise of humanism, the recognition of the inherent dignity and of the equal and unalienable rights of all members of the human family, is here modified by values springing from man's experience of nature. It is the art of the *via media* and *vita activa,* based on the knowledge of nature's ways and moderated by the awareness of limitations inherent both in nature and in society. The 'eco-' prefix, we may say, protects humanism from its own excesses.

The eco-humanist tradition of knowledge is forged less by the lore of the city and more by the 'wisdom of the open air': it promotes realism rather than extravagance, equality rather than hierarchy and, though it launches organic, holistic perceptions of nature, it measures the value of the environment and culture in individualist and utilitarian rather than in romantically idealist terms. After all, pragmatism, as William James remarked, 'means the open air and the possibilities of nature, as against … dogma, artificiality and the preference of finality in truth' (James 1975: 13).

The attempt to identify an 'ecohumanist' strain in Scandinavian cultural history is not merely to de-romanticise a tradition which still employs Nature as its central image; it is to suggest that the dominant system of values which in the last two hundred years empowered social change in countries like Norway, Sweden and Denmark has been based on a particular worldview and a corresponding code of action. Although there is no doubt that this code was not shared equally by all social groups, it has nevertheless constituted a crucial axiological reference system. Nobody who has aspired to political or cultural leadership could afford to ignore it in the past century.

We might add here that it is the same Nature of Scandinavian Enlightenment – one that was allowed to flourish in cultures largely spared the experience of social debasement and bestiality – which goes some way to explain the terrible beauty of Arne Næss's deep ecology. Notwithstanding Næss's own insistence on the influence of Spinoza, Gandhi and Advaita Vedanta on his work, there is an invisible tradition that nourishes his green utopia – invisible by virtue of the mere fact that Næss is so completely immersed in it and so unconsciously in dialogue with it. As I have argued elsewhere, central to Næss's ecological work is the notion of the proper cosmic humility of humankind (Witoszek 1997). This is the old 'Håvamåleasque wisdom'. The distance between the ancient Scandinavian *codex naturae* and Næss is nothing like the distance between, say, Beowulf and Sir Alfred Ayer. In the Norwegian case the values of moderation and respect for the elements that were codified in 'Håvamål' and then incubated for centuries were simply re-canonised by Næss – and with them, the pragmatic tradition that gives priority to action over the word, experience over fixed principle, practice over theory. Its discourse and its worldview are, on the whole, rather wintry, unresponsive to the power of passion, the metaphysics of evil and the lure of eroticism. Ultimately, it rests on a belief in a cosmic whole where every organism, from the King to your local friendly wolf is a good, self-restrained Protestant citizen.

Conclusions

In the above I have tried to compare some aspects of the mythical and ethical biographies of modern Western European cultures that shared – and later invoked – a similar story of origins but nonetheless ideologically diverged from one another. It is a hazardous comparison. One has to take into consideration the radically different environments involved. In one case we deal with a relatively homogenous society – both religiously and ethnically – and one, which, by comparison with Germany, has been largely spared the trepidations and devastations of wars and revolutions. In the other case we are confronted with a multi-cultural, multi-religious mosaic of communities, which were continuously traumatised in the course of history and hence were naturally more prone to reach for consolatory narratives and ideological salvage kits. In one tradition individual rights had been brutally quenched by authoritarian rulers, in the other, the rights of the subject were basically respected, even under absolutist kings such as Charles XII (Roberts 1967). What was significantly absent from the Norwegian and Swedish countryside was the experience of serfdom and of the dehumanising machinations of state bureaucracy and officialdom on a scale comparable with the rest of Europe. What was present – and unique in comparison with other peasant societies – was the sense of individual rights and freedoms fostered by the allodial property system. For centuries the legally free peasantry – even under tenancy conditions – had felt themselves to be answerable only to God and King. Freedom, democracy and egalitarianism were ideas which may not have had a strict institutional basis at the beginning of the nineteenth century but, as has been frequently noted, they were prefigured for centuries prior to the Norwegian Constitution of 1814 in the social practices and communal ethos of countless villages and valleys (Østerud 1979: 129).

These political and economic differences cannot, of course, be ignored. Yet cultural values and their shaping influence have an – as yet – unacknowledged power. At the turn of the century, the Germans, the Norwegians and the Swedes resorted to nature to define their identity. But they employed two nature stories – and consequently two opposing identities – whose sources lay in respective traditions. One has been hierarchical, emotive and violent, the other egalitarian, prosaic and rational. One opposed Nature to Reason, the other has conflated them. One has celebrated a Faustian *Übermensch,* the other has preferred a humanist survivor. One has presided over the *entgültige Lösung,* the other has supported the gentle despotism of the mediocre and the insecure. As I have argued elsewhere, the workings of the opposing legacies – and the corresponding ethics – were especially manifest in the strategies to tackle the Great Crisis of the thirties (Witoszek 2002). The Scandinavians embraced an 'ecological' approach – ecological in the sense of giving priority to adaptability and survival. Unlike the German dichotomising of Romanticism, the Nordic conciliatory, pragmatic stance was not just an ad hoc strategy of the political leaders, but a 'group-think', the roots of which lay in the native tradition.

By suggesting that the birth of national communities in Scandinavia should be reconsidered in the context of continuity, and vis-à-vis the tradition of Christian Enlightenment rather than by drawing analogies with European Romanticism, I hope to draw attention to a value system which, I believe, informed not only much of nineteenth century cultural and political developments but established a cultural legacy which bears on the present. The ancient semiosphere – alloyed later with the Enlightenment ideas of nature – was usurpatory in the sense that it comprised not only a vast amount of newly created, translated and interpreted texts, but a programme for generating future texts (Lotman 1990: 14). Most significantly, it created an influential representation of Scandinavia (Norway in particular) as an outpost of ecological awareness and humanist values, an image that the Scandinavian countries largely assimilated to themselves and cultivated in the past century. This representation, and the legacy behind it, may today be a source of frustration – if not virtual bewilderment – to the outside world. It is especially those who insist on seeing whale hunting in the romantic rather than pragmatic light, that miss the deeper cultural weight of the tradition which has empowered Scandinavian images of and attitudes to nature over the past millennium. The fact that a 'moral community' that has yielded ecophilosophy insists on consuming a mammal that has become a totem animal of international environmental movements, testifies not just to the economic interests involved, but to the durability of values that remain active in the Jurassic Park of culture.

NOTES

1. The quotations come from 'The Sayings of Hár: Hávamál' in *The Poetic Edda*, trans. Lee M. Hollander. Austin: University of Texas Press, 1978.

2. *Vidar*, a noteworthy journal of the Norwegian Intellectual Party in the 1830s devoted most of its columns to an extensive critique of the new aesthetics and the correspon-

ding worldview. Leading Norwegian writers and historians (A. Schweigaard, J.P. Welhaven, J. Collett and P.A. Munch) who were also the trend-setters of the day, spilled a great deal of ink condemning almost everything European Romanticism prized: the priority of emotions (read 'emotional muddle'), formal experimentation (read 'formlessness'), fascination with evil ('moral licence') and spirituality ('indulgence in hypochondrias'). See the debate in *Vidar* (Kristiania), especially issues 1-9 (1832-1834).

3. After a research trip to Berlin, Schweigaard complained about the *überschwenglich Nonsens* and *Charlatanisk bombast* of the academy and insisted he had never seen 'so many sublime trivialities and indigestible crudities growing in that part of Germany that calls itself most urbane and educated'. His lecture in the Studenterforbundet (Student Society) in 1833 on 'falske Idealer, Systemtvang og Goethes Kunstbestrebelse som begge modsat' elaborated some of his critique. See L.M. Aubert (ed.), *Anton Martin Schweigaard's barndom og ungdom: 1808-1835, breve og erindringer* (Kristiania: Mallings Forlag, 1883) p. 137. See also Anton Martin Schweigaard, *Ungdomsarbeider* (Kristiania: Aschehoug Forlaget, 1904), p. 243.

4. The concept of 'eco-humanism' is used here in a metaphorical sense; it designates a set of phenomena which were prior to the proper discovery of the environment and the establishment of the science of ecology. As such it is a result of a struggle to name, and thereby to come to terms with, a distinctive tradition of knowledge which was heavily influenced by the dynamics of man's relationship to nature.

REFERENCES

Aall, A. 1811-1911. *Filosofien*. Det Kongelige Frederiks Universitet, Vol. II. Oslo: Aschehoug.

Aubert, L.M. (ed.) 1883. *Anton Martin Schweigaard's barndom og ungdom: 1808-1835, breve og erindringer*. Kristiania: Mallings Forlag.

Baudelaire, C. 1962. *Curiosités estethiques. L'art romantique et autres oeuvres critiques*. Paris.

Bruun, C. 1898. *Folkelige Grundtanker*. Kristiania: Al. Cammermeyers Forlag.

Burton, R. [1929]. *Anatomy of Melancholy*. In Floyd Dell & Paul Jordan Smith (eds.). New York: Farrar & Rinehart.

Camus, A. 1991. *The Rebel: An Essay on Man in Revolt*. New York: Vintage Books.

Carlyle, T. 1911 [1840]. *On Heroes and Hero Worship*. Melbourne and Toronto: Ward, Locke.

Caspari, T. 1917. *Lore. Norsk naturfølelse i det nittende århundrede*. Kristiania: Aschehoug Forlaget.

Castren, G. 1910. *Norden i den franska litteraturen*. Stockholm.

Danstrup, J. 1949. *History of Denmark*. New York: Wivels Forlag.

Dietrichson, L. 1866. *Omrids af den norske poesis historie. Norges bidrag til felleslitteraturen.* Copenhagen: Gyldendalske Boghandel.

Goethe, J.W. v. 1969. *Goethe's Gesprache.*, Vol. 1. W. Herwig (ed.). Zürich.

Herder, G. (n.d.) Ideen zur Philosophie der Geschichte der Menschkeit. In *Deutsche nasjonal Litteratur,* LXXVII, ch. 4, book 18, J. Kurschner (ed.). Stuttgart.

Hölderlin, F. 1929. Hyperions Jugend. In *Sämtliche Werke,* Vol. III, Friedrich Beissner (ed.). Stuttgart: J.G. Cottasche Buchhandlung Nachfolker.

Holmsen, A. 1966. *Gard, Bygd, Rike.* Oslo: Universitetsforlaget.

Holmsen, A. 1976. *Nye studier i gammel historie.* Oslo: Universitetsforlaget.

Hobsbawm, E. 1995. *Age of Extremes.* London: Abacus.

Isbell, A. 1994. *The Birth of European Romanticism: Truth and Propaganda in de Staël's De L'Allemagne.* Cambridge: Cambridge University Press.

James, W. 1975. *Pragmatism.* Harvard University Press.

Janion, M. & M. Zmigrodzka 1978. *Romantycyzm i Historia.* Warszawa: PIW.

Jordanova, L. 1976. *Languages of Nature: Critical Essays in Science and Literature.* London: Free Association Press.

Kålsrud, O. 1958. *Norges Kyrkjesaga.* Oslo: Aschehoug.

Lotman, J.M. 1990. *Universe of the Mind: A Semiotic Theory of Culture.* London: I.B. Tauris.

Lovejoy, A. 1948. *Essays in the History of Ideas.* Baltimore: The John Hopkins University Press.

Paasche, F. 1979. *Norges litteraturhistorie,* Vol. 3. Oslo: Aschehoug.

Roberts, M. 1967. *Essays in Swedish History.* London: Weidenfeld and Nicolson.

Sannes, H.J. 1959. *Patrioter, Intelligens og Skandinaver: norske reaksjoner på skandinavismen før 1848.* Oslo: Universitetsforlaget.

Schelling, F. 1856-61. Ideen zu einer Philosophie der Natur. In *Sämtliche Werke,* Vol. II. Stuttgart: Cotta'Scher.

Schiller, F. 1967[1795]. *On the Aesthetic Education of Man.* Oxford: Clarendon Press.

Schlegel, F. 1975 [1812]. Über nordische Dichtkunst. In *Charakteristiken und kritiken,* Vol. II, H. Eicher (ed.). Munchen: Verlag Ferdinand Schöningh.

Schweigaard, A.M. 1904. *Ungdomsarbeider.* Kristiania: H. Aschehoug Forlaget.

See, K. v. 1972. *De Gestalt der Håvamål. Eine Studie zur eddischen Sprachdichtung.* Frankfurt/Main: Athenahm.

Schama, S. 1995. *Landscape and Memory.* London: Harper and Collins.

Short, J.R. 1991. *Imagined Country: Society, Culture and Environment.* London: Routledge.

Steblin-Kamenskij, M.I. 1953. *The Saga Mind.* Odense: Odense University Press.

Staël' Mme de. 1968 [1813]. *De L'Almagne.* S. Malay (ed.). Paris.

Treschow, N. 1927. *Philosophiske Forsøg og andre Skrifter*. Oslo: Aschehoug.

Treschow, N. 1963. *Menneskeværd og Mennesekevel*. Oslo: Tanum.

Turville Petre, G. 1974. On Skaldic Poetry. *Medieval Scandinavia*, Vol. 7.

Wax, R.H. 1969. *Magic, Fate and History: the Changing Ethics of the Vikings*. Lawrence: Colorado Press.

Weber, W. 1996. Nordisk fortid som chiliastisk fremtid. Den 'norrøne arv' og den sykliske historieopfattelse i Skandinavien og Tyskland omkring 1800 og senere. Unpublished manuscript.

Witoszek, N. 1997. Arne Naess and the Norwegian Nature Tradition. *Worldviews*, Vol. 1, No. 1.

Witoszek, N. 1998a. The Unromantic Romantics: The Norwegian Nature Tradition. In *Nature in the History of Knowledge*, R. Porter & M. Teich (eds.). Cambridge: Cambridge University Press.

Witoszek, N. 1998b. The Fugitives from Utopia: the Scandinavian Enlightenment Reconsidered. In *The Cultural Construction of Norden*, B. Strath & Ø. Sorensen (eds.). Oslo: Scandinavian University Press.

Witoszek, N. 2002. Crisis and the Politics of National Community: Germany and Sweden 1933/44. In *Culture and Crisis*, N. Witoszek & L. Trägårdh (eds.). Oxford: Berghahn Books.

Wolfstonecraft, M. 1796. *Letters Written During a Short Residence in Sweden, Norway and Denmark*. London: J.J. Johnson, St. Pauls Church-Yard.

Østerud, Øyvind 1978. *Agrarian Structure and Peasant Politics in Scandinavia*. Oslo: Universitetsforlaget.

The duality of indigenous environmental knowledge among the Fulani of northern Burkina Faso

Bjarke Paarup-Laursen & Lars Krogh

Introduction

In the interface between anthropology, development studies and human geography one of today's buzzwords is 'indigenous knowledge'. Policy makers and development workers have increasingly realised that the incorporation of an indigenous knowledge component in soil and water conservation projects gives insight into farmers' conceptual models of nature and their priorities, and thus facilitates development of new or adapted technologies, which are attractive and viable for local populations (Mazzucato & Niemeijer 1997). This also applies to the sub-Saharan region of West Africa, where soil and water are some of the most constraining resources for sustainable agricultural development (Eswaran et al. 1997). In this process of political recognition indigenous knowledge has been reified, in that it is 'often viewed as the latest and best strategy in the old fight against hunger, poverty and underdevelopment' (Agrawal 1995). The question is whether indigenous knowledge is a specific field that we can outline, substantiate and activate in development plans?

The analysis of indigenous knowledge has a long tradition in anthropology, and during the last forty years this field has increasingly become central in development studies. However, the theoretical understanding and value assigned to indigenous knowledge has changed dramatically during the period. Expressed simplified, in the sixties, Modernisation Theorists and Marxists considered indigenous people as conservative and indigenous knowledge was often perceived as the main obstacle to 'rational' modern development (Bendix 1967; Kahn 1985; Agrawal 1995). Over the last decade or more the general perspective has changed and a number of studies have attempted to show the ecological wisdom of indigenous knowledge (e.g.

Rappaport 1968; Brokensha, Warren & Werner, 1980; Richards 1985; Breemer 1992; Croll & Parkin, 1992), and today indigenous knowledge is considered the very platform of sustainable development (Richards 1985; Chambers 1993).

Although most studies of indigenous knowledge are somewhere between these extremes, it is our objective to demonstrate that it may be possible or even necessary to hold both positions at the same time. We believe that ecological rationality and wisdom, or the opposite, cannot a priori be assigned to specific ethnic groups, but must be substantiated through thorough analysis (Reenberg & Paarup-Laursen 1997). The argument is based on a study among the Fulani of northern Burkina Faso.

The Fulani of northern Burkina Faso have an intimate and dynamic, experimentally derived knowledge of their natural environment, and at the same time they have certain inflexible concepts of it, which are intimately linked to their ethnic and social identity. The latter type of perception seems not to be compatible with the experimentally derived knowledge. Our problem is thus: How are we to understand both the experimental character of indigenous knowledge and the traditionalist or anti-modernist attitude of the same ethnic or social groups?

In order to reach our aims it is relevant analytically to distinguish between different aspects of indigenous knowledge of the natural environment with different headlines, like knowledge and classification, knowledge and practice, and knowledge and identity. All knowledge is presumably generated and regenerated by the same type of cognitive processes. However, this does not necessarily mean that knowledge is consistent, and the segmentary character of knowledge is evident if we look upon the different domains of human life. The three-tier distinction is in line with the transformational model Descola outlines to 'account for the largely implicit schemes of praxis through which each society objectifies specific types of relations with its environment' (Descola & Pálsson 1996). Each local cultural construction of nature results, he argues, 'from a particular combination of three basic dimensions of social life' (ibid.) The three dimensions are: modes of identification, modes of interaction, and modes of classifications (Descola 1996). Descola relates each dimension of social life to principles specific of each dimension in an attempt to make a general classification of our relation to the environment. We do not consider the outline of a general classification a central priority but consider the applied distinction between three types of knowledge an ad hoc model developed to account for the obvious contradiction encountered among the Fulani of both dynamic experimental knowledge and inflexible positions. We therefore limit ourselves to apply the model in the analysis of different aspects of knowledge of the environment in the Fulani society. We want to stress that we do not consider this model part of a distinction between Western and traditional knowledge systems, but consider the model relevant for any social group with an identifiable identity/culture (Agrawal 1995).

The study uses a multidisciplinary approach combining anthropology and physical geography, thus allowing us to deal with the great range of topics we believe necessary to include in the analysis.

Materials and methods

Study area

The study area includes two Fulani villages in the tropical, semi-arid Sahel zone of northern Burkina Faso in West Africa; Bidi in Oudalan Province and Petacole in Seno Province, separated by a latitude distance of 50 km. The two villages serve as study sites for the SEREIN project (Reenberg, 1995) and this article is therefore based on fieldwork carried out there. Both villages were established in the second half of last century by Fulani immigrants from Mali. Bidi counts approximately 300 inhabitants (Reenberg and Fog, 1995) and consists of thirty to forty households. Petacole has approximately 300 inhabitants, divided into thirty to forty households. In ethnic terms the people of the villages are Fulani (French: Peul). About twenty-five percent are FulBe, formerly an aristocrat subgroup (Peul Noble) who based their livelihood on nomadic livestock rearing, while the remainder are RimayBe, the former slaves of the FulBe. The two subgroups coexist but the former division between masters and slaves still influences their relationship. During the droughts of the 70s and 80s large herds of cattle were lost and it is generally assumed that the percentage and number of sedentary farmers in the area has increased (Claude et al., 1991). Today all households are depending on subsistence millet cultivation although many households have a small number of cattle.

Investigation methods

The fieldwork was carried out between March and August 1995 and January and February 1996. The methods used for the investigation were open-ended qualitative interviews, conducted in French, Hausa and Fulfulde, with the aid of an experienced translator, involving the leaders, elders and active farmers. When appropriate, interviews were combined with field visits where discussions concerning soils, land-scape and environmental resources were held on the basis of boring samples, maps and air and satellite photos.

Results

Fulani knowledge of their natural physical environment

The Fulani hold perceptions of their natural physical environment on various levels and in various contexts. As for knowledge and classification we will limit our outline to Fulani perceptions of landscape and soil.[1]

Knowledge and classification

The Fulani language, Fulfulde, does not include a term similar to the Western concept 'landscape'. The term landscape is here used as an etic term to cover the most general expression of the perception of natural features. It is general because it covers the classification of various physical features of nature in abstract, i.e. non-socio-centric terms and because it includes the syntagmatic relationship of different specific natural features; rivers and dams as well as different botanical or physical features like forests, hills, etc. The most general and central of Fulani classifications of their environment are the distinction between *seno* and *koladde*. *Seno* (pl. *senore*) is a term applied for the huge transverse dune bands, which run east–west with approximately 30km separation across northern Burkina Faso. *Koladde* (singl. *kollangal*) is a term for the pediplain. *Seno* and *koladde* characterise, together with *cheki,*[2] (singl. *chekol*) (an unspecific term for rivers and riverbeds) the central types of landscape in Seno and Oudalan provinces.

The Fulani also assign meaning to the central categories of the landscape. To the Fulani, *seno* is the central element of the landscape as indicated in the name of their province in Burkina Faso. In relation to agriculture the Fulani perceive *seno* as the ideal area for farming, while *koladde* is principally perceived as pastureland. The Fulani farmers esteem *seno* high because *seno* as farmland is easy to cultivate. The manual operations associated with millet cultivation on *seno:* clearing, sowing and weeding, demand less work input than on clayey pediplain soils due to the loose consistency of the sand. Furthermore, yields are not so dependent on a threshold rainfall, as infiltration is rapid and the water retention characteristics are favourable compared to those on clayey soils.

The two main types of landscapes are associated with specific soil materials. Thus *seno* indicates a sandy soil and *koladde* indicates a clayey soil. Apart from being distinguished according to clay content, soil is also classified according to colour. Five colours were mentioned; *boderi* (red), *buneri* (black), *boleal* (grey), *orlal* (yellow) and *daneri* (white). This classification cuts across *seno* and *koladde* distinctions in that both types can be classified as, for example, red. The colour classifications are very much based on specific local experience and related to its use value in brick production, agricultural soil etc. Classification of colour and the above classifications related to different types of landscape feature, do not seem to interlink. The two were considered by informants to be different perspectives on the same reality.

Knowledge and practice

The knowledge tied to practice is evident in relation to agriculture and more specifically in relation to the cultivation of millet. In this respect, a number of subdivisions of *seno* and *koladde* emerge that are based on criteria such as the depth of sand and the clay content of sand. The terms are descriptive, specifying the quality of *seno* and *koladde* for millet cultivation.

The characteristics are termed hot and cold. Hot and cold are relative categories referring to the fertility of the soil as well as to the texture of the soil. *Seno* tends to be cold, while *koladde* tends to be hot. The classification also refers to the amount of rainfall the soil needs to be productive. Water adds coldness to the soil. Hot soil (clay soil) needs a lot of water to make it colder. Cold soil (sandy soil) does not need much water, as it will make it too cold for the crops to grow. Cold soil can be made hotter by applying manure. Hot and cold soils not only need different amounts of rain, but also different intervals between rainfalls. Cold soil can do without rain for several weeks, while hot soil needs rain at least every eight days. Likewise, the planting of the seeds is carried out at different times in the two types of soil. In the cold *seno* soil, planting has to take place after the first good rain. If replanting has to take place late in the season the soil often becomes too cold due to heavier rainfall. In the hot clay soil this is not a problem as the soil will rarely be too cold for plants to grow.

Similarly, Fulani farmers have knowledge of a number of crops and crop varieties, as well as vast meteorological knowledge. They make a number of choices during the agricultural season depending on the type of soil, rainfall and the time of the season, all linked to an intimate knowledge of their natural environment and the changes that have taken place in recent years.

Knowledge and identity

The Fulani also view their natural environment in socio-centric terms. The environment is viewed from the human settlement and the perception of the relationship between village and natural environment reflects a specific human identity. The Fulani distinguish, as is common (Croll & Parkin 1993), between the human settlement, *wuro*, and the natural environment, the bush, *ladde*. The term *wuro* not only designates a village, but any settlement, even a compound in the bush (see also Riesman 1977). The relationship between *wuro* and *ladde* is thus not one of a fixed spatial distinction between a dense settlement/village and a non-inhabited bush, but *wuro* and *ladde* are relative terms characterising the relationship between any human settlement and a non-cultivated bush.

While *wuro* is the place of human life, *ladde* is the area outside human control, i.e. the place of animals. *Ladde* is the home of various non-human powers first and foremost the animals. The most central of the animals related to *ladde,* and the one identifying *ladde,* is the lion. The name of the lion is not called directly but through the eufemenon, the cat and the dog of the bush (see also Riesmann 1977). The relationship to the lion is one of fear. In numerous stories man's relationship to the lion is described as one of fear, often causing a complete breakdown in the behaviour associated with humans. Confrontations with the lion cause an inability in a person to orient himself, and the general response to the encounter is temporary insanity. 'A man became so scared when he saw a lion that when he entered the village and he got water to drink, he did not drink it, but put it in his pocket' (Interview in Petacole, 1995). The relationship to the lion is similar to the relationship to wizards and jinns also inhabiting the bush and also causing insanity, a condition rather common in Fulani society. As has been described for many other ethnic groups, the dangers of the bush are most active at night and at noon.

The border between *wuro* and *ladde* is not marked. There are no markers at the entrance to the village or compound that guard the village against the forces of the bush. This has to do with the fact that the distinction is relative. To the FulBe the delimitation of the bush is not spatial and linked to society, but individual. Rather than being a spacial distinction in society it is a distinction linked to the identity of being FulBe and is closely bound up with the concept of *pulaaku* (true FulBeness). In short *pulaaku* mean 'qualities appropriate to the Fulani' (Riesman 1977). It includes physical qualities such as being light-skinned and slender, and socio-cultural qualities like a sense of shame and the mastering of one's needs and emotions.

The socio-cultural qualities of *pulaaku* are central in the establishment of a relationship to the bush. In the encounter with the forces of the bush, such as jinns and the lion, it is central for a FulBe to be able to control his emotions. Lack of control of emotions – as expressed in fear – cause sickness, mainly insanity. Thus the relation to the bush is relative, and individually related to identity as a FulBe.

The lack of delimitation of the bush is also related to the fact that the *ladde* is not only a dangerous domain. The bush is a positive domain because it is the central resource, both as potential farmland, but even more so as pasture for the cattle. FulBe identity is closely linked to cattle, and moving with the cattle in the bush is a kind of initiation into the FulBe way of life. The bush is, at one and the same time, the central resource and a space of freedom – both as a way of life where the FulBe can earn his living on the basis of a more or less open access to the bush, being free to move anywhere, and also for the individual shepherd who is free from the social control of the village (Paarup-Laursen 1996). The bush is also highly valued as a space for reflection, a quiet space outside the disturbance and demands of the village, often used to reflect on the nature of God. The bush is thus central to FulBe identity both as an economic resource and as a space for individual freedom and reflection. Also as a negation of the pleasures of social life, the bush is central to the FulBe. In youth while wandering with the cattle, it shapes the hard and enduring personality the Fulbe relate to *pulaaku*.

Thus the clear-cut distinction between village and bush as the human and non-human space is not present. And there is no communal spatial marking of this distinction. The delimitation of village and bush is not primarily a communal problem but an individual one. The individual shows his FulBeness (*pulaaku*) by being able to handle the negative forces of the bush. The dangers in relation to the bush are not to be avoided, but the effects are to be controlled. Not controlled through communal rituals, but through the individuals control of his emotions.

Discussion

The three types of knowledge outlined above can be described as part of a more general field termed culture. In the last decade the general trend in social studies have been to focus on culture as practices rather than culture as ideas. Barth (1995) suggests that we recognise 'knowledge as a major modality of culture' (see also Barth 1975, 1987, 1993). Here knowledge refers to 'what people employ to interpret and act on the world: feelings as well as thoughts, embodied skills as well as taxonomies and other verbal models' (Barth, 1995).[3] The focus on knowledge rather than culture stresses the fragmentary character of the world we live in (Barth 1989) and may make it relevant to talk of different types of knowledge with different characteristics. Barth focuses on the open and transitive character of knowledge, but tends to focus less on the hegemonic character of certain kinds of knowledge. Also Cohen (1993) focuses on the segmentary character of knowledge. He argues that knowledge is central to self-identification, both in the external relations of a society as in a local versus expert discrimination, as well as in the 'internal' positioning of every member of society. The outline of segmentary knowledge and its importance to the introduction of new knowledge is highly illuminating. But we find that Cohen, just as he criticises others, homogenises knowledge (1993: 37-38). His analysis is based on a society where knowledge, identity and practice,[4] although multiplicite (op. cit. 32), can all be said to belong to a common 'field'. In some societies self-identification refers to a field that is outside daily practice and in many societies social groups are not free to define themselves, but are defined by dominant groups or classes. Thus there is not always an intimate and open relationship between practice and self-identification.

We therefore find it relevant not only to talk about knowledge of the environment as segmentary but to distinguish between different modes of knowledge of the environment such as knowledge related to classification of the environment, knowledge related to specific practice in relation to the natural environment and knowledge linked to identity.[5]

FulBe and RimayBe

As stated in the introduction in ethnic terms the people of these villages identify themselves as Fulani, but at the same time acknowledge a division into an original and aristocratic subgroup (Peul Noble) here termed FulBe, and the RimayBe, the former slaves of the FulBe. In the villages studied the two groups share more or less the same general classifications of the environment as seen in the relationship between *seno* and *koladde,* although they may evaluate them differently. The same is the case for the conceptions relevant in agricultural practice as in the specifications of soil. On the other hand, it is evident that the relation between *wuro* and *ladde* is perceived differently by the FulBe and RimayBe. Where FulBe focus on the relation to the bush as linked to individual identity and in more general terms to FulBe identity, then the RimayBe perceive the relation between village and bush as a relation between the social and the non-social in the line of most ethnic groups in Africa (Croll & Parkin 1992). To the RimayBe, *ladde* is productive, but linked with various dangers. *Ladde* does not carry the positive connotations to individual life and is not closely linked to control of emotions.

The identity of the FulBe is well described in the literature (Stennings 1959, Dupire 1970, Riesman 1977). Apart from the concept of *pulaaku*, the FulBe define themselves through their relation to their cattle (Riesman 1977: 158). Even when the FulBe have no cattle, cattle are still central to their identity. The relation to the cattle encapsulates the characteristic of themselves, that is, as a free and aristocratic people in control of themselves, dependent not on physical work, but on the exploitation of an essentially unlimited bush through wandering and interrelation with their cattle. Thus the FulBe have a well-defined identity not linked to any specific space, and this is the case even though many FulBe no longer have any cattle. FulBe identity is therefore not only, or primarily, a result of everyday social practice, but the result of a relation to a tradition no longer practiced (independence, power, cattle).

Neither are the RimayBe defined only, or primarily, by their everyday social practice. They were, and still are, defined in opposition to the FulBe as people without *pulaaku* and without cattle, whether or not they actually practice *pulaaku,* or today may have more cattle than the FulBe. As former slaves the RimayBe were tillers of the land and were linked with a place. Through physical work they transformed the bush and gained an income. Today the RimayBe are in the process of being – at least formally – integrated in a general FulBe identity, although without taking over its concepts of *pulaaku*. They speak the Fulfulde language, practise a number of FulBe customs, are identified by government as FulBe and share the same living conditions as the FulBe. But they are not accepted as FulBe by the 'real' FulBe (Peul Noble) as this is associated with *pulaaku*, inherited through the mother. In relation to identity the RimayBe are in an indeterminate position. Thus the original FulBe have a very fixed identity linked to a conception of the environment as an open space, i.e. any area relevant for cattle. The RimayBe have an indeterminate identity linked with a limited and fixed space, the village farmland (see also Paarup-Laursen 1996).

Knowledge and development

In relation to their integration with various development projects this difference is highly visual. The FulBe find it difficult to participate in development projects as the rationales of these projects often run counter to their own. Various projects have tried to change the practice of cattle rearing, basing it more on rational productive principles, like the selling of bulls, the sale of milk to dairies, the gathering of hay for the cattle to eat in the dry season, etc. The FulBe object to any fundamental changes of their cattle rearing practice, whereas the RimayBe generally show great interest in projects suggested by development authorities. To the FulBe many of the suggested projects run counter to a way of life, to central aspects of their construction of identity. At times the Fulbe have to succumb to new strategies due to drought, but as soon as it is possible the Fulbe will often try to return to a 'traditional' FulBe way of life.

The Fulani have very detailed knowledge of their environment, and apply an experimental approach in individual dealings with their environment as is seen in agriculture. The same is the case in their movement with their cattle to new pastures, in recent years to new areas in southern Burkina Faso. In this sense knowledge is constantly re-evaluated in practice. The Fulani also have a set of classifications of their environment that is linked to a specific space. The central categories are in Sahel the distinction between *seno* and *koladde*. When the Fulbe settle in southern Burkina Faso, the opposition of *seno* and *koladde* are no longer central to the characterisation of the local space. Without much ado, other categories take their place. Among the Fulani in general, these classifications of the natural environment are not in conflict with scientific categories, and neither are they central to the construction of Fulani identity. Thus they have no central importance for the success or failure of development projects. With the knowledge linked to identity the situation is quite different. Even minor changes in the knowledge related to identity are not considered possible, and when forced on the FulBe they cause a major outcry. In general, knowledge related to the constitution of identity cannot easily be changed. It has a hegemonic character (Williams 1994) implying that it cannot be contradicted nor overruled by practice, but only reframed by a new and higher evaluated knowledge as is often considered the case when the FulBe become settled in major towns. Thus there is a differing rationality in the management of natural resources depending on what type of knowledge is activated.

In the perspective outlined here, the relevance of indigenous knowledge depends on what aspect of knowledge we consider. The knowledge linked to agricultural practices, i.e. the evaluation of signs in the natural environment and the production plans that follows, may be of central importance to a development intervention. Here development planners can become acquainted with the local conditions and the very complex strategies followed by local farmers. As the farmers already evaluate various agricultural interventions, this knowledge can also be relevant for the farmers' evaluation of new methods and crops.

The knowledge linked to classifications of space are a general framework for the relation of external agencies to these societies and they can in many contexts define the areas relevant for development. Here we may see a great difference in the importance of categories of space among pastoral and agricultural cultures.

The type of knowledge essential to the success of development projects is the knowledge related to the constitution of identity among the relevant population. The social importance of identity is often far more central to any population than any economic or other incentive offered by development projects.

Thus the modernists of the sixties and the ecologists of the nineties may not disagree on the relevance of indigenous knowledge after all, as outlined in the beginning of this paper. They may just be talking of different types or aspects of knowledge.

NOTES

1. For a more detailed description of this field see (Paarup-Laursen 1996, Krogh and Paarup-Laursen 1997).

2. Chekol also means a cut, tear or gash in relation to the human body.

3. Barth's argument for introducing 'knowledge' as the central modality of culture is that culture understood as linked to an assemblage of customs integrated into a locally shared way of life leads to exoticising and disempowering people. In the study of indigenous and local knowledge we can see that knowledge in many cases is understood as a factor of central relevance to development concerns, but we also see a fetishising of indigenous knowledge not much different from the exoticising criticized by Barth. Thus the focus on knowledge rather than culture may not solve all the problems Barth outlines.

4. In Cohen's terms. In our terms, modes of interaction, modes of classification and modes of identification do not constitute each other.

5. Scientists tend to assume that local knowledge is consistent, probably because we view it in terms of scientific knowledge and the strict demands on consistence applied here.

Whether it is our own everyday knowledge or African farmers' knowledge of their environment, local knowledge is highly contextual.

REFERENCES

Agrawal, A. 1995. Dismantling the Divide between Indigenous and Scientific Knowledge. *Development and Change* 26: 413-39.

Barth, F. 1975. *Ritual and Knowledge among the Baktaman of New Guinea.* New Haven: Yale University Press.

Barth, F. 1989. *Cosmologies in the Making: A Generative Approach to Cultural Variation in Inner New Guinea.* Cambridge: Cambridge University Press.

Barth, F. 1993. *Balinese Worlds.* Chicago: University of Chicago Press.

Barth, F. 1989. The Analysis of Culture in Complex Societies. *Ethnos* 3-4: 120-42.

Barth, F. 1995. Other Knowledge and Other Ways of Knowing. *Journal of Anthropological Research* 51: 65-68.

Bendix, R. 1967. Tradition and Modernity Revisited. *Comp. Stud. Soc. Hist.* 9: 292-346.

Breemer, J.P.M. van der 1992. Ideas and Usages: Environment in Aouan Society, Ivory Coast. In *Bush Base: Forest Farm. Culture Environment and Development,* E. Croll, & D. Parkin (eds.). London: Routledge.

Brokensha, D., D.M. Warren & O. Werner 1980. *Indigenous Knowledge Systems and Development.* Washington: University Press of America.

Chambers, R. 1993. *Challenging the Professions: Frontiers for Rural Development.* London: IT Publications.

Claude, J., M. Grouzis & P. Milleville. 1991. *Un Espace Sahélien.* La Mare d'Oursi. Paris: ORSTOM.

Cohen, A.P. 1993. Segmentary Knowledge: A Whalsay Sketch. In *An Anthropological Critique of Development. The Growth of Ignorance,* M. Hobart (ed.). London: Routledge.

Croll, E. & D. Parkin 1992. Cultural Understandings of the Environment. In *Bush Base: Forest Farm. Culture Environment and Development,* E. Croll & D. Parkin (eds.). London: Routledge.

Descola, P. 1996. Constructing Natures: Symbolic Ecology and Social Practice. In *Nature and Society. Anthropological Perspectives,* P. Descola & G. Palsson (eds.). London: Routledge.

Descola, P. & G. Pálsson 1996. Introduction. In *Nature and Society. Anthropological Perspectives,* P. Descola & G. Pálsson, (eds.). London: Routledge.

Dupire, M. 1962. *Peuls nomades: étude descriptive des WoDaaBe du Sahel Nigérien.* Travaux et Memoirs 64. Institut d'Etnologie, Musée de l'Homme, Paris.

Eswaran, H., R. Almaraz, E. van den Berg, P. Reich 1997. An Assessment of the Soil Resources of Africa in Relation to Productivity. *Geoderma*, 77: 1-18.

Gadiere, A.H. (n.d.). *Dictionnaire Fulfulde-Francais*. Dori.

Guilaud, D. 1993. *L'ombre du mil. Un système agropastoral en Aribinda (Burkina Faso)*. Paris: ORSTOM.

Kahn, J.S. 1985. Peasant Ideologies in the Third World. *Annual Review of Anthropology* 14: 49-75.

Kintz, D. 1981. Le perception de leur environnement par les populations sahèliennes. UNESCO, Distribution limitèe.

Krogh, L. & B. Paarup-Laursen 2003. Indigenous Soil Knowledge among the Fulani of Northern Burkina Faso: Linking Soil Science and Anthropology in Analysis of Natural Resource Management. *GeoJournal*, 43(2), 187-97.

Mazzucato, V. & D. Niemeijer 1997. *Beyond the Development Discourse: Dynamic Perceptions and Management of Soil Fertility*. Publication de l'Antenne 39, l'Université Agronomique Wageningen, Pays-Bas.

Paarup-Laursen, B. 1996. *Perceptions of the Environment and their Importance to Resource Management among the Fulbe-Rimaybe of Northern Burkina Faso*. SEREIN Working Paper No. 19.

Rappaport, R. 1968. *Pigs for the Ancestors: Ritual in the Ecology of a New Guinea People*. New Haven: Yale University Press.

Reenberg, A. 1995. SEREIN – A Short Historical Introduction. In *The Sahel – Ethnobotany, Agricultural and Pastoral Strategies, Development Aid Strategies*, A. Reenberg, & H.S. Marcussen (eds.). SEREIN Occasional Papers 1: 161-66, Copenhagen.

Reenberg, A. & B. Fog 1995. The Spatial Pattern and Dynamics of a Sahelian Agro-ecosystem – Land Use System Analysis Combining Household Survey with Georelated Information. *Geojournal* 37: 489-99.

Reenberg, A. & B. Paarup-Laursen 1995. Determinants for Land Use Strategies in a Sahelian agro-ecosystem – Antropological and Ecological Geographical Aspects of Natural Resource Management. *Agricultural Systems* 53: 209-29.

Richards, P. 1985. *Indigenous Agricultural Revolution: Ecology and Food Production in West Africa*. Boulder: Westview.

Riesman, P. 1977. *Freedom in Fulani Social Life. An Introspective Ethnography*. Chicago: University of Chicago Press.

Stenning, D. 1959. *Savannah Nomads*. London: Oxford University Press.

Williams, R. 1994 Selections from Marxism and Literature. In *Culture/Power/History. A Reader in Contemporary Social Theory*, N.S. Dirks, G. Eley, & S.B. Ortner (eds.). Princeton: Princeton University Press.

People-nature relations:
Local ethos and ethnic consciousness

Björn Bjerkli

This essay[1] focuses on 'people-nature relations' in a sedentary Coastal Saami community, named Manndalen, in the county of Troms, Norway. In the essay it is argued that local exploitation and management of natural resources, and conflicts related to this, have contributed to the production of a local ethos, which has led to an increased consciousness and expressions, of being Saami. Despite the strong efforts of the Norwegian state to eradicate the Saami culture and language in the first half of the twentieth century, such demonstrations of identity have emerged and remained visible in Manndalen. In many other sedentary Saami communities the efforts of assimilation have resulted in an abandonment of Saami identification. Only in the past twenty years, due to a shift in politics, have these communities seen an ethnic revitalisation. Comparison between local communities that historically have been similar in ethnic composition reveals differences in contemporary expressions of Saami belonging and identity. Current explanations of Saami revitalisation have related it to modernity and globalisation. Although such explanations have some validity, they cannot explain all observable local variations. These variations are embedded in complex social ecologies. One important factor in accounting for these variations is what I call 'people-nature relations'. Such considerations are in general important for understanding aspects of consciousness and revitalisation movements.

Understanding Coastal Saami society

Ethnographic writings on Coastal Saami adaptation from the mid-twentieth century report – almost without exception – of a non-visible Saami society (Falkenberg

1941; Kolsrud 1955). Coastal Saami culture was to a large extent treated as almost extinct or lost; the people had become Norwegians due to assimilation. A census from 1950 reporting very few Saami people on the coast, also gives the impression of a disappeared people (Bjørklund 1985). Other perspectives maintained that Coastal Saami culture still existed, but was not visible because it had gone backstage, or could only be found in secluded or non-visible structures (Eidheim 1971; Paine 1957, 1965, 1988, 1994). This development had occurred as a result of the considerable stigma attached to being Saami, produced through the state induced Norwegianisation process partly based on Social Darwinist theories and eugenics. Paine (1965, 1988) describes coastal Saami society as ruled by a prevalent ethos of *non-involvement,* which meant that the assimilation efforts made by the Norwegians, where met by a withdrawal from confrontations on the part of the Saami people. Obviously, such an ethos would also make the Saami people take measures of precaution in openly expressing Saami traits.

The discussion in this essay is based on the empirical study of a small hamlet called Manndalen. Norwegianisation efforts were clearly at work also in this community. One ethnographer who visited Manndalen in the mid-1950s reported about a previously-Saami society that, by then, could not be distinguished from the Norwegian societies in the region, and that almost no ethnic differentiation could be observed inside the community (Schjøtt 1958). Such views obviously had a theoretical foundation in substantial/essensialistic points of view. However, as will be described in this essay, the people of Manndalen to some degree showed more resistance against assimilation than people in most other Coastal Saami areas. The data collected also indicate a reconsideration of the ethos of *non-involvement* as a general feature of Coastal Saami society. In Manndalen, confrontations with the authorities, especially in connection with property relations and extensive use of natural resources, have never been far away. Uses of commons have a special place in this connection. The locals have been able to preserve a self-regulating system for use of the commons, despite state authorities' attempts to control the resource utilisation. Such confrontations have a long history in Manndalen and can be documented both in later years and in the period between 1880 and 1950 when the authorities' policy of Norwegianisation was implemented with great force. This history of confrontation supports the argument that non-involvement is not a general feature in Coastal Saami societies. If it does exist, it is generated through evolving mind patterns due to people experiencing relations with each other locally and with the surrounding world, natural and social/political. As such, the confrontation-al ethos that is prominent in Manndalen, is also a result of the locals acting on their surroundings.

The most influential theories on Saami ethnic revitalisation and identity man-agement connect it to identity politics launched in the 1950s and 60s (Bjerkli 1997; Eidheim 1971, 1993, 1997). Here Saami ethnic identity is connected to a general discourse initiated by an educated Saami elite. Within this field of action and signifi-cation, a master-paradigm on how to understand one's ethnic self has been pro-duced. As such it is recognised as a modern phenomenon with strong international connotations, where Saami people became globalised by increased communication with other indigenous people, and shaped their self understanding as a fourth (or first) World People. This analytical paradigm is clearly inspired by the work of Fredrik Barth (1971), whose focus was turned to border generating processes be-tween ethnic groups. Ethnicity became the aspect of inter-group transactions that maximised cultural difference.

Even though ethnic consciousness in Manndalen clearly has other sources than modern identity politics (Zaretsky 1995), the analytical paradigm of border-gener-ating processes through the maximising of cultural differences can easily be applied to my material. During the meetings with Norwegian authorities who wanted to regulate the Saami society according to Norwegian standards, the locals defended their ways by resorting to ethnic values. Hence ethnicity became instrumental in achieving other goals. When people experienced that such means did have an effect, their ethnic sentiments were strengthened, among other things by becoming aware of how they were different. Cultural difference as such was maximised through the repeated confrontations.

The prevalence of ethnic instrumentality is well documented in ethnographical writings and quite a few have used such theoretical perspectives (Banks 1996; Oka-mura 1981). Certainly, Saami revitalisation is part of the ethnic argument that can be heard in Manndalen today. These perspectives do unravel some insights, but there are further questions to be asked. Is the use of natural resources solely to be under-stood as instrumental in consumptional need, and as such converted into ethnic value in inter-group relations – where such arguments have some validity – by the creation of a legitimate field of indigenous politics? Even though the perspective is on generating borders, it has a certain functionalist flavour. I will instead argue that ethnic consciousness can also be embedded in people's relations to their local environment. In my view, the main reason that Manndalen people have, in general, a higher consciousness of their Saami belonging than people in other Coastal communities with a Saami past, is connected to certain ways of organising the exploitation of natural resources. I must emphasise that it is not the use of resources itself that is particularly Saami, but the accumulated experience connected to it is in certain situations transformed into a consciousness of being Saami. People in Manndalen have actively protected the 'uses of nature' based on values of equality and autonomy. Such areas of usages are still very important in the community, and more so than in other Coastal Saami localities, where there are only remnants of such usage. By successfully protecting this area of values and self-determination, a more confrontational ethos among people in Manndalen was fostered. When Saami ethnopolitics became legitimate in the sphere of state and global politics in the 1970s and the 80s, the stage was set for Manndalen as one of the leading Coastal Saami societies.

Before continuing the theoretical discussion I will give a short description of the community of Manndalen, and make an outline of actions and events that my argument is based upon.

Place and history

The community of Manndalen, literally the Valley of Men, is situated in the municipality of Kaafjord, located within a fjord district in the northern part of Troms county in Northern Norway. The valley is narrow with steep mountains reaching up to 1,300 meters with birch-forests on the lower parts. Approximately one thousand people live in the valley, with housing spreading from its estuary, which leads into a branch of the greater Lyngen fjord and approximately thirteen kilometres into the interior. The community is sedentary with small-scale farming as the most common form of livelihood. Around seventy farms bring incomes of various sizes to their owners. Some of these farms are full-time family run enterprises, and others are part-time farmers in combination with other forms of employment in the local or regional workforce. Farming is based on meat production, mainly from sheep rearing – which in addition is a source of wool for use in the homecraft industry – and on the production of milk from cows and goats. A combination of small-scale farming, fishing, and the exploitation of natural resources from the outlying fields, constituted almost the sole means of livelihood for all of the people in the area up to

World War II. This type of adaptation goes several hundred years back. Modernisation and integration into a wider commodity market, and the societies' integration into the Norwegian welfare state, has since then set the agenda for a change both in economic adaptation and cultural orientation. Considering these changes, it is remarkable that small-scale farming still has an important place within the community. In 1990, one out of three persons in the valley was occupied in small-scale farming, while the average for the whole municipality was one out of eight. In a neighbouring valley, with approximately the same number of people and a similar history of adaptation, one out of six were then occupied in small-scale farming (Statistics Norway 1991).

Until the beginning of the nineteenth century nearly the whole population in Manndalen were Saami. In the official 1900-census they were classified as Saami, and because of their occupations as fishermen and farmers, they differed from the nomadic reindeer-holding Mountain Saami. During the nineteenth century, Finnish speaking people, the so-called Kvens, from the northern part of Sweden and Finland, moved into the area and mixed with the Saami through marriage. In the latter half of the nineteenth century a small number of Norwegians also settled in the area, some marrying into the community, others not. However, in 1900, around eighty percent of the population were still classified as Saami, despite the fact that some intermarriage between the groups had taken place, and despite the increasing Norwegianising efforts by the state authorities. These efforts to assimilate the Saami (and the Kvens) were carried out through a consistent policy that lasted until World War II, and continued as the welfare state's policy of integration until around 1980. This process was in part responsible for the loss of the Saami language in most of the Coastal Saami districts.

A substantial number of the current population in Manndalen have a Saami past, and it is one of the places within the Coastal Saami districts where the affiliation to Saami life and ideas has its strongholds. Manndalen has become *the* Coastal Saami place. Quite a few people are actively engaged in Saami cultural and ethnopolitical work through associations with areas of ethnic activity that are connected to the officially instituted Saami Parliament.[2] Today, many of the locals are engaged in the realisation of a Coastal Saami centre in the valley. The proposed centre will serve as a focus for the promotion and general development of Coastal Saami societies, with emphasis on cultural, social, educational and economic aspects.

Even though many people in Manndalen actively look upon themselves as

Saami and engage in ethnopolitical matters, the ethnic affiliation is questioned by others. The question of mixed descent (Thuen 1989, 1995) for example, is today used by some of the inhabitants as an argument against being Saami. Expressions like, 'we are not Saami, we are descendants from three different kinds of people, Norwegian, Saami and Kvens, and now we all are Norwegians', can be heard. Others are satisfied with being Norwegians and regard Saami revitalisation as a step backwards. To them, being Saami means being poor, and there is a considerable negative stigma attached to this option of identity. However, this area of analysis is very complex and touches on many issues. This stigma probably is treated differently today, compared to how it was interpreted in the 1950s and 60s, when according to Eidheim (1971), 'being Saami' was expressed backstage in closed private spheres. Today, however, many people openly talk about the lives they lived under poor conditions as Saami, thus admitting having a Saami past.

Anyway, the focus in Manndalen on Saami values and on 'being' Saami, is to some extent remarkable compared with other communities in the region with a similar background. A neighbouring valley in the same municipality has a similar population and is also recognised as being a Saami community. During the 1900 census it was even reported to have a greater Saami population than Manndalen. The majority of today's population are descendants of these very people, just as they are in Manndalen. But in this neighbouring valley only a few persons are actively engaged in ethnopolitics in general, or in bringing Saami considerations into their daily lives. One example of this is the recent introduction of the Saami language curriculum into primary school education. It is stated in Norwegian law, that six municipalities, of which Kaafjord is one, are considered Saami language core areas. In Kaafjord, however, the Saami language curriculum is optional. Approximately half of the pupils in Manndalen have chosen Saami language instruction, in the neighbouring valley less than ten percent. This can serve as an illustration of the communities differing degrees of orientation towards Saami values, being Saami or expressing it.

Why is this? People in the region are aware of these differences and the most popular explanation is seclusion. Geographically, Manndalen is somewhat secluded, enclosed by high mountains, and until the early 1960s it did not have any road connections. Hence, the popular theory goes, people were less in contact with the outside world and better protected against Norwegianisation, thus it was easier for them to preserve the Saami ways. Anthropological theories suggesting that the

Saami people are more attached to their own communities than Norwegians, due to the obstacles they have met in Norwegian society in general, could support this popular seclusion theory (Eidheim 1958).

However, a critical view on the historical development of the community of Manndalen indicates that this popular theory has some weaknesses. Before 1940 there were almost no roads in the region. Communication was by boat, a method of transportation that prevailed well into the fifties. Manndalen was well served by sea connections, and the local school, the postal office, and other national services were not inferior to institutions in comparable locations.

Historians and anthropologists alike have further proposed a theory that portrays Coastal Saami fisheries in general as based on local fish resources with low-capital investments (Falkenberg 1941; Kolsrud 1955; Paine 1957). Such theories also support the view of the Coastal Saami in general as a people attached to specific areas. When engines were introduced in fishing vessels at the beginning of the twentieth century, larger boats were built, and mobility increased. It has been argued that the Coastal Saami did not participate in this development, due to structural and cultural obstacles in obtaining capital for the necessary investments. The investment systems required, among other things, knowledge of Norwegian cultural codes. Similar explanations about the former coastal Saami societies have become confirmed truths by means of extensive committee reports and political documents produced during the last ten to fifteen years, reflecting a new direction in Norwegian ethnopolitics (e.g., NOU 1985: 14). I am not suggesting that such assumptions are totally without merit. There is, however, a tendency to take such models at face value, as for example Hovland (1996) does. Such descriptions do not apply to Manndalen. A few years after the switch to motorised fishing vessels, five of the common coastal type of boats were in use in Manndalen. These boats were all managed by Saami owners, and were operated mostly by a locally recruited crew. Depending on the type of seasonal fisheries, thirty to fifty men took part in the general coastal fisheries all over Northern Norway. Until 1940, Manndalen was a bustling fishing community with a modern coastal fleet. Evidently people also fished regularly from open boats in their local fjord, using inexpensive equipment. This combination could be found in most of the places where investment in larger vessels had occurred.

World War II changed Manndalen in many ways. In the autumn of 1944, when the German army retreated from the northern parts of Norway, they used scorched earth tactics. Every house, every construction in Manndalen was burned down and the people were forced to evacuate to southern parts of the country. Fisheries in their pre-war form did not recover. However, in the decade following the war, quite a few people earned a living by commuting to seasonal work. One of the main activities for men was logging in Sweden and in the south of Norway. Even whole families would leave Manndalen for shorter or longer periods.

The general picture of the community of Manndalen, in the period when state-induced attempts at assimilation were at their most intense, is surely not one of a people in a secluded valley with little contact to the outside world.

Local ethos

When I started my fieldwork in Manndalen, some people asked me in jest if I dared to do fieldwork in the valley: 'You know, people here are not always easy to handle'. Statements like this were never explicit as to what exactly I ought to be afraid of, or what people actually were up to. However, such comments ceased after a while, except when I myself reintroduced them into the conversation. I did not interpret such statements as open warnings. I saw them rather as some kind of statement about how people perceived themselves, and as such bearing on some ontological property.

This also became evident in special cases, especially when people found that local values – or something valued in the community – were threatened. One example is related to the re-organisation of the national postal system, which has been undergoing major structural changes in Norway during the last years. As a result of this process, postal services have been centralised, and small offices in the rural districts have been shut down. In the winter of 1997/98 ramifications of this process reached Manndalen. People's normal reaction to such closures in small communities is often one of disappointment and resignation, arguing that those in power do not care about ordinary people's needs or opinions, hence there is little they can do.

In Manndalen, however, the reaction was different. When it was reported that the post office would be shut down, people got together and established an action committee. They contacted the media, and invoked local and regional newspapers and radio stations. Big headlines in the leading regional newspaper in Northern Norway, announced a rebellious community, reporting that people would fight for their post office to the bitter end, and that the postal service in its attempt to accomplish the reorganisation, had come to the wrong place. Among other things, a blockade of the main road was discussed. Their determination was emphasised by a reference to a story from the past where they had chased away the rural police when authorities had tried to impose regulations against the will of the locals.

The exact course of events in this story was never explained, and when investigating the basis for such stories I realised that people in general had little detailed knowledge about it. The purpose of such stories was not of course to point to historical events as such, or to openly threaten the postal authorities. I see it more as an expression of a local ethos and, hence, of symbolic value. Behind the expression lie 'assumptions, values, and meanings which underlie particular and varying expressions of cultural behaviour' (Epstein 1978: 122). As such it connects threads of continuity to the consciousness of belonging to a group that exists in time. These expressions are related to a local ontological narrative (Somers 1994), depicting the people as unafraid, confrontational, action oriented and defending their own ways. People locally are aware that these qualities especially pertain to people from Manndalen. A much-used phrase locally is 'between ourselves there is much quarrelling, but when we feel threatened from the outside we stand together'. People from neighbouring places also point to the people from Manndalen as being slightly different. Particularly in earlier times, such characterisations or stereotypes often had slightly negative connotations. When people from other places heard stories about chased policemen, the usual comment would be that they are a wild bunch in that valley.

Use of nature

These rather vague statements of earlier confrontations surely have a substantial counterpart. A closer look at the local use of natural resources in Manndalen, historical and contemporary, and how this use has been integrated (or disintegrated) by local customs and the various frameworks set by both the locals and central authorities, reveals more than a century of fighting, actions and resistance against official efforts to control and set the premises for local exploitation of natural resources. Though people usually do adapt to new laws and regulations because of the rather unbalanced power relations at work within the nation-state, local opposition against state directives and regulations is not that unusual. Success in influencing the political agenda normally depends on being connected to nationwide pressure groups. In Manndalen, however, there are several cases of local success in opposing external pressure through persistent actions. This success has strengthened the local ethos, and more so, because the resistance has a direct bearing on continuity. It is not only a continuation of ethos, it is also a continuation of a specific form of organising the use of nature that goes way back in time.

Before the mid-nineteenth century, the small-scale farmers who lived in the region were leaseholders, but with a rather high degree of self-determination. Among other things, they themselves regulated succession to the land they occupied by their own rules of inheritance. As such, they could also split up the land. The kinship system was bilateral and both males and females had rights to the land occupied by their parents. The landowner's interest in the land was mostly to extract fees and taxes, since it could not be treated as a commodity. This system of land usage also included outlying fields, which were used as commons by the people connected to the area. Exploitation of natural resources from outlying fields has been one of the distinguishing features for sedentary people in this region. The main use has been fodder exploitation, animal grazing, use of the birch forests for building constructions and fuel, hunting, fishing and berry picking.

The system of inheritance in the traditional sedentary Saami society has generally been described as ruled by principles of ultimogenitur (Solem 1933). The youngest son (or daughter) inherited the property from the parents; but prior to that, older siblings would get their share when they established families and were in need of land. In principle, both males and females could forward claims on land. This inheritance practise contributed to an increasing subdivision of land and a concurrent fragmentation of the land holdings, resulting in a system of strip farming.

In the second half of the nineteenth century, the landholding system changed. The land was sold to the leasers who then became private holders. During this process, outlying fields in common use were either privatised – with the former users dividing the land between them, or the state bought commons from the former landowner. In Manndalen, part of the commons was privatised in 1879, when equal shares where divided among the farmers, and in 1885, the remaining part was presumably sold to the State with no encumbrance on the part of the locals. As such, locals, in principle, had no usufruct to this land.

Reality, however, took another path. Local people continued to use the presumed 'state land' as their commons, and in their own way. It is still extensively used.

In the past years, thirty to forty families have collected birch wood in the area. Summer pastures provide grazing for two to three thousand sheep. In addition, nearly one thousand goats belonging to nine mountain dairy farms established on the commons graze here. It can easily be documented that the locals have extracted natural resources in different ways and by different means during the past hundred years. In connection with this use they have built structures like goat barns and summer cabins, hunting cabins (sodhuts) and cable lines to take logs down from the steep mountainsides, and so on.

However, the type of land-use has shifted over time. Logging for sale ended in the late 1940s. Today logging is for subsistence only and there is a tacit agreement that logging for sale will not be tolerated. Hay foraging in the area ended in the beginning of the 1950s. Goats were introduced into the area in the mid-1950s, and sheep were actively led to graze the pastures in the 1960s. Before that, only some roaming sheep would visit the area. The use of the land can be characterised as varying and dynamic due to, among other factors, changes in the more general conditions the larger society has provided for local adaptations.

At times the locals' exploitation of the natural resources has been rather intensive. From the 1920s, reports state that large parts of the area were deforested due to logging for private use and for sale. The forest recovered, but in the late forties the regional forest office again reported the beginning of deforestation due to uncontrolled local logging. Both in the 1920s and in the late 1940s there were confrontations between local people and state authorities attempting to stop the logging. The authorities were not very successful.

What has to be emphasised is that none of the natural resource extraction activities have been granted by legal permission of the authorities. In general, the local principles for gaining access to the commons seem to be based on concepts of collectivity, equality and autonomy. Everyone living in the community, whether he or she is a landowner or not, seems to have the same right to use the commons for their own purposes. In this way no one is in a position to monopolise resources at the expense of others. Only by using does one's use become legitimate. If one person withdraws, others can take over. As such it is regarded as a collective right. This implies a certain amount of competition, operating on a 'first come first served' principle. This point takes us to the principle of autonomy. This has two aspects: first, community autonomy. The local majority consider the use of the commons to be the community's own responsibility. If the state or other authorities are called upon, it is to provide service, not as controlling or managing institutions. The second aspect is connected to individual autonomy. If you want to use the natural resources in the commons in one way or the other, it is up to you. There are no codified rules as to how the use should be exercised. If there is any main principle guiding individual use, it is linked to the idea of equality. That means that you should not do anything that could put severe limits on other people's use. In this way, the two principles balance each other and have kept the local use and management relatively stabile. Internal conflicts have been very few.

Defending local use of nature

There have, however, been several confrontations between locals and the authorities, some of them serious, resulting in police investigations. Since the state looks upon the commons in Manndalen as state land where the locals have no usufruct, the resource exploitation by the locals has been classified as an infringement on state land and thus illegal. The confrontations have occurred when authorities have tried to take control over the resource exploitation. This has mainly been done by prohibiting use, such as bans on logging or by demanding leasing contracts specifying use and location on the commons. Attempts at implementing leasing contracts have also resulted in conflicts among the locals. In the 1920s, some of the locals went into a dialogue with state authorities and leased land officially for the purpose of fodder extraction. People in general did not accept that some of their neighbours seemingly accepted state ownership in this way, and infringed on the leased land by cutting the grass. By this action they questioned the legality of leasing, and leasing as a system was efficiently stopped, even though the 'trespassers' were sued and the police investigated the case. However, a verdict was not given. There was also some local disagreement on the issue, when state authorities unsuccessfully tried to introduce leasing contracts for the goat barns in the mid-1980s.

Apart from the last war, when there was Nazi rule, the majority of the people have never accepted bans and propositions from the authorities. Another example is an incident that took place in the winter of 1946-47, when logging for firewood was rather intense at times. The regional forest office feared deforestation if the logging was not stopped. After announcing a general ban on further logging, with no result, the activity was reported to the rural police. A police officer that came to the valley and caught people in the act of chopping, declared the activity illegal and demanded that it should stop immediately. He reported later that people did not obey the command. Instead they continued their work even more eagerly than before while they all joined in a *joik* (a special Saami chanting). Later that year, the police and the regional forest office came back on a new visit. They came upon local people with around twenty horses engaged in transporting wood from the commons. The police ordered them to stop and unload. One of the leading men took an axe and rammed it into a piece of wood so hard that the leading horse became scared and ran off. The others followed and the police had to jump aside and let them go. When the policeman later reported that he had been threatened with an axe, things turned serious. After this incident many of the users were put under investigation. The outcome was meagre for the authorities and a success for the locals. The investigation concluded that the state's position concerning the locals' usufruct to the commons was questionable. The prosecution claimed that before a verdict on illegal use could be delivered, a settlement of rights was required. Such a settlement never took place, and people continued their use of the commons as before.

In 1993 the state announced that the whole 'use and rights' complex was to be taken to court in order to settle the dispute once and for all. This was based on a special tribunal appointed by the Norwegian Parliament in 1985 to deal with disputes on land rights in the Nordland and Troms counties in the northern part of Norway. The purpose of the tribunal was to judge what land was state owned, settle the borders between state and privately owned land, and assess if there were any other user rights on state land than those of the state. When the announcement came, the reaction in Manndalen was the same as when the postal office tried to reorganise their services: action, mobilisation and headlines in the newspapers describing a rebellious group of people claiming that the commons belonged to the people of Manndalen and that the state had no good case. A majority at a local meeting in the community discussing the new situation, also claimed this to be a Saami indigenous rights case. Statements of this kind have obvious connections to the new ethnopolitical field of politics, but the oppositional actions point to a prevailing local pattern.[3]

In the following I will comment briefly on the system of strip farming. This is a type of farming that for the most part has been abandoned in Norway.[4] During the past century the national agricultural authorities have promoted a more efficient and rational organisation of production. Strip farming has been looked upon as outdated and not compatible with modern farming principles, and programs to promote land-strip exchange were put to work. This has in general been applauded by farmers and looked upon as a positive action taken by the authorities. In Manndalen, however, the old strip-farming system is still going on. Few places in Norway today, if any, are divided in such a complex pattern of properties as we can find here. Around eighty per cent of what is defined as agricultural land is divided into strips ranging in number from three to more than ten. The distribution of these strips makes it even more complicated, since the strips belonging to one farm may be spread all over the valley. Although some of the farmers look upon strip farming as somewhat burdensome, and it is characterised by the authorities as outdated and inefficient, Manndalen is probably the most dynamic farming community in the region, which is also indicated by the great number of people engaged in farming, as I mentioned at the beginning of this essay.

After World War II, when programs for rebuilding the country where implemented, the authorities also felt it was the right time to modernise the system of land ownership. In the late 1940s a surveyor was sent to Manndalen to investigate and prepare for an exchange process.[5] The locals heavily opposed the work of the surveyor. They chased him off, put him on a boat and escorted him to the other side of the fjord. The surveyor reported that he had been threatened by people armed with stones, sticks, knives, scythes and dung forks. The incident ended up in court, where four men were convicted of having committed an offence against a civil servant. In a higher court they were discharged, however. One argument was that they were Saami, hence the court assumed that difficulties in communication led to misunderstandings on both sides.

The strip farming system did continue. As such it is part of the same system of use of natural resources that has been described in the collective use of the commons. Both have roots in the Saami past, they are locally organised and regulated systems, and are based on their own cultural values. In both cases we find incidents of resistance against the efforts of the central authorities to control and regulate the use. However, it should be underlined, that agricultural property holdings and land-use are strongly regulated by law in Norway today, and farmers in Manndalen in general also follow these regulations. For example, agricultural land is not divided by the former inheritance rules anymore. However, as strip farming is not forbidden, it gives a special quality to farming in Manndalen and links it with a local ethos, as indicated in the incident with the surveyor.

Continuity and discontinuity of ethnic consciousness

As indicated in the introduction, a consciousness of being Saami and activities connected to the modern sphere of ethnopolitics, is much stronger in Manndalen than in neighbouring communities with approximately the same background. The examples of conflict I have given also show that ethnic related strategies have been used in confrontations with the authorities. This comes clearly to the surface in the late 1940s, which is somewhat remarkable because it is in this time period that reports from Coastal Saami societies tells of a non-visible culture where Saami expressions were a back-stage phenomenon, if not more or less extinct due to assimilation.

In analysing the Manndalen case, it might be useful to look at what is said about Saami ethos in general. Robert Paine (1965, 1988) is probably the anthropologist who is most explicit on the matter. Based on fieldwork in a Coastal Saami society in the 1950s he uses the characteristic of *non-involvement* as a most basic quality among these people. He also postulates this as a general characteristic pertaining to Saami people before Norwegianisation was launched as an intentional policy in the mid-nineteenth century. He uses the Batesonian (Bateson 1949) concept of *steady state* to describe a prevalent ethos among Coastal Saami people. It is characterised by need satisfaction instead of need maximation, and by tendencies of withdrawal from situations that are experienced as threatening. This is not a static condition, but is described as a state of dynamic equilibrium. Tensions build up and have to be relieved by certain means, such as ritual actions. This is a type of society that contrasts to societies based on competition where relations are symmetrical. Competitive society can also be asymmetrical, as in hierarchically organised societies. Such asymmetrical relations are characteristic for ethnic majority/minority relations. Paine's point is that when intra-relations in Saami societies were organised by principles of a steady state, the relations between Norwegians and Saami were of a competitive asymmetrical kind. Again referring to Bateson, this asymmetrical relation is seen as schismogenetic. That means that relations of dominance and submission were escalating. The general ethos of non-involvement among the Saami fuelled this escalation when the Norwegian authorities intensified their assimilation efforts. His point is clarified when he explains that Saami people found relief from this intolerable situation in the religious movement of Laestadianism, and through it turned the ethnic interrelations into a symmetrical one in the sphere of religion. However, in general economic life the asymmetrical relations continued. Laestadianism is named after its founder, Lars Levi Laestadius (1800-1861), a man of Swedish/Saami origin who served as a priest in the Swedish state church in the Saami districts in northern Sweden in the middle of the nineteenth century. He promoted a pietistic, Protestant religious revival that spread rapidly among Saami and Finnish-speaking people in the northern parts of Sweden, Finland and Norway. One of its main characteristics is the egalitarian authority structure with emphasis on a relatively autonomous role for local congregations. Laestadianism is still an important factor in organising religious life, as well as life in general, in many local communities.

The picture that Paine is drawing does not entirely fit in with my material. Admittedly such patterns can be traced in some areas of life. For example, no clear opposition against the school system, which was one of the most important assimilation devices, can be traced locally in the pre-revitalisation period. But when it came to substantial economic questions such as the exploitation of natural resources, the people in Manndalen clearly did not slip into a state of non-involvement. The pattern is oppositional or symmetrical, to use Bateson's concept. Local ways of doing things, and values, were continuously expressed as preferable to those imposed by the authorities. Their values were deeply embedded and protected, and there was a clear tendency towards escalating symmetrical schismogenetics. Until recently, relations have generally been cooled down by withdrawal or non-involvement on the authorities side.

This raises a fundamental question about the reliability of the hypothesis that Coastal Saami society before assimilation could be said to be of a steady state kind, ruled by general principles of non-involvement. I do not renounce this as a valid characteristic of some Coastal Saami societies after the assimilation effort had had its affect on people and produced a social stigma. Laestadianism, that grew in importance parallel to the politics of assimilation, could obviously also foster a non-involvement ethos, at least in non-religious matters, by its emphasis on the virtues of being humble and justifying, and by accepting the hard conditions of life.

In the Manndalen case we find a society that, even though it is just as modern and integrated in the welfare state system as the rest of rural Norway, has preserved some basic principles of natural resource exploitation. These clearly were important organising principles in the pre-assimilation era, when people were Saami without the kind of self-reflection that characterises modernity. Within regulating frames of equality and autonomy, competition connected to exploitation of natural resources in the commons was clearly at work. This can be observed both in the 'first come, first served' principle, and in special cases such as the one mentioned before, where actions by the people who had accepted the authorities' regulating principles were not tolerated by the local majority if it went against their view.

If Laestadianism fuelled a non-involvement ethos in non-religious spheres, the question of its standing in Manndalen must be raised. A hypothesis of a relative absence of Laestadian impact would seem reasonable, but is, however, a dead end. Laestadianism is, mainly due to principles of congregational autonomy, divided into different branches. Modernity and shifting relations to the outside world continuously place the congregations in dilemmas over their religious principles, sometimes resulting in a split-up (Eggen 1998). The regional branch of Laestadianism, the so-called 'Lyngen-movement', has its roots in Manndalen. Its founder and incontestable leader for more than two generations (1860s up to 1940) lived as a small-scale farmer and fisherman in Manndalen and had scarcely any formal education. He is remembered with the highest respect in the local community for his vision of a dignified life and justice for ordinary people. Erik Johnsen (1843-1941) as his name was, figures in police investigation reports from 1922 as one of the locals that opposed the authorities' attempts at regulating the locals' use of the commons.[6] He was labelled 'the little Lap (Saami)' in contemporary Norwegian society. He openly and strongly opposed the theology of the state church and even met with central church authorities on their home ground at national church meetings to discuss theological matters. The police investigations tell us about a man who did not refrain from getting involved in matters of a non-religious character. As such, Laestadianism cannot entirely be seen as promoting a non-involvement ethos in non-religious matters. It has to be seen in a larger context.

The conditions in Manndalen points to collective fields of interaction that still were experienced as important. When justice – as the locals perceived it – was at stake, it led to action. The use of commons was obviously such a field. In this context Laestadian notions of humility and acceptance of the hard life, could be transformed to oppositional symmetrical relationships even in spheres of economics. Laestadianism's accept of the hard life was probably not only a device for tolerating and enduring unjust conditions, but could also be a device for claiming a just treatment under hard conditions.

Obviously the material I have presented makes a further development of theoretical perspectives on Saami ethos and ethnic consciousness necessary. Perhaps it would be better to explain the competitive ethos and the increased ethnic consciousness in a more phenomenological way. If we are to relate ethos and ethnic consciousness to uses of natural resources, we must take as a starting point that people actively act upon their surroundings, and it is through the experiences of these actions that meaning evolves. When people act upon their surroundings, meaning does not need to be explicit, but special forms of use can be embodied as 'our way of doing', and one is able to recognise that other ways can be different. This can be developed through bodily experience and not necessarily as a conscious reflection of the mind. As such it would be wrong to propose that certain ways of using nature is particularly Saami or ethnic. However, as a conscious reflection through metaphor and/or metonymy, it can be given such labels. This is the case with reindeer herding, which today serves as the most important symbolic label for Saami ethnicity, even though less than 10 percent of the Saami people are engaged in it. Such prosesses are obviously at work at special events, events that can be regarded as emplotments (Somers 1994) that inform narrative, hence self-understanding. When people refer to 'chasing of the police' in very general terms and without explicit time/space reference, it can be understood as an ontological expression where the actual events figure more as emplotments that connect different parts of people's social experience to a 'constructed *configuration* or a *social network* of relationships composed of symbolic, institutional, and material practices' (op.cit.: 616), than referring to the event as sense-making in itself. Events having the quality of emplotments bind together meaning in ethos and consciousness.

This view is also inspired by Tim Ingold's perspectives on *building, dwelling, living* (Ingold 1995). By referring to Heidegger, he discusses the relations between building and dwelling. Contrary to the notion that we build a house in order to dwell, i.e. a conscious preparation for living and acting, Ingold argues that in order to be able to build and be conscious of our actions, we first have to dwell in the world. The forms that appear 'rise within the current of their involved activity, in the specific relational contexts of their practical engagement with their surroundings' (op.cit.: 76).

In Manndalen the commons are a specific part of the people's surroundings, with special qualities. The dwelling perspective comes clearly to mind when investigating the use. It is based on a non-ordered system in that the use and management do not follow codified rules of specification about who, where and what. Out on the commons people act on the basis of some very general principles. The actual context sets the premises for what is done. Changes occur, reflecting the inherent flexibility of use. If certain uses are misconceived, this mainly appears only after such uses have been implemented. People's knowledge of usage probably exists more as an non-conscious enskillment obtained through activity, than as a preconceived mind-set. This becomes clear when people are asked about specific management rules in the commons. Answers are very elusive, like 'we have our own ways'. In order to understand people's actions we cannot only consider persons as self-contained individuals in relation to other persons, but have to understand people as part of their environment.

The people in Manndalen have utilised the commons in special ways. Through equal access and a large degree of individual autonomy, and through a successful struggle to preserve their own ways of doing things up to the present, they have been able to keep intact a field of natural resource exploitation that has clear connections to a Saami past. Although there is little doubt that the confrontations with the authorities must have increased the people's sense of 'Saami-belonging' to a renewed level of consciousness, there is reason to believe that some pre-existing basics of ethos and ethnic consciousness have been at work. It is difficult to specify such basics precisely. There is no clear-cut body of traits and values that define and firmly establish people's ethnic affiliation and way of being. Instead we can identify some general principles of value, like equality and autonomy. These are not ethnic values as such, but are connected to peoples feeling of integrity as self-constituted individuals. Such values, which have guided activities on the commons, have been preserved through the period of assimilation policy right up to modern times. As such they have served as vehicles for self-consciousness, both when it comes to being action-oriented and being Saami. In the Coastal Saami localities outside of Manndalen that adapted to Norwegian imposed regulations, these unconscious levels of knowledge, which connected people to a Saami past, have faded away. Of course, a possible *non-involvement* ethos induced by the assimilation efforts did not help the situation, on the contrary. But in Manndalen these persisting people-nature relations helped restore a consciousness of being Saami.

NOTES

1. This paper was first presented at the second Baltic-Scandinavian Research Workshop in Tartu, Estland in May 1998. In revising the paper I would like to thank the participants of the workshop for highly useful comments and discussions. I would further like to thank Nils Bubandt, Wendy Gunn, Per Mathiesen, Andreas Roepstorff and Trond Thuen for their help and comments.

2. In accordance with a Norwegian law of 12 June 1987, the first Saami Parliament was constituted in 1989. The Parliament has 39 members, three from each of the thirteen voting districts. Since the first election in 1989, elections have been held in 1993 and in 1997. Manndalen belongs to a voting district consisting of six municipalities and four of the six elected members of the Parliament from the district have been from Manndalen.

3. The verdict was delivered by Utmarkskommisjonen (the tribunal) on 5 March 1999. The state was declared owner of the commons. The people of Manndalen were given rights to use the forest and the pastures.

4. Strip farming, however, is returning in a modern form, due to the increase in land size that is demanded in modern farming. Scattered plots of vacant land are in different ways added to the larger farms.

5. A further description and analysis of the event with the surveyor is to be found in Bjerkli (1997).

6. Report of an investigation written by Lensmannen i Lyngen (a local officer with police authority), 2 June 1922. Troms Forestry Administration's Property Archive.

REFERENCES

Banks, M. 1996. *Ethnicity: Anthropological constructions*. London, New York: Routledge.

Barth, F. (ed.) 1969. *Ethnic Groups and Boundaries. The Social Organization of Cultural Difference*. Oslo: Universitetsforlaget.

Bateson, G. 1949. Bali: The Value System of a Steady State. In *Social Structure: Studies Presented to A. R. Radcliffe-Brown*, M. Fortes (ed.). New York: Russell & Russell.

Bjerkli, B. 1997. Landskapets makt: Sted, ressursutnyttelse og tilhørighet i en sjøsamisk bygd. *Norsk antropologisk tidsskrift* 8 (2): 132-56.

Bjørklund, I. 1985. *Fjordfolket i Kvænangen. Fra samisk samfunn til norsk utkant 1550-1980*. Oslo: Universitetsforlaget.

Eggen, Ø. 1998. *Troens bekjennere. Kontinuitet og endring i en læstadiansk menighet*. Universitetet i Tromsø: Hovedoppgave i sosialantropologi.

Eidheim, H. 1958. *Erverv og kulturkontakt i Polmak*. Samiske Samlinger, Vol. IV(1). Oslo: Norsk Folkemuseum.

Eidheim, H. 1971. *Aspects of the Lappish Minority Situation*. Oslo: Universitetsforlaget.

Eidheim, H. 1992. *Stages in the Development of Sami Selfhood*. University of Oslo: Working Paper No. 7.

Eidheim, H. 1997. Ethno-political Development among the Sami after World War II: The Invention of Selfhood. In *Sami Culture in a New Era*, H. Gaski (ed.). Karasjok: Davvi Girji OS.

Epstein, A.L. 1978. *Ethos and Identity. Three Studies in Ethnicity*. London: Tavistock Publications.

Falkenberg, J. 1941. *Bosettingen ved indre Laksefjord i Finnmark*. Oslo: Nordnorske samlinger II, Vol. I (2).

Hovland, A. 1996. *Moderne urfolk. Samisk ungdom i bevegelse*. Oslo: Cappelen Akademisk Forlag.

Ingold, T. 1995. Building, Dwelling, Living: How Animals and People Make Themselves at Home in the World. In *Shifting Contexts*, M. Strathern (ed.). London: Routledge.

Kolsrud, K. 1955. *Sjøfinnane i Rognsund*. Oslo: Studia Septentrionalia Vol. VI.

NOU 1985: 14: Samisk kultur og utdanning.

Okamura, J.Y. 1981. Situational Ethnicity. *Ethnic and Racial Studies*, 4(4): 452–65.

Paine, R. 1957. *Coast Lapp Society I. A Study of a Neighbourhood in Revsbotn Fjord*. Tromsø: Tromsø Museums skrifter IV.

Paine, R. 1965. *Coast Lapp Society II*. Oslo: Universitetsforlaget.

Paine, R. 1988. Grace out of Stigma. The Cultural Self-management of a Saami Congregation. *Ethnologia Europaea*, XVIII: 161–78.

Paine, R. 1994. Night Village and the Coming of Men of the World: The Supernatural as a Source of Meaning among Coastal Saami. *Journal of American Folklore*, 107 (425): 343–63.

Schjøtt, T.B. 1958. *Bosetning og erverv i Manndalen*. Samiske samlinger, IV-2. Oslo: Norsk Folkemuseum.

Solem, E. 1933. *Lappiske rettsstudier*. Oslo: Institutt for sammenlignende kulturforskning, serie B. skrifter XXIV.

Somers, M.R. 1994. The Narrative Constitution of Identity. A Relational and Network Approach. *Theory and Society*, 23: 605–35.

Statistisk Sentralbyrå 1991. Folke- og boligtelling 1990. Kommunehefte 1940 Kåfjord. Oslo.

Thuen, T. 1988. 'Mixed' Decent and Ethnogenesis – Some Comparative Considerations of Contact Situations in the North. *Acta Borealia*, 6 (1): 52–71.

Thuen, T. 1995. *Quest for equity. Norway and the Saami Challenge*. Memorial University of New Foundland: Social and Economic Studies No. 55.

Zaretsky, E. 1995. The Birth of Identity Politics in the 1960s: Psychoanalysis and the Public/private Division. In *Global Modernities*, M. Featherstone, S. Lash & R. Robertson (eds.). London, Thousand Oaks, New Delhi: Sage Publications.

Networking the nomadic landscape: Place, power and decision making in Northern Mongolia

Morten A. Pedersen

Introduction

This paper[1] explores how nomadic people perceive their landscape as a heterogeneous network of powerful places. More specifically, the paper is about how the reindeer-herding *Tsaatang* people of Northern Mongolia dwell and move within their landscape in ways that, on the one hand, produce strong attachments between the Tsaatang and particular places in their environment and, on the other hand, govern the structuration of Tsaatang spatial sensibilities.

Following an introduction to the Tsaatang people and their landscape, and some necessary theoretical clarifications, the paper sets up the hypothesis that the Tsaatang landscape is a nomadic landscape, as opposed to the sedentary landscape of Danish agriculturists. People for whom the landscape is nomadic, it is proposed, highlight places at the expense of spaces, whereas people whose landscape is sedentary highlight spaces at the expense of places. This opposition also implies that, whereas sedentary landscapes are homogeneous and bounded, nomadic landscapes are heterogeneous and infinite.[2] However, the differences between the present landscape of the Tsaatang nomads and that of the Danish agriculturists do not arise from two radically different cultures constructing their own natures, a Tsaatang and a Danish one. Rather, the differences between the two landscapes result from certain historical transformations, both at a particular level in terms of social and technological changes within the societies in question, and at an universal level in terms of figure-ground reversals within a perceptual hierarchy of place and space.

After having established a model for the spatial economy of the Tsaatang landscape, the paper moves on to an analysis of the ritual aspects of Tsaatang movement.

It is proposed that, submitted to the infinity of a nomadic landscape, the Tsaatang, through their very movements within their environment, carry out a number of ritual actions that structure their spatial sensibilities in various ways. The paper concludes with the proposition that, while Tsaatang migration rituals definitely serve to fixate perceptions of an infinite nomadic landscape, they also make possible perceptual intimations of spatial finitude.

In terms of theory, the paper aims at bringing together Bruno Latour's 'actor-network-theory' with recent takes on the anthropology of landscape, such as the writings of Tim Ingold, Philippe Descola and Caroline Humphrey. The crux of the argument is that an analysis of the Tsaatang landscape not only contributes to ongoing debates concerning the phenomenology of environmental perception; it also provides a novel example of what an actor-network may look like in a non-western context.

The Tsaatang people

The Tsaatang ('reindeer people') are a group of approximately 500 ethnic Tuvinians inhabiting the Tsagaan Nuur district situated in the north-western part of the Mongolian Xövsgöl province. Half of the Tsaatang live in the village Tsagaan Nuur, together with Mongolian *Darxad* and Xalx people, and the other half are dispersed over two large territories of Siberian-style *taiga* where they practise reindeer- and horse-breeding, and hunting. The latter group – the primary focus of this paper – are fully nomadic. They move camp 10-15 times during a year, using their reindeer as pack- and riding-animals. The nomadic Tsaatang are divided in two major groups – an eastern and a western one – and both groups trace themselves back to a particular region in The Tuvinian Autonomous Region of Russia, from where they immigrated to Mongolia 200 and 50 years ago respectively (Wheeler 2000). The families of both groups live in tepee-like dwellings (*orts*), and during the year they live together in family-groups (*ail*) of shifting composition and size. A traditional clan system is still functioning among the Tsaatang (c.f. Vainsthein 1980); the two original groups are split up in five different, exogamous clans (see Dioszegi 1963; Badamxatan 1987). Descent is patrilineal, and each family, or *ail*, is headed by a elderly male (informal) leader (c.f. Pedersen and Højer 1997). The Tsaatang's first language is Tuvinian, a Turkish language, but they all speak Mongolian fluently with a strong Darxad accent.

The Tsaatang have a strong shamanist tradition, and practising shamans (*böö*) live among the two groups in the taiga, and also in Tsagaan Nuur. Especially among the more mongolised Tsaatang, who live in Tsagaan Nuur among the Darxad and the Xalx, Mongolian Buddhism has had an influence as well. For example, the annual ceremonies performed by mountain cults (*ovoony bayar*) are now headed by Buddhist lamas, although they are clearly of shamanic origin.

The Tsaatang landscape

Let us take a closer look at the Tsaatang landscape, and the various manifestations of powers believed to inhabit it. The Tsaatang dwell in the northernmost part of the Republic of Mongolia. This area – known as the *Darxadyn Xotgor* – is characterised by its many forests, rivers and lakes, its abundant wildlife, and its inaccessibility. High mountains – up to 3500 m – tower all around a large depression, and between this upper alpine land and the lower steppe land, large forests make possible the Tsaatang's reindeer-nomadic subsistence. Among the (Buddhist) Xalx Mongolians, this area is known for its wild and beautiful 'nature' (*baigal*), and for its fierce and poor population of Tsaatang and Darxad people. Tellingly, an English speaking city-dweller of the Mongolian capital Ulaanbaatar calls the area 'The Dark Valley', a name referring not only to the rugged mountains and the deep forests of Siberian Larch that surround it, but also to the numerous legends about its violent shamans of 'black faith' (*xar shashin*).

Being shamanist, or could we say animist,[3] the Tsaatang regard their landscape as animated by both human and nonhuman agents. For the Tsaatang, the environment is full of powerful spirits manifested in particular objects of nature, such as certain mountains, trees, rivers and animals. This 'animist geography' plays a significant role in many of the Tsaatang's everyday practises. Hunting, for example, is a task that for a given Tsaatang man cannot be carried out successfully without proper knowledge of the landscape, and, for the Tsaatang, this includes any skilful hunter having to be aware of where and how to deal with the spiritual entities of the landscape (see example below).

The Tsaatang landscape, in other words, is not simply made up by the physical contours of the environment that surrounds the nomadic camp. Firstly, the camp does not define an enclosure of cultural space on the other side of which its inhabitants encounter a natural landscape; a wilderness. 'Wild' spaces can be found inside the camp, just as 'tame' places can be found outside it. Secondly, the Tsaatang land-scape-ontology can be rendered as a combination of a spiritual background-reality and a physical foreground-reality (c.f. Hirsch 1995). It is important, however, to keep in mind that this distinction is largely analytical; for the Tsaatang themselves, it seems, the background and the foreground of their landscape are always collapsed into a simultaneously spiritual and physical *presence* of spirit-'owners' (*ezed*). Each of these spirits are believed to control or indeed *own* something within the total envir-onment of the Tsaatang, be that the fireplace inside a nomadic dwelling, the wild animals moving around in the landscape, or the barren peaks of the high mountains. Let us look at a concrete example. Among the Tsaatang, most prominent mountains are believed to have owners; that is, intentional nonhuman 'persons' with whom humans have to engage in a friendly and submissive manner in order to avoid trouble. One such mountain is called *Agaya* and, during fieldwork, I heard many stories about this place. Special spirits, the so-called *avlin*, are believed to inhabit or own this particular mountain. Usually the *avlin* are invisible to humans, but a few hunters claim to have seen them. When the *avlin* show themselves to man, they always do it in the *half* shape of something. One hunter tells that he saw them in the form of half-people (humans with only half of the face, the whole body being sliced in a vertical direction), another claims to have encountered them in the form of deer with only half of their antlers.

In principle, the *avlin* are benevolent; they harm neither man nor beast. Thus, the story goes, a group of children once got lost near the mountain, and had to spend the night alone in the taiga. The next morning their parents found them near the camp, without a scratch. The children were not able to give any details of what had happened, but they remembered being fed with candy and kept warm by 'someone' during the night. However, later the encounter turned out to be danger-ous, because it was followed by an unusual amount of deaths among the families involved in the incident. Another story is about domesticated reindeer disappearing near the Agaya-mountain, only to be found days later. When discovered, the rein-deer had twisted and colourful antlers, and when later milked, wild flowers were found in their milk.

Also the wild animals belonging to the Agaya-'owner' are being watched over by the *avlin*. Once a hunter had been tracking down a wild reindeer for several days. He finally managed to kill it, and only then realised that he was near the Agaya mountain. The mountain was angry and said to him: 'why did you shoot my animal here?'. The hunter became very scared, but as it was late evening, he had no choice but to spend the night on the spot. When he woke up at dawn, he caught a glimpse of a group of half-people climbing up the mountain near its peak. As the hunter turned around, he saw the wild reindeer rising from the spot where he had killed it the previous day. It had been healed by the *avlin*. He then looked up the mountain again, and at the very moment the half-people reached the top, a blizzard broke out. After this event, no one has been hunting near the Agaya mountain, people claim. Instead, hunters go there and present various offerings to its 'owner'.

This is not the place to carry out a thorough interpretation of the above stories. Instead, we shall concentrate here on the fact that they illustrate what seems to be a general Tsaatang understanding of the landscape as different powerful fields defined by significant places. To use the term field is very adequate, I believe, because it conveys a core aspect of the Tsaatang landscape-ontology: the idea of a focal point from whence beams of this point's quality somehow radiate, thus creating what may be called a field of power. Indeed, one of the central aims of this paper is to develop an adequate theoretical vocabulary for this particular Tsaatang ontology of landscape.

Other Tsaatang stories could be retold here showing that, while the present Tsaatang landscape has many different powerful places, they all fulfil the field-like properties described above. As already mentioned, these places are not necessarily mountains, but are just as often special trees or other particular locations in the forest or on the steppe. Often, the significance of these places turns out to be the result of shamans' actions, either in the form of places for family- or clan-worship defined by shamans, or in the form of burial-places for deceased shamans, who decided for these particular locations before passing away. Other places again are powerful because of their connection to evil or unusual events that took place within particular families who used to dwell there. Thus, the past actions of hunters have created spatial qualities in the Tsaatang landscape, but so have the past actions of shamans and of particular domestic groups. Moreover, certain places in the landscape have qualities *as such*, simply because they are beautiful, frightening or odd, such as the highest mountain, the strongest river, or the lone tree on the steppe.

The Tsaatang landscape, in other words, is *heterogeneous*. This should be understood both in the weaker sense, as a landscape consisting of different fields of powerful places, and in the stronger sense, as a landscape whose present spatial qualities originate from the past actions of different social agencies, be they human or non-human ones. Within the Tsaatang landscape, not only the various types of sacred places add up to a heterogeneous blend, also the different spiritual qualities of these places constitute what may be called an ontology of heterogeneous powers (c.f. Humphrey 1996).

Theorising the Tsaatang landscape

As already mentioned, this paper takes its departure from recent anthropological writings on how people engage with their environment. One good example is Tim Ingold's 'dwelling perspective' (1995: 75-77), which emphasises that human beings are part of their landscape, are *embedded* in it; as opposed to the more culturalist renderings promoting the existence of arbitrary 'cultural constructions of nature' (c.f. Ingold 1992; 1993a). As I see it, this is first of all a phenomenological perspective, that is, it takes its analytical departure from actual human experience. Seen in relation to the Tsaatang case, this means that, if a Tsaatang hunter says he encountered a mountain 'owner', then this statement must be analysed literally, not metaphorically. More generally, the point is that animism is best analysed as an active way of being in the world, and not merely as a passive representation of it. This leads on to the second aspect of Ingold's perspective, the ecological one, which stresses that the particular *means* of engaging with the environment structure the overall perception of it (Ingold 1993b). This implies that, given their particular reindeer-nomadic mode of existence, the Tsaatang's life on the move is likely to have a great influence on how they perceive their environment as a whole.

Keeping the above in mind, a key question must be how best to understand the relationship between the two phenomena of animism and nomadism. If we, following Ingold, accept that Tsaatang animism should not be conflated with an ideology which is simply executed in nomadic practises, and, vice versa, that Tsaatang nomadism neither should be conflated with the simple practice of executing animist ideology, then the lesson to be learned boils down to the fact that animism and nomadism are best analysed, not as ideology and economic practice respectively, but as two deeply interrelated Tsaatang 'ways of perceiving the environment' (c.f. Ingold 1993b). As such, both animism and nomadism *structure* Tsaatang spatial perception, just as neither can be described as being determined by the other.

While newer anthropological writings on landscape constitute the overall theoretical background for this paper, Bruno Latour's so-called 'actor-network theory' provides the particular theoretical topology whose territory I shall occupy in order to carry out my analyses. While this is not the place to summarise what Latour's perspective is all about, it is worthwhile to highlight a few major points of particular relevance for the present analyses.

Firstly, in this perspective, an actor is defined semiotically; an actor is basically anyone or anything – be that a human or a nonhuman – 'granted to be the source of an action' (Latour 1996: 374; see also Latour 1993: 62-65). Secondly, a network is neither merely a social structure, nor is it just a technological thing. A network is rather a kind of fragmented totality crosscutting the domains of society (humans) and environment (nonhumans), because it is constituted by all the connections that can be traced between a given constellation of human and nonhuman actors (c.f. Latour 1996). Thirdly, and perhaps most importantly, an actor-network is never homogeneous, it is always heterogeneous. A given actor-network is not confined to a finite, homogeneous territory demarcated by clear-cut boundaries; it rather carries a potential of infinite expansion made possible by an unproblematic incorporation of all actors, however different from each other, it may mobilise (c.f. Latour 1993).

Now, if we paraphrase one of Latour's (negative[4]) definitions of an actor-network by substituting the term 'networks' with the term 'Tsaatang landscapes', the following baseline understanding of the Tsaatang landscape arises:

[Tsaatang landscapes] are simultaneously real, like nature, narrated, like discourse, and collective, like society (Latour 1993: 6).

If we look back upon the ethnographic information provided earlier on, this general description of the Tsaatang landscape is very satisfactory. Clearly, the Tsaatang do conceive their landscape as an arena of intentional nonhuman actors; that is, the landscape as a quasi-social *collective*. The example with the *Agaya* mountain illustrate that, while the Tsaatang obviously do not conflate humans with nonhumans, they definitely incorporate a number of nonhumans – e.g. the mountain 'owners' – into their sociality. Further, the Tsaatang landscape is the object of a constantly accumulating number of stories; that is, the landscape is a *narrative*. The ongoing narration of these stories is not only inseparable from, for example, what makes a hunter a good hunter, it is also constitutive for the coming into being of the Tsaatang landscape as such, because, for a large number of people (notably the women), hearing these stories is all they will ever experience about certain places in the landscape, such as the *Agaya* mountain. And, needless to say, the Tsaatang landscape is also very *real*. The magnitude of the mountains, the strong currents of the rivers, the bitter cold of the wind from the North; these all give rise to strong bodily experiences and thus very particular conceptions of the landscape (e.g., that the highest mountains have spirit 'owners') which are hard to overestimate.

In sum, the analytical framework provided by Latour renders possible an understanding of the Tsaatang landscape which can fruitfully employ the heterogeneous ontology of the actor-network, and this without contradicting the important lesson provided by Ingold. Put differently: if Ingold's writings allow us to understand the *phenomenology* of Tsaatang perceptions of the environment, then Latour's perspective makes it possible to understand the *topology* of the Tsaatang landscape. With these theoretical clarifications in mind, we can now move on to a closer anthropological analysis of the particular characteristics of Tsaatang spatial perception.

Place and space in the Tsaatang landscape

The most striking characteristic of the Tsaatang perception of the environment is their focus on places at the expense of spaces. For the Tsaatang, each powerful field radiating from a nonhuman entity in the landscape has a well-defined centre, but its boundary seems correspondingly ill-defined. The Tsaatang sacred mountains, for example, fit this description. As already shown in the example with the *avlin*-spirits of the *Agaya*-mountain, a sacred mountain is believed to have a particular spirit-owner (*ezen*) – an intentional, often moody nonhuman being with whom the Tsaatang hunters, for example, have to interact 'socially'. Nothing, however, in the stories about the *Agaya*-mountain has to do with spatial boundaries. It is true that the man who went hunting for wild reindeer suddenly realised that he was near this mountain, but it is difficult to establish any exact demarcation of the owner's domain from his story. This also goes for other Tsaatang stories about the mountain. What really seems to matter in all these stories is the fact that something unusual happened and that this event was linked to the mountain-spirit, not where it happened.

Once I asked a young herdsman, Amra, to draw a map of the landscape surrounding him. We were standing on top of a hill, and Amra was very careful in his depiction of all the features of the various mountain peaks in the horizon. Many of them had spirit owners, and each of these mountains/spirits had a particular (nick)name. Asked about possible boundaries/borders in the landscape (*gazaryn xil*), Amra insisted that there were no boundaries to be seen *at all*. Somewhat perplexed by this answer, I asked him whether a highly sacred mountain-pass, which we could see in the far distance, did not in fact represent a boundary of some kind. After all, I added, people on the two sides of the mountain-pass call themselves by different names, just as the two areas belong to different political units. But Amra persisted: his land was boundless (*xilgüi*), and the political distinctions were merely names (*ner*) of the land, not boundaries in the land. Finally I pointed towards a river at our feet, crosscutting the whole view towards the west, and asked him whether this river did not define a boundary in the land. But again Amra stressed the lack of spatial boundaries; in fact, judging from his laughter, my question about the river as a spatial boundary did not seem to make much sense to him at all.

In sum, it is my impression that, whereas no Tsaatang will doubt that the locus of the spirit owners is at the very centre of the mountains (the peaks), people will either disagree or perhaps not even know where the possible boundary between one mountain owner's spatial realm and another mountain owner's spatial realm is located in the landscape. And, as the above example illustrates, this lack of spatial boundaries not only refers to the spiritual aspects of the landscape, it refers to physical, ethnic and political aspects as well (to the extent that such a conceptual atomisation into discrete landscape 'aspects' makes sense in the Tsaatang case at all). Put differently, many domains of the Tsaatang landscape are not 'owned' by anyone in particular, be that humans or nonhumans. At the same time, however, many particular locations in the landscape are believed to have 'owners', be that particular trees, lakes or – as we have seem – mountains. Hence, whereas a number of *places* are imbued with particular qualities (spirit powers), most of the *spaces* in between these places are 'empty', that is, they are devoid of any such quality. This, of course, does not imply that these spaces are not perceived at all; it only means that they do not qualify as loci of powerful nonhuman entities. This difference is also revealed in the different toponymical systems used for places and spaces. As already mentioned, sacred places such as mountains are usually known under diminutive names, because uttering and indeed knowing their real names is conceived as dangerous, why these matters solely are left for the shamans to deal with. Names of spaces, on the other hand, such as administrative districts, are unproblematic to speak of and are regarded as common knowledge.

Nomadic and sedentary landscapes

I will now analyse the particular spatial economy of the Tsaatang people in light of their nomadic existence, and thus, adopting Latour's theoretical framework, generalise the Tsaatang case to the wider one of nomadic people as such.

Why do the Tsaatang highlight places at the expense of spaces? One possible answer is that an spatial economy of spaces and boundaries is not workable when people often move from one place to another. The effect of a spatial boundary, one may argue, is exactly to separate one finite space or domain from another, and the wider effect of such a demarcation seems to be the denial of frequent movement between such finite spaces. Put differently: what, if any, is the use of spatial boundaries when your nomadic lifestyle implies their continuous crossing?

Think about the herdsman, Amra, who was asked to make a two-dimensional representation of his landscape in terms of the different spirit-owners inhabiting it. The result was quite unlike a political map consisting of distinct territories with their own special colour. It was rather a representation consisting of many different dots, in between which there were large gaps of unqualified space; a kind of spiritual no-man's-land, if we pursue the analogy to the political map.

Now think of a Balinese landscape with terraces of rice fields, or, even better, the typical agricultural landscape of the Danish countryside with different, and well-demarcated fields, each consisting of a single and pure crop. Imagine an aerial photograph of such a sedentary landscape. What you are likely to see is a pattern consisting of different, finite spaces that are internally homogenous and externally heterogeneous. Then imagine moving around inside this spatial pattern. Movement within such a sedentary landscape would seem to give rise to a feeling of spatial discontinuity; of jumping from one pure domain to another.

Sedentary landscapes, I therefore propose, are characterised by finite, homogeneous spaces with clear-cut boundaries in between them. For the Tsaatang and possibly also for other nomadic people, however, an alternative spatial economy characterised by places and boundlessness is much more meaningful given their life on the move. Unlike the boundary-producing economy of finite spaces found in sedentary landscapes, the economy of places found in the Tsaatang *nomadic landscape* produces neither boundaries nor finite spaces. Instead, the Tsaatang economy of places produces something very different, namely a number of spatial centres – or points of reference – from each of which an infinite spatial realm takes its beginning.

A given Tsaatang nomadic camp, for example, constitutes a unique place from where vectors point towards the unique sacred mountains towering around this camp. From one camp, the vectors will mainly point toward, say, the mountains A and B, and from another camp the vectors will mainly point towards, say, the mountains C and D. However, neither camp is for that reason located within a distinct, finite space, nor is there a clear-cut boundary marking the transition from the one camp site to the other. Rather, the two camp sites are distinguished by the difference between the two particular configurations of powerful places that their locations give rise to. In other words: what matters in the Tsaatang's nomadic landscape is the *impure* blend of unique places, not the *purity* of distinct spaces.

This brings us back to Latour and the nature of actor-networks. A given such network, we may recall, consists of different points – actors – from which threads towards different directions take their beginning. In principle, following Latour, a network knows no ending; it has no boundaries. Each position is the starting point of its own unique network, but one such network is not qualitatively different from the network defined by another position, rather it is a potential part of it. Movement within a network thus implies continuity; or what Latour calls a *translation* from one network to another, either of which were never pure. Indeed, in Latour's words, 'a network has no outside' (1996: 373).

And indeed, the place defined by a Tsaatang nomadic camp is the starting point of a particular network of places, of human and nonhuman powers, and this network does not differ in kind from the one constituted by a neighbouring Tsaatang camp; it only differs in degree. A given Tsaatang camp is just one place among a large number of places (e.g. camps) where the human actors, who temporarily dwell there, engage with the nonhuman actors, who permanently dwell there. A given Tsaatang camp can thus be said to constitute a social network of particular humans, who are embedded or indeed *placed* within a particular animist configuration of powerful nonhuman actors, and who must therefore work upon this actor-network in order to facilitate their particular actions.

The spatial modalities of place and space

It is important to emphasise that the proposed differences between the Tsaatang and the Danish landscape do not stem from two cultures being radically different in kind. What differs in kind is rather two *modalities* of spatial perception – the economy of place and the economy of space – which seem to characterise the Tsaatang and the Danish landscape phenomenology respectively. An inherent tension between these two modalities, I propose, structure the coming into being of both the Tsaatang nomad's and the Danish farmer's landscapes, just as this tension between place and space govern spatial perceptions within *any* society on earth. Neither spatial modality, I therefore propose, is restricted to particular human cultures. Rather, both spatial modalities represent a universal potential which may or may not be highlighted in a given society within a given environment. As such, the two modalities stand in a structural relationship to each other. This does not mean, however, that the two modalities are aspects of the mind (c.f. Descola 1996: 86-87). Instead, they could be called patterns of perception, that is, structures of spatial sensibility constituted in the very relationship between human beings and the environment.

The difference between the Tsaatang nomad's landscape and the Danish farmer's landscape, then, is due to an inversion of the hierarchy between the place-modality and the space-modality within the two societies, not to a lack of one of the two spatial modalities in either society. But what makes such perceptual figure-ground reversals between place and space possible? Not surprisingly, the answer must have something to do with historical transformations, that is to say, the history of societies as well as landscapes (c.f. Ingold 1993a). The space-economy of the present Danish sedentary landscape is inseparable from Western processes of modernisation, rationalisation and secularisation, just as the place-economy of the present Tsaatang nomadic landscape is linked to the complex history of Inner Asia as a whole; in Mongolia notably the great transformation from tribal shamanism into state-Buddhism which was followed by a change into planned socialism and, most recently, by the emergence of a post-socialist capitalist society and various re-traditionalised nomadic modes of existence.

However, this is not the place to write either the history of the Tsaatang landscape or that of the Danish countryside. Instead, I shall conclude this section by looking at the cityscape of London as a spatial environment which produces a re-activation of the place-economy – and consequently a de-activation of the space-economy – in a Western context. Thus, when travelling around in London, notably with the Tube, one's perception of the environment is highly place-oriented. Imagine taking the Tube from, say, Piccadilly Circus to King's Cross. Even for a person who has lived for a long time in London, the experience of these two domains of the total London environment is likely to be defined by his or her popping up from the ground at the two Tube stations respectively. Following an initial lack of spatial orientation, one will focus on a significant place near or at the station – such as a high building – and literally move on from there. The cityscape of London, I therefore propose, is not a landscape characterised by its bounded spaces (the parks being a notable difference), it is rather a constellation of significant places, such as Tube stations, from whence particular networks of both human and nonhuman actors take their beginning.

The ritual aspects of Tsaatang migration

We shall now look at what happens in terms of spatial perception when the Tsaatang are moving. If we accept the hypothesis that the Tsaatang landscape is of the nomadic kind, and that it therefore fulfils the characteristics of an actor-network, then an interesting question arises: how does the Tsaatang economy of places work *while* they are on the move? In other words: how do the Tsaatang network their landscape in the course of moving through it?

We shall concentrate here on Tsaatang migration, that is, the moving from one campsite to another. (Obviously, the Tsaatang move within their landscape in many other ways, such as when they are hunting, herding reindeer, or collecting firewood or nuts in the forest). Migration among the Tsaatang is highly ritualised. When the Tsaatang move camp, they begin by packing down all their belongings in a very specific order, and when they arrive at the new camp-site, they end the trip by unpacking these things in exactly the reverse order. On either occasion each family also makes a sacrifice to the mountain owners believed to preside over the given camp site. It is also significant that the Tsaatang do not tear down their tepees completely. Rather, just before departure, the men carefully take down the wooden poles of the tepee one by one and put these on the ground next to it, only to leave a tepee-skeleton consisting of three poles. After that, the women carefully clean the inside ground of each tepee. Indeed, when one travels through the Tsaatang landscape one often notices these abandoned campsites, which, were it not for their characteristic tripartite wooden structures, would be indistinguishable from the surrounding landscape.

Why are the Tsaatang so keen on carrying out these highly structured practises; why don't they just move? Obviously, to move camp is, though it happens frequently, a significant event. The day of migration is a special day, and thus potentially a dangerous day. Things may go wrong; the spirit owners, for example, of both the new and the old campsite may become offended by peoples' various wrongdoings (such as forgetting to present them with a sacrifice). On a more abstract level, the ritual practises taking place in the new as well as in the old camp are also a celebration of place, or rather, a celebration of the transfer from one place to another. Basically, my thesis is that when the Tsaatang are carrying out the same formalised practises, but in reversed order, in the new and in the old camp respectively, they thereby effect the necessary transfer of the 'home-ish' quality of their previous camp into the site of the new one. The Tsaatang's careful cleaning of the campsite to be abandoned also supports this argument. However, due to the presence of the wooden tepee-skeletons at former campsites, it would be wrong to say that the Tsaatang, when moving, reduce their former places of dwelling to general 'empty' space, that is, cut them out of a network. Rather, the abandoned campsites continue to be places; but their home-ish qualities, through the above ritual practises, are now reduced to potentials inherent in these places. In fact, the Tsaatang often return to an old campsite after a couple of years, thus making possible a reversed transformation from what is potentially a home into a real one (*ger oron*), that is, re-activating a network.

The Tsaatang, then, are not merely packing down their various belongings for a while to later unpack them again at the new campsite, they are actually packing down their whole *sense of where their current place is*, to borrow a term from Feld & Basso (1996), so they can unwrap this spatial sensibility later, at the moment they have reached their new home. The practices constituting Tsaatang migration, however, cannot be analytically divided into two fundamental kinds of action; a practical and a symbolic one respectively (*contra* Leach 1976). My Tsaatang data does not present itself so that an opposition appears between expressive animist ritual, on the one side, and instrumental nomadic behaviour, on the other. For the Tsaatang, carrying out a sacrifice to the spirit owners is as practical an endeavour, it seems, as the cleaning of their former campsite is a symbolic one. We are, in other words, not faced with a purely expressive layer of animist ideology resting independently on top on a purely technical basis defined by a nomadic subsistence economy. Instead, the above practises may best be understood phenomenologically; that is, as particular Tsaatang techniques of transferring their sense of belonging from one place to another by means of formalised action.

A home away from homes

Turning now to spatial movement itself: while on the move the Tsaatang will ride in a certain order, just as they will follow particular tracks and make great efforts not to stop, except at the particular places where – as they say – 'people usually halt'. Among these places, the *ovoos* are particularly interesting in light of the present analysis. An *ovoo* basically is a cairn of mainly stones, but also animal bones, used bottles, etc., usually located on the top of a mountain or a mountain pass, but sometimes also at places where unusual events are reported to have happened.[5] When people travel in Mongolia, including the Tsaatang, they will usually stop at any *ovoo* they encounter on their way. Ideally, people will then pick up three stones and circumambulate the *ovoo* three times, each time throwing a stone on the *ovoo*, and sometimes also making a prayer to the particular spirit it incarnates (*ovoo taxix*). As such, the *ovoos* are part of the networks of sacred places described earlier on in this paper. An *ovoo* is basically the locus of an 'owner'; a peak of power. If an *ovoo* is not actually located on the very top of a mountain, then the place where it is built nevertheless becomes mountain-like. Again, this should be understood literally, not just metaphorically, for the very shape of an *ovoo* may be described as a miniature mountain and, as we shall see below, in terms of its structuration of spatial perception, an *ovoo* fulfils the same properties as a sacred mountain (c.f. Humphrey 1995, n.d.)

My concern here is not to analyse the various systems of belief (if we can call them that) connected with the *ovoos*. Rather, the aim is to look at what effects the ritual actions – carried out in the *ovoo* rituals – may have on the Tsaatang's perception of their environment. Basically, my point is that the very bodily practises carried out at the *ovoo* sites produce a continuous re-evocation of the economy of place outlined earlier. The fact that the Tsaatang circumambulate the *ovoo*, I think, underlines the general point about their landscape being characterised by places as opposed to spaces. Thus, when the Tsaatang make a stop at an *ovoo* while moving camp, what they basically do is to momentarily create a fixed point of reference resembling that of a given campsite. The *ovoo* ritual, in short, constitutes a place within a context of empty space. Or, in Caroline Humphrey's wording, 'the ritualised journey is ... a spatial liminality, into and out of the otherness of "travelling that is not travelling" – paradoxically which serves to reassert the nomadic way of life – thereby negating movement in the everyday world' (1995: 142-43).

Framed in terms of nomadic existence, the *ovoo* can thus be described as a home away from homes. However, like all homes, which are not real homes, the site of the *ovoo* is not a place of dwelling, it is a temporary place of rest. Now, my point is that the Tsaatang, in order to enter such a state of rest while being on the move, must engender perceptions of spatial finitude. I therefore propose that the ritualised movements constituted by the *ovoo* circumambulations, which are taking place within the larger framework of spatial movement, momentarily untangle the Tsaatang from the infinite nomadic landscape in which they are otherwise constantly entangled, while on the move.

Intimations of finitude

We have already seen why the Tsaatang landscape may be described as infinite. Amra, the herdsman, insisted that his land is boundless. More generally, we saw that the animist qualities of the Tsaatang landscape, together with the negation of bounded spaces inherent in nomadic practises, made possible a characterisation of the Tsaatang nomadic landscape as an actor-network. As also pointed out, this analogy is analytically fruitful because of the resemblances between two topologies, the topology of the Tsaatang landscape and that of an actor-network. In both topologies, finite spaces and boundaries are downplayed, whereas places and boundless networks are highlighted.

Strictly speaking, however, the infinity of an actor-network is relational, not spatial. For Latour, networks are not suspended in a space with *distances* expressed for example as 'near' and 'far'. Rather, the idea of an actor-network implies a special topology in which the *extent* of a network must be measured vector-like in terms of whether it is 'long' or 'short' (Latour 1996). An actor-network, in other words, is not suspended in something, such as empty space, it rather encapsulates itself, creating a boundary which does not demarcate anything, and thus exists independently of notions of what is inside and what is outside (ibid.). In consequence, a given actor-network should not be described with reference to the category of space at all, because what counts is the number of actors, or places, which stand in relationship to each other.

Turning now to the infinity of the Tsaatang landscape, this however is clearly measured in terms of spatial limitlessness. Undoubtedly due to the specific contours of the Mongolian landscape, with its wide-open spaces and rugged terrain, the

Tsaatang perception of the environment is highly grounded in the faculty of vision. In the Mongolian language, concepts for looking and seeing are more numerous, and seem to play a wider role in everyday language, then those for hearing, for example. For all people in Mongolia, shamanists and Buddhists alike, one of the greatest powers conceivable is the sky (*tenger*), which is praised in countless prayers, songs and tales. The concept of *tenger* stands as something that is – at one and the same time – constantly present and infinitely distant (see also Humphrey 1996: 78-84). Small wonder that, immersed in a landscape of limitless views, and living under an eternal blue sky (as they would put it themselves), the nomadic people of Mongolia seem to have come to despise spatial confinement. When told about the size of Denmark, for example, and at the same time confronted with its number of inhabitants, my Mongolian friends, looking terrified, seemed to imagine a people who constantly must avoid bumping into one another.

My point, however, is that exactly this love of boundlessness is likely to render necessary the Tsaatang (and, more generally, the Mongolian) celebration of particular places. The above differences between the topology of a nomadic landscape and that of an actor-network put aside, the similarities between the two topologies still make room for an understanding of this need to deal with – what may be called – the Mongolian problem with infinity. Following Marilyn Strathern (1996; 1997), I would strongly insist on the fact that human beings cannot tolerate constantly to be part of an infinite actor-network. In other words: if Latour teaches us that human action is about 'networking networks', then Strathern tells us that human action is also about *cutting* such networks. Phrased in terms of the present discussion, this implies that, if the Tsaatang nomadic landscape can be described as an infinite network, then the Tsaatang need ways of cutting this network. And this is exactly what the *ovoo* rituals, among other things, enable them to do. In fact, the *ovoo* ritual has a double effect in terms of Tsaatang control over their engagement with the environment. On the one hand, the Tsaatang's movements around the *ovoo*, as we have seen, create a fixed point of reference; an anchored spot from which the totality of the environment can be apprehended – a place from which people can *loop into* the infinity of the landscape, so to speak. On the other hand, the ritual circumambulation of the *ovoo* makes possible an inverted process of *looping out* of the infinity of the nomadic landscape, namely the coming into being of an invisible circle within which a finite, sacred space is intimated (see also MacDonald 1997).

This may sound unduly abstract, but try to imagine moving 360 degrees around an object, clockwise, as the Tsaatang do in the *ovoo* ritual. If you look straight ahead, you are part of the motion. If you turn your head towards left, you *fall out of* the motion, towards an infinite void. If you look right, however, as the Tsaatang do when throwing stones at the *ovoo*, you *fall into* an inner, finite space, towards the very axis of your circumambular motion. This latter phenomenon is exactly what I refer to in the term 'looping out of the nomadic landscape'.

Interestingly, both the Tsaatang and the Mongolian nomads actually live in round dwellings. The nomadic Tsaatang live, as already mentioned, in tepees (*orts*), whereas the Mongols live in felt yurts (*ger*). The different designs of these dwellings put aside, the overall spatial layout of their insides are very similar, just as highly for-malised rules govern the way both the Tsaatang and the Mongols are supposed to move around as well as place themselves within these miniature landscapes. In fact, one may anticipate whether a phenomenological analysis of the spatial perceptions taking place inside these round dwellings is not likely to reveal a tension between the bounded and the limitless, the finite and the infinite, which is analogous to the one I have tried to lay bare in this paper.

Conclusion

Four main points have been made in this paper. Firstly, that the Tsaatang landscape is of the nomadic kind as opposed to the sedentary kind. The Tsaatang, being animist nomads, highlight places at the expense of spaces, as opposed to modern sedentary people, who highlight spaces at the expense of places. Following Latour, the Tsaa-tang landscape may be characterised as an infinite actor-network of heterogeneous places devoid of spatial boundaries, and not as a pattern of finite homogeneous spaces with boundaries in between them, as found in the modern Danish agricul-tural landscape.

Secondly, that the established opposition between nomadic and sedentary land-scapes is analytical, in that it refers to two fundamental modalities of human spatial perception, a place-oriented one and a space-oriented one. Far from belonging to particular human cultures, and equally far from being faculties of the human mind, these two modalities are constituted in the very relationship between human beings and the environment. Standing in mutual opposition to each other from a structural point of view, either of the two modalities becomes highlighted at expense of the other as they are constituted in shifting historical processes involving both human and nonhuman actors.

Thirdly, that the Tsaatang's nomadic movements involve certain ritual actions that serve the purpose of structuring the Tsaatang perception of the environment. A number of ritual practises taking place both before departing from the old camp and after arriving at the new camp, enable the Tsaatang not only to move their belongings when migrating, but also their *sense* of belonging. Moreover, although no Tsaatang migration involves the crossing of boundaries between finite spaces, every Tsaatang migration involves the celebration of particular places (*ovoos*) – or points of reference – from where the infinity of their landscape can be apprehended in a 'safe' manner.

Fourthly, that some ritual aspects of Tsaatang movement enable them to 'loop into' their environment, whereas other elements facilitate the Tsaatang's 'looping out' of their environment. The Tsaatang's ritual movements at the *ovoo* site, for example, give rise to two mutually opposed transactions within their economy of places. Thus, the Tsaatang's circumambulations of the *ovoo* make possible the double process of both anchoring certain Tsaatang perceptions within an infinite landscape *and* of intimating other Tsaatang perceptions towards a finite realm, namely the inside of a magic circle.

NOTES

1. The final version of this paper has benefited from the many helpful comments received from the participants in the Second Baltic-Scandinavian Research Workshop, in particular the editors of this volume. I would also like to thank Caroline Humphrey, Martin Holbraad, Peter Marsh, Nikola Dimitov, Hürelbaatar and Alan Wheeler for their perceptive comments on earlier drafts of the paper. Special thanks to Lars Højer for his constant support.

2. After the editorial deadline for this paper I discovered that a similar theoretical framework has been used by Deleuze and Guattari in their essay on 'Nomadology' (see 1999). Indeed, the present analysis of 'nomadic landscapes' may be seen in continuation of Deleuze's work on the 'ontology of difference', although my own findings about Tsaatang spatial perception have been reached independently.

3. The meaning of the two terms 'shamanism' and 'animism' suffer from their long history within anthropology, where they – wrongly – have been defined either substantially or

formally (c.f. Pedersen 1997). In this paper, therefore, the two terms are used as analytical concepts, not as empirical objects. That is to say, neither the term 'shamanism' nor that of 'animism' refer here to particular institutions or cosmologies, either existing as pure types or not at all, in various societies worldwide. In Humphrey's words, '...[shamanism is]... the ways of being in the world which suggests quite simply that "we need to have shamans"' (Humphrey 1996: 4). Likewise, the term animism here denotes a universal 'mode of identification' (Descola 1996: 87), that is, as a general term for describing any society which 'endows natural beings with human dispositions and social attributes' (ibid.; see also Pedersen 2001). In the Tsaatang case, shamans, among others, make possible the ongoing creation of a sociality partly constituted by animist entities. As such, the Tsaatang landscape may be described as both shamanist and animist.

4. Like many advocates of new ideas, Latour is far better at describing what his idea is *not,* than what it actually *is.* The present quotation is a good example. It very clearly conveys Latour's idea of an actor-network, but paradoxically so by phrasing it in the language of what Latour calls the 'modern constitution', against which he fundamentally objects (Latour 1993: 46-48). As a matter of theoretical principle, Latour denunciates the modern project of singling out ontologically pure aspects of the world, such as 'the real', 'the collective' and 'the discursive' (Latour 1993: 3-8). And yet he nevertheless employs this very 'modernist' language to make what is a negative, though very precise, description of the ontological impurity of actor-networks.

5. *Ovoos* can be found, but under different names, at significant places all over the Inner Asian region. The origin of the *ovoo* ritual is obscure, but it is widely assumed to stem from the ancient shamanist societies of Inner Asia. In areas where Tibetan Buddhism, or for that matter socialist atheism, have later had an impact, the official meaning of the *ovoo*-rituals has been re-interpreted so as to fit the ideology in question (see also Humphrey 1996; Heissig 1980).

REFERENCES

Badamxatan, S. 1987. Le mode de vie des Caatan éleveurs de rennes du Xövsgol. *Études mongoles. ... et sibériennes* (18).

Descola, P. 1996. Constructing Natures: Symbolic Ecology and Social Practice. In *Nature and Society. Anthropological Perspectives*, P. Descola & G. Pálsson (eds.). London: Routledge, 82-102.

Deleuze, G. & F. Guattari 1999. *A Thousand Plateaus. Capitalism and Schizophrenia.* London: The Athlone Press.

Dioszegi, V. 1963. Ethnogenic Aspects of Darkhat Shamanism. *Acta Orientalia Hungaria* (16), 55-81.

Feld, S. & K. Basso 1996. Introduction. In *Senses of Place*, S. Feld & K. Basso (eds.). Santa Fe: School of American Research Press, 3-12.

Heissig, W. 1980. *The Religions of Mongolia*. London, Routledge & Kegan Paul.

Hirsch, E. 1995. Landscape: Between Place and Space. In Hirsch, E. and M. O'Hanlon, (ed)., *The Anthropology of Landscape: Perspectives on Place and Space*, Oxford: Oxford University Press, 1-30.

Humphrey, C. 1995. Chiefly and Shamanist Landscapes in Mongolia. In *The Anthropology of Landscape – Perspectives on Space and Place*, Hirsch & O'Hanlon (eds.). Oxford: Clarendon Press, 135-63.

– (n.d.). Some Thoughts on the Glamour of Mountains in Mongolia. Unpublished manuscript.

Humphrey, C. with U. Ongon 1996. *Shamans and Elders – Experience, Knowledge, and Power among the Daur Mongols*. Oxford: Clarendon Press.

Ingold, T. 1992. Culture and the Perception of the Environment. In *Bush Base. Forest Farm*, E. Croll & D. Parkin (eds.). Routledge, London, 39-56.

– 1993a. The Temporality of the Landscape. *World Archaeology* 25, 152-74.

– 1993b. Hunting and Gathering as Ways of Perceiving the Environment. In *Beyond Nature and Culture,* K. Fukui & R. Ellen (eds.). Oxford: Berg.

– 1995. Building, Dwelling, Living. How Animals and People make Themselves at Home in the World. In *Shifting Contexts – Transformations in Anthropological Knowledge*, M. Strathern (ed.). London: Routledge, 57-80.

Latour, B. 1993. *We Have Never Been Modern*. London: Harvester Wheatsheaf.

Latour, B. 1996. On Actor Network Theory. A Few Clarifications. *Soziale Welt* 47(4), 369-81.

Leach, E. 1976. *Culture and Communication. the Logic by which Symbols are Connected*. Cambridge, Cambridge University Press.

MacDonald, M. 1997 (ed.). *Mandala and Landscape*. New Delhi: DK Printworld.

Pedersen, M. 1996. Totemisme, animisme og identitet – nye svar på gamle spørgsmål om relationen mellem kultur og natur. M.Phil. Thesis, Dept. of Social Anthropology, University of Aarhus.

Pedersen, M. & L. Højer (n.d.). Når fortiden trænger sig på. En historie om mødet mellem etnografisk og mongolsk re-traditionalisering. Paper Presented to The Danish Ethnographic Society, Copenhagen, March 1997.

Pedersen, M. 2001. Totemism, Animism and North Asian Indigenous Ontology. *Journal of the Royal Anthropology Institute* 7 (3), pp. 411-27.

Strathern, M. 1996. Cutting the Network. *Journal of the Royal Anthropology Institute* (N.S.) 2, 517-35.

— 1997. A Return to the Native. *Social Analysis* 41(1), 15-27.

Vainsthein, S. 1980. *Nomads of South Siberia – the Pastoral Economies of Tuva*. Cambridge: Cambridge University Press.

Wheeler, A. 2000. Lords of the Mongolian Taiga: An Ethnohistory of the Dukha Reindeer Herders. MA Thesis, Dept. of Central Asian Studies, Indiana University.

The horizontal architecture,
or how we locate ourselves inside nature[1]

Sabine Brauckmann

> *On a été horizontal, j'ai envie l'être vertical.*
>
> LÉON PAUL FARGUE

After some introductory remarks about the Kantian theory of space and its ecological interpretation by Uexküll, this chapter will sketch the conceptual relationship between place and environmental space. Contrary to the abstract term *space*, places have a personal and concrete connotation, because we experience them by walking around inside nature as if we qualitatively measure the surroundings. The objective of the chapter is to combine the specific horizontal geometry of modern architecture, as linked to the body-centred orientation, to the movements inside the environment, our man-made world. In the second part I will illustrate how our ambivalent attitude towards nature is expressed in the world of our dwellings by analysing two famous buildings, the *Villa Savoye* by Le Corbusier and *Fallingwater* by Frank Lloyd Wright.

Architecture and biology

When trying to grasp the horizontal shape of two famous houses, the Villa Savoye by Le Corbusier and Fallingwater by Frank Llyod Wright, which have fascinated visitors and connoisseurs of Euclidean rectangularity for decades, some resemblances of my early childhood come to mind. I refer here to the Kindergarten plays where one tried to construct a grid of horizontal and vertical lines, or to draw circles with a pencil and a pair of compasses. Another memory is the time when my father taught me about orientation during our strolls through the landscape. He would accompany his remarks with space-encompassing gestures, the tools being his left and right hands. Thus, I learned that we can only orient ourselves inside nature's environment if something like a conceptual coordinate system is placed onto the boundless space of the outer-world. My father also explained how houses should be placed on a site – or inside the landscape – to be ideally suitable for our life's purposes. Fallingwater and Villa Savoye, these two classic icons of modern architecture – both erected around 1930 – illustrate in very different ways how buildings can be set into nature either as an integrated component of, or as a counterpoint to, their natural surroundings.

As a trained philosopher of science, my research is mainly focussed on holistic theories of developmental biology that claim the importance of an all-embracing view on life in general, and living beings in particular. One of the most controversial issues of embryology is how the shaped organism emerges from a shapeless embryo; particularly, how organic cells and tissues configure themselves to spatial patterns. The organic forms are often admired for their harmony and complexity, which are features one can observe in architecture, too. The many allusions to organic forms in these two houses, and the conscious treatment of the natural environment i.e., the horizontal line, are obvious. At a first glance, the architecture of the houses appears to establish an interrelation between two very different worlds; the organic and the architectural. However, as the philosopher Suzanne Langer emphasised it some time ago:

In reading the works of great architects with a philosophical bent ...one is fairly haunted by the concepts of organic growth, organic structure, life, nature, vital function, vital feeling, and an indefinite number of other notions that are more biological than mechanical. None of these terms applies to the actual materials or the geographical space required by a building (Langer 1953: 99).

In my opinion the last sentence is not altogether correct. I acquainted myself with architecture, its theories, and, most important of all, its interpendencies with our spatial perception through links to the natural environment. To understand a discipline that is not one's own, one becomes a traveller who explores unknown territories and places, visiting them again and again to become acquainted with their nodal points and intersections. In this way one meets, at least partially, the naturalists's demand to perceive nature in all its spheres. It was not obvious when my journey started from theoretical biology to the unknown territories of architecture – which I had left behind a long time ago in my childhood – that my educational training in philosophy would come to serve as a *cicerone*. It would allow me to decipher the hidden signs that map an intuitive geometry of the houses in which we live. Thus, the walk went beyond any narrow disciplinary boundaries straight out into the domain of cultural aesthetics. Right from the beginning it was astonishing that, just like the developmental branches of biology, architecture also is preoccupied with the shapes of its objects, whose spatial structures very often imitate forms of nature. Both disciplines suggest that the number of geometrical forms that attract human awareness and interest is rather small. However, two spatial dimensions, the horizontal and the vertical, are fundamental for sectioning the empty space surrounding us. My focus in this chapter is on ourselves, on the human inhabitants and their specific habits, and on our ways of occupying the natural space that we, little by little, convert into a place called our environment. I will concentrate on the architectonic images that we create by interlocking our intuitive geometry with the world *out there*. In the first part the Kantian philosophy of space will be roughly outlined, later interpreted by Uexküll's ethological comprehension. The second part depicts our ambivalence towards nature by illustrating our movements inside the interior space of two famous buildings. Thus the abstract space of our perception, which focuses towards the vanishing point, will be compared with the finite, lived place of our dwellings. Obviously, our specific body-centred perception helps us to localise ourselves as elements of nature, and, at the same time, it demarcates us from the surroundings by a non-visible grid of horizontal and vertical lines. Thereby, we have ordered our phenomenal space into a seemingly flat plane, vaulted by a concave horizon. In a similar way, we cover a sheltering membrane around ourselves when we build domiciles that protect us from an exterior, which very often is hostile towards helpless creatures such as ourselves. However, except for the primitive huts of our ancestors, or some post-modern kitsch boxes nowadays, our buildings are characterised by an angularity that apparently has forgotten the semicircular beginnings of architectonics.

From the body-centred space to the environmental place

On first approximation, Kant determined the horizontal as the plane on which our body is positioned as a vertical. Since humans are distinguished as the mammal that walks in an upright position, our bodies function as the perpendicular to the two-dimensional ground on which we stand. As soon as we have internalised this standpoint, we can distinguish between top and bottom, up and down. Then, we are qualified to differentiate into front-back and right-left axes in conformity with the structure of the body. Moreover, we can conceptually arrange a sequence of vertical planes, which intersect our field of vision. One of these vertical planes divides our body into two similar halves by which we localise two other directions, namely, left and right. The other one cuts our phenomenal space into *in front* and *behind* of the visual horizon. Thus, we humans know how to orient in space since we determine our location relative to the body. In a lecture on physical geography Kant extrapolates our apprehension of orientation in space to our knowledge of geography in general:

The same holds true of geographical, indeed of our most ordinary knowledge of the position of places; such knowledge is of no help to us, so long as we are unable to place the so ordered things and the whole system of reciprocally related positions, according to regions, through the relation to the sides of our bodies (Kant 1770: 379-80).[2]

Implicitly presupposed here is the three-dimensionality, which orders the position of the spatial segments, and an inherent chirality as well. For Kant, the three-dimensionality meant a constraint, serving us to define incongruent counterparts or figures (Janich 1996: 59). To translate it into modern terms, two three-dimensional figures corresponding in all their relations can be distinguished alone by their (incongruent) chirality. Due to chirality, an essential feature of nature as Kant stated, we can constitute the directions and, by it, we order our phenomenal space. Together with the four directions, being fixed relative to the sun, they guide us in locating ourselves inside nature (Kant 1786: 269).[3] As soon as our experience has corroborated such interdependencies of spatial perceptions, which are linked to tactile relations, we can acquaint ourselves to nature's space (Jammer 1969). Concretely, distances, lengths, and forms are not observed in reality, but they are based on figures drawn from past experiences, and they are equalised to the qualitative measurement of the here and now. To say it in the words of cartography, the human mind has built into itself a spatial schema, analogous to the grid of a map projection (Richards 1974: 4).

In this century the French mathematician Henri Poincarè has again emphasised and generalised the Kantian approach when he stated, that space is necessarily referred to a system of axes invariably bound to our body (Poincarè 1946: 257). Or, as the Chinese philosopher and ethnologist Yi-Fu Tuan once wrote, vertical-horizontal, top-bottom, front-back and right-left are positions and coordinates of the body that are extrapolated onto space (Tuan 1976: 34f). When applying the epistemic perspective to the real world where we move from one place to another, this philosophical theory of space factually furnishes us with the certitude that we are born with an apperception of the surface of the earth, on which the sense data are mapped when we walk around our environment (Ingold 1993: 36). Whether the statement is correct and can be confirmed by cognitive research will not be discussed here. However, the theory departs somewhat from the Kantian idea of space. Immanuel Kant exemplified his theory of space by tactile tools, namely, our hands, and not by the feet that are our means of moving around; the means to leave a place and to walk towards the open space lying in front of our field of vision. It is precisely this locomotion ability that has pre-equipped us to obtain a practical knowledge of our environmental topology.

As one of the first biologists, Jakob von Uexküll, who investigated the environments of living organisms like the ticks and the *homo sapiens*, construed the Kantian space by ethological reasoning. The main difference between the philosopher and the biologist is that Uexküll focused on the animal kingdom in general, while Kant's philosophy concentrated on the ideal of the *homo scientificus* who possessed the know-how of an experienced mathematician (Pobojewska 1993).[4] As opposed to Kant who, in effect, based his theory on the knowledge of physics of his time, Uexküll's point of departure was the organismic world. This was a holistic place of phenomena, whereas the physic's space consisted of singular elements influencing each other through a spatial continuum. Thus, while the biologist studies the actual visual space of organisms, the physicists are calculating the abstract entity of space-time.

However, Uexküll's space owes its existence to our internal organisation that converts sensory signals into spatial images – an understanding of the process not unlike that of Kant. In this conceptualisation of the relationship between body and space, the space outside our body remains motionless while the system of planes shifts at once, when our head is moving. We orient ourselves in space by changing the external direction signs, horizontal and vertical, into internal ones like front and back. According to Uexküll, we perceive our locomotions, their directions and dimensions even when we move our limbs with closed eyes. For instance, with our hands we explore our surroundings and make pathways into the open space. When we now divide our inner space – still with eyes closed – into left-right, up-down, front-back domains, we realise that these three planes cross each other near the tip of our noses. These planes apparently part that tactile-visual space which we encompass, into eight equal segments that build up the Euclidean coordinate system (Uexküll 1922: 297). Thus, we create the *Wirkraum*, or the space of action (Uexküll 1956: 31):

We cut the space which is situated out of our body by three planes of which the cross junction is inside our head … Every local sign informs us about the position of our body, however, just the internal direction signs determine the spatial location of our body (Uexküll 1920: 15f).[5]

This space of action is not merely a domain of movements constructed by the paces we take, rather it is controlled by a system of vertical planes, a matrix of coordination that establishes the constraints of phenomenal space. A dynamic maze is configured by this direction matrix without fixing the positions of the separate planes permanently. To create such a dimensional tool, we make use of an inherent mental cluster of rectangularity. With it, we perceive our environment anew everyday and in different shapes. In Uexküll's approach, this bounded space of our environment represents the fixpoint and, simultaneously, a kind of shelter. It functions as a tool which allows us to feel secure against the infinite space of the universe. Obviously, the interactions between our environment and the physico-chemical surroundings of the earth have a decisive impact on our sense of being protected from nature's imponderabilities.

As soon as we have established a relationship between the data of our surroundings and our mental matrix of spatial measurement, we have identified our world as the environmental tube or *soap bubble*, which encompasses every living organism. We realise that everybody is surrounded by a bubble-like membrane that is smoothly integrated, as it consists in effect of a whole system of subjective signs. As a consequence, space *per se* does not exist, it is always tied to a subject, which constructs its own environment by perceiving its surroundings. In other words, the environment, or *Merkwelt*, to use Uexküll's term, is the conceptual model that allows us to comprehend and to explain our contacts with an exterior world. For instance, when walking through a landscape or going around the inside of a building, we can feel as if a sixth sense measures the distance to every object and every sign in our peripheral vision and sets them in relation to sounds echoing from objects and surfaces near and far (Crowe 1995). This continuous process shapes and structures the *espace vècu*, the perceived, lived space (Minkowski 1933: 403).

Moreover, there is the continuous, embodied response to the authority and balance of bilateral symmetry that helps us to feel the location and motion of our own body. This sense of balance is an unconscious perceiving of the Earth's gravity by an encompassing sense of balance that involves our eyes, ears, and our skin. When we move our body, the bubbles inside our sense organs are shifted simultaneously. It stimulates the balance organs and informs our body about its specific position. As long as we are standing in a vertical position, balance is maintained by an interplay between the eye, the sensibility for depth as exhibited by muscles and joints, and the balance organs themselves. These organs function in an analogous way to Uexküll's 'schemata' that are determined by our sensory *Bauplan* and imprinted in our mind, the same way the future house is hidden in the blueprint of the architect. All of it helps us to perceive, to observe, and to comprehend the space outside of our bodies.

For Uexküll's ethological aesthetics, the space of vision performs the visual cue, which plays a great part in our understanding of the environment. This fact was already known to Berkeley who, in his new theory of vision, mapped the space of vision to the phenomenal signs of the tactile space (Berkeley 1975). Evidently, our orientation in space is a visual-tactile interrelation for which we need our hands as tools for grasping and as tools for measurement. However, we also need our eyes to perceive things, to negotiate a passage between them until we have fixed the horizon that encloses our spatial environment on all sides like an impenetrable wall. That boundary sphere, closely related to our sense of spatial depth, shifts like a kinematic reference. From a scientific point of view, the horizon encircles the flat surface of the earth from the sky – in the centre of which the observer is located; in more poetical words, it is the celestial vault in which the earth seems to rest.

In a further development of Uexküll's approach, James Gibson claimed that from the perspective of an ecological optics the relevant data about our environment are picked up directly from the surroundings. Our perceptive states relate directly to the outer-world without consulting any sensory data, thus, nature's invariants are perceived without any internal or deductive mechanisms of reasoning (Gibson 1966).[6] For Gibson, information is embedded in the environment, a statement which resembles Uexküll's ethological model of *Merkwelt* and space of action. Due to our perceptual ability to soak up information from our surroundings we selectively structure our environment and discover both its extension and our local position within it; or to say it in philosophical terms, from the depth we arise, and into the depth we vanish (Gölz 1970: 222).

Inside the *Merkwelt*, a place that in its ancient Greek origin means *broad way* and *movement*, is the soil of all our experience. For, it represents a specific, personal, bounded, unique and concrete substrate, maybe even the substance of all of our environment (Walter 1988). On the one hand, the space of action is topologically arranged into specific places indicating to which location a phenomenon belongs, at least preliminarily. On the other hand, it is split into geographical regions as a coherent grid of places that cannot be localised anymore to a specific domain. However, it is accessible by the objects being situated in it (Bialla 1997: 166).

As we possess a tacit knowledge of places, which corresponds to the inherited knowledge of three-dimensionality, we can respond to specific environments instantaneously. This might be the main reason that *place* becomes established in and through whatever stable object catches our attention. Anthropology later extrapolated the reasoning on spatial fixpoints to a place theory (*topistics*) that comprehends places in the natural and built world as characterised by cultural evolution (Walter 1988). This sense of place refers to the demand we have for familiar landscapes, like refuges sheltering us from the unknown, from the sometimes terrifying prospect of being set adrift in a dimensionless, timeless, and chaotic world (Crowe 1995). In our environment we always see a qualitative space in front of us, in which our activity develops (Lawrence & Low 1990). The anthropologist Eugene Walter summarised the experience of places:

People do not experience abstract space; they experience places. A place is seen, heard, smelled, imagined, loved, hated, feared, revered, enjoyed, or avoided. Abstract space is infinite; … and repetitive and uniform. It has no shape, though it possesses logical form (Walter 1988: 18f).

Why do we like to imbue places with qualitative properties? Topistics approach this question through the analogy of the Roman belief in *genius loci*. For the Romans certain places revealed spirits, which reflected the uniqueness of a place and distinguished one place from others with which it might be confused. Maybe, it might be rational to state that a kind of atmospheric mentality characterises places, which are contrasted to space as the three-dimensional organisation of single elements. In transcending *topophilia*, Norberg-Schulz even argues that the influence of both the natural and the built environment is undeniable in the formation of a people's national and ethnic character when people become a component of their places on Earth (Norberg-Schulz 1980: 11f).[7]

In fact, we make places more suitable for our survival when we try to change an environment that is sometimes hostile to human living. To convert the surroundings of space into an environmental place, we cultivate nature to a landscape and fill it up with buildings that defend us against coldness, heat, or wetness and simultaneously please our sense of beauty. This is an essential feature of our style of life, particularly since we are not as fortunate as snails or turtles, who are able to produce dwellings out of their body material. An existential purpose of buildings, therefore, is that we convert a landscape into a familiar domain called a home, and, in so doing, take the environment into our possession.

Thus, the domain changes into a scenery. As opposed to the scene of pictorial art, or the kinetic volume for the sculpture, the ethnic domain becomes the basic abstraction of architecture (Langer 1953: 94f). Here the architect deals with a spatial sphere – created mainly by drawing boards and protractors – and extends the space from a phenomenal place to the virtual scene of a house, which symbolises the area in a box, or *interior space*. When we recognise our own place in a building, then architecture has produced a human environment that may even mutate into an icon of culture, as has happened in the case of these two houses. The theory of place outlined here and its close relative, the concept of ethnic domain, might be successful conceptions when applied to architecture and cultural anthropology. To sum up my argument thus far, one could interpret the place theory with its emphasis on ethnic domains as a cultural fusion of Kant's transcendental philosophy of space with Uexküll's ethological approach.[8]

The following is a brief sketch of Le Corbusier's Villa Savoye and Wright's Fallingwater, both erected for the daily use of their inhabitants. Of course, both houses are actually luxurious images rather than models for a family home. Thus, it would be unfair to condemn these architectural naturalists for their very specific style, or to praise natural dwellings whose function is quite another one, namely, to provide a temporary shelter before walking away and searching for a new place. Since most of our life takes place outside of nature's world, modern houses act as blueprints for our locomotions inside their walls. Therefore, the sense of place, or the assumption of place theory in what has been called environmental memory (Quantrill 1987), might be better grasped, when related to tilt places and our movements inside interior space.

The main question posed in this essay, is how these houses have dealt with our locomotion, which spread out a grid of horizontals and verticals, and how they have solved the crucial issue of relating dwelling space to the surrounding environment. Hence, to think about space is to think of the environment we inhabit and to ask which kind of environment we inhabit first. The simple answer, particular when looking at the two icons of modern architecture, is that we live inside houses that feature the rectangularity of our spatial images. Through sense organs like our eyes we know the architectural space, which is finitely limited by walls and the ceiling. We can move our heads to the side or from top to bottom and with these movements, we may perceive, for instance, the horizontal lines of a freely floating cantilever, or the vertical presence of a fixed column. Moreover, we may turn our bodies or transport them on our legs through rooms or even up spiral stairs – at least for a while until we become dizzy. All this depends, however, on our ability to move around – on our locomotion – that fundamentally distinguishes us from the surroundings that are static and positioned. In extending Poincare's statements, we can establish an analogy between our instinctive procedure of creating sensory space, and the mental activity of the housebuilder who determines by a system of axes the skeleton of his work.

The architectonic place

The two houses, Villa Savoye and Fallingwater, that were both built around 1930, have inspired many subsequent building designs with their emphasis on a strong horizontal line. Whether this was a good inspiration for modern architecture can be questioned. However, this crucial issue will be left for the trained historian of architecture as this essay focuses instead on the habituè of these houses with the environmental space they occupy.

Both buildings were expressively designed as polemical statements of an ideal relationship to nature based on cultural factors; but they should not be seen as cases of ecological reasoning examining our attitude towards the environment.

The houses feature the open plan as developed by Mies van der Rohe who, conversely, adopted the *sukiya* style of Japanese classical architecture. *Sukiya* shows a translucent object avoiding clear directions and continuous axes, an attitude that perfectly fits the Japanese sense of place (Nitschke 1986). The Japanese house reveals an artificial image of simplicity and accidentalness with its raw and delicately tilt wood, loamy walls and paper windows, which are inconspicuously assembled to set a dwelling inside the environment and to distinguish a man-made place against the landscape. Due to the open plan, the inside and the outside are demarcated ambiguously from each other by movable walls, which simulate a floating spatial situation. In the Japanese open plan several rooms lead from one to the next chamber, 'lightly insulated from one another by screens of opaque or possible translucent or transparent materials' (Blake 1974: 31, see also Speidel 1983 for further discussion of Japanese architecture).

As a counterpoint to Western architecture, a Japanese building displays a parallel perspective that belongs to Asian art in general. This conveys a holistic worldview, which situates humans inside the very nature of which they are elements. In this perspective, the observer's view is frontal, wandering in segments from one plane to another until an image of bounded space is established without attaching particular importance to the vanishing point on the horizon. Conversely, the Western eye that is trained in observing the central perspective, will converge *ad infinitum* towards the horizontal depth.

Besides the adaptation of the *sukiya* style, the open plan of modern Western architecture emerged from a more feasible technology based on steel frames, reinforced concrete, and pre-cast elements. As a practical consequence, the emphasis shifted from the vertical column to the horizontal slab, facilitated by the steel-concrete frame, which supports a structure that holds up floors and the roofs above. In particular, the reinforced concrete revolutionised the aesthetics of construction because it suppressed the roof, and replaced or supplemented it by terraces that project to the outside. The accent does not run from top to bottom of the upward movement of former centuries, but floats horizontally, from left to right as Le Corbusier or Wright enforced it (Scruton 1994:10). The new statics did not need load-bearing screens of massive stonewalls anymore, and the new design opened up and enlarged the interior space. When buildings are erected by the pre-cast elements of ferroconcrete, they consist of a few slender columns spaced widely apart as, for instance, the Villa Savoye exemplifies it with its pilotis. Another consequence was that the modern architect left the sketchbook aside and became an engineer.

Paradoxically, however, this does not hold for Le Corbusier nor for Wright. They never stopped to sketch their ideas – with strong reminiscences of plant-like shapes – on paper.

For Le Corbusier, who coined the conception of *life in space*, architecture meant first and foremost the manifestation of man who creates his own universe that incorporates the principles of gravity, pressure and tension for simulating nature's shaping. According to his architectonic theory, nature itself is ruled by mathematical laws since it exhibits the same charisma as the geometry of curves and straight lines. Based on this Platonic perspective, Le Corbusier aimed at transferring the harmony of nature's universals inside the *machine mouvoir*, as he once termed his style of building. Since engineers at the time were considered superior to architects, it would seem only natural that cars – the icons of modernity in Le Corbusier's time – provided the ideal for buildings. Nevertheless, and consistent with the cubistic affection for mathematics, his architectonic ideal was the Parthenon, a pure creation of the Euclidean mind, and – ironically – a building that orders the landscape by subduing nature.[9] Finally, his approach led to a topological view that reduces space to a two-dimensional field of horizontal forces instead of distinct figures which are combined into a structured whole by our perception of interior space.

This, then, is how a highly abridged version of Le Corbusier's theory might sound, and indeed this is how the history of architecture has described it over the last decades. There is, however, another dimension to this history, which the history of architecture tends to neglect. This dimension is connected with LeCorbusier's upbringing in the Swiss Jura where the houses were often painted milk-white, a colour that symbolises purity and simplicity. The geometrical structure of the Alpine plants also had a strong impact on him, as the many drawings of the spruce or the yellow gentian illustrate.

LeCorbusier's Villa Savoye (Figure 1), which was designed for Monsieur Savoye, a rich insurer between 1929 and 1931, is composed like a white cube without a facade, perfectly presenting the Cartesian dictum of *clarité* and *sobrieté*, and resembling one of the ideal geometric figures the architect admired.[10] When looking at its living area and hanging gardens, which are raised above the columns so as to give views right to the horizontal line, one is reminded of an abstract modification of the classic atrium of Roman architecture. Further, it exemplifies a counterpoint to the skeleton cover and the internal dividing walls of the blueprint *Dom-ino*, the small apartments that were designed for low-income families a few years earlier. Here

Figure 1. Le Corbusier's Villa Savoye, 1929 (Courtesy Fondation Le Corbusier).

environmental place and interior space are interspacing each other on different levels, supported by pilotis, a spiral staircase and a ramp. Thereby, the open plan and its steel skeleton allow perfect control of the dominant horizontal line of the inside (Besset 1968: 86). Like a hostile fortress that faces in all four directions, the Villa Savoye stands on a green, encircled by a belt of trees that do not approach the house's inhabitants who apparently live in a world apart. Since the internal gardens face the south and the main entrance opens to the north, the human occupant wanders through the darkness of the entrance into the bright light of the interior space leaving the landscape behind.

The pilotis that consist of reinforced concrete, relieved of the static function that characterised the static columns of past centuries, support the whole facade. They playfully allude to the verticals, as it were, lift the weight of the building from the ground, and complement the sunroof. When one looks from the pillar to the main slab, it seems as if the pilotis visually lengthen the building through the vertical to the ground. The thin pilotis are contrasted to the mass of the roof-level service stacks, and likewise both are transformed into enigmatic statues resembling the vertical. Except for the red entrance doors, the polychromy of Le Corbusier's later buildings is limited to the eye-catching white of the outer walls as another colour would have been one too many for the well-ordered composition where nothing is left to chance. The box of the outer membrane and the superstructure of the sunroof compose the interior space completely.

The inside of the Villa Savoye exhibits a unitary volume, divided into two by the main floor, and not a composition of isolated cells. On the first floor the living rooms with glazed sliding walls overlook the internal gardens. Unlike Wright, LeCorbusier opted for a two-floor living room in which humans can comfortably breathe. When Uexküll compared our monadic style of life to an existence inside a soap bubble, he also thought of architectural space as a bubble. If the bubbles are sufficiently spacious, their inhabitants breathe freely, and their eyes are able to wander within the boundaries of the walls. To avoid the restrictions of this boundary and realise his ideal of infinite visibility, Le Corbusier, together with Pierre Jeanneret, developed window friezes that guide the view to the outside and fit his objective to imagine infinite visibility. The ribbon windows slit the exterior surface and run unbroken from corner to corner to preserve the integrity of the sides of the square (Trachtenberg & Hyman 1986). Furthermore, the perception of the environment outside regulates the specific composition of the inside, since the outer walls act as a sheltering membrane that lets in the light and permits the inhabitants to look out onto nature's world.

The bedrooms, reduced to a minimum of space, resemble the narrow sleeping cabins of a train, and are innervated like extremeties into a body. A spiral staircase leading from the basement to the sunroof is the main vertical in a composition of the prevailing horizontal. On a ramp, which is situated behind the outer wall, beginning at ground level, one slowly glides upwards in a meandric movement to the main living floor and the sunroof. This ramp represents the *promenade architecturale*, a recurring feature of Le Corbusier's building style. Together with the spiral stairs and curved walls, the ramp connects the floors and establishes the vertical dimension inside this cubistic space. This provides the two-legged animals, who dwell within the house, a sense of being able to move without obstacles.

Nowhere is the movement disturbed or interrupted by chairs, tables, or rugs, as the furniture is built in. To sum up, the impression that the Villa Savoye imparts on the visitor is that of a horizontal white box. It looks as if it has landed on stilts, or, as Frampton states, like a ship floating above the landscape from which it will walk away in the next moment (Frampton 1983: 344). Thus, it illustrates pure dynamics, as opposed to the static image of Fallingwater, in which a stroll around its interior was not intended.

Frank Lloyd Wright who disliked all the paraphernalies of the Renaissance, worked under the carefully chosen image of *Taliesin*, the Welsh hero who sees Nature, who has a heart for Nature, and who has the courage to follow Nature. He postulated an organic architecture where beautiful buildings are organisms configured by the best available technology and inspired by our imagination. Le Corbusier also saw buildings as organisms, but the organisms that the two architects saw as their models were two quite different specimens. Whilst Le Corbusier thought of the modern man of the machine age, Wright considered the need of a place to rest, to step away from the bustle of daily life and to comfort oneself inside a house.

Wright's houses often appear to be tucked into the landscape. Thus, in a much stronger manner than applies to Le Corbusier's architecture, a dominant horizontality and the importance of the roof characterise nearly all of Wright's buildings. Another remarkable characteristic of his architectonic style is that the buildings show a strong and close relationship to the landscape which surrounds them. In effect, they often turn to the landscape itself, as Wright opted for an interdependency between the building and the soil on which the houses were erected. Wright inspected a site, studied the outline of the piece of land, its visual aspects, its colours, and its orientation, until his imagination visualised the *genius loci*. He tried to preserve all that he liked about the site when, for instance, placing the house in a particular corner. A special property of the site, like a stone, a forest, a spectacular view, or a waterfall, became the key element of his blueprint and finally formed the image of the building (Brooks Pfeifer 1987: 37). The house was built into nature, but never, as the Villa Savoye, faced nature like a hostile fortress.

Wright's ecological alternative wanted to intensify the specific quality of the natural site, as with Fallingwater – the house built for the Kaufmann family of Pittsburgh – which was placed over a cascading river.[11] Instead of turning the house into a platform for an architecture of the woods, the waterfall was incorporated into the basement of the house. Compared to other modern architects, for example, Le Corbusier or Mies van der Rohe, who were, in some ways, more inclined to occupy nature's site with their structures, this specific attitude towards nature was something genuinely different. It might be the reason why Wright's dwellings formed a unity with the terrain in accordance with his lifelong slogan: 'I do not know where the environment starts and the interior space stops'.

Figure 2. Fallingwater. Fall southeast elevation. Photo by Thomas A. Heinz.
(Courtesy Western Pennsylvania Conservancy).

For Fallingwater, Wright used sandstone quarried on the property, and used local craftsmen to build it. Furthermore, its colour scheme repeats shades that refer to the colours of the environment, for instance the Cherokee red of the window frames connects the house to autumn's foliage. Wright initially wanted to cover the concrete of Fallingwater in gold leaf, a 'kitsch gesture' from which the good taste of his client saved him, and decided finally to paint the surface in apricot (Frampton 1983: 398). Nevertheless, just the idea to paint a house inside a forest in glittering gold, is thrilling. When one looks at Fallingwater, a building thrown into the forest, it resembles an image of anchoring in nature (Figure 2), partly supported by the extended horizontal slabs that seem to anchor it in the ground.

The same slabs venture into the open space like huge trays carried on stone piers of native sandstone, which on the left side look like a sturdy mast. The main house is massed high at the back, and the accumulated weight counters the great projection over the stream. In short, the statics of construction is based more on tenuity-continuity than on the conventional formulas of pillars and beams. As a consequence, the theme of the house oscillates between ledge-cantilevering and floating cascades, which are repeated through the whole design. Everywhere, on the outside as well as the inside of the house, there are many more allusions to the overall theme of ledge and cantilever repeating the image of water, which runs over sharp stones. For instance, the stairs, inside and outside the house, are designed to reflect the cascading nature of the site. They look like gateways, which should hide the entrance of a sheltering dwelling and evoke, when inside the interior space, the image of a cave. This refers also to one of the main differences between the two houses, which is suggestive for our topic. In Fallingwater one will not find the gliding motion that Le Corbusier mastered. Here even the naked stones of the walls behave like sharp angles that seem to prevent an undisturbed locomotion up and down. However, one does not miss the motion. Instead one feels at rest in this house. This feeling is supported by the comfortable sofas and chairs of the huge living room, inviting you to lie down in the horizontal position.

Conversely, the vertical element is given back to nature, namely, to the trees, whilst the horizontal line is limited to the living space of the human occupants. Wide stones extend that horizontal image. Like Le Corbusier, Wright reduced the size of the bedrooms to a minimum. At Fallingwater they serve as antechambers to their terraces, which function to increase the horizontal volume. This is further emphasised by a low ceiling level of just two meters. Without his ingenious treatment of the sunlight the building complex would have felt like a dark cage. As it is, the sun sneaks into the house through porthole-like windows, while elsewhere it illuminates the interior through glass gates. The wandering light beams animate and transform the interior space into a stage for the spot-like intrusions of natural light.

The most significant feature of Fallingwater, as of nearly all of Wright's houses, is the architect's ambivalence towards the new technology of reinforced concrete, a material Wright regarded as 'an illegitimate stuff with little quality in itself' (Frampton 1983: 398). The window details exemplify this at best. Wright normally preferred wood to steel as he could customise window frames of wood. The Kaufmann house, however, has steel windows that he modified to emphasise the horizontal joints by omitting the fixed vertical rail at the joining of the two operable window pieces. If one opens the two windows, which meet each other at one corner of the wall, the rooms lose this corner, and the inside and the outside pass over into each other. The same ambiguity holds for the point where window and wall merge into each other. There, the vertical rail is set directly into the stone with only a space to bear the glazing compound (Ford 1990: 341f).

To compare these two buildings in a few catchwords, one could state that Le Corbusier's Villa Savoye exhibits an architecture of the concrete tension between a cube on pillars and our gliding movements through interior space. Wright, however, set Fallingwater apart when he stressed the horizontal aspect in a much more progressive way than Le Corbusier. When looking at the Villa Savoye, one could even recall the dead nature of *arte povera* that the Italian futurism claimed in the first decades of this century. When discovering Fallingwater in the woods, one is reminded of a dark cave protecting us from all of nature's imponderabilities.[12]

Conclusion

The two houses are random examples of contrasting views on the relation between the man-made world of architecture and the natural world that surrounds us with all its invariants. The discussion of whether we can change this relation essentially, or whether we can just try to exploit it for our purposes, will be left to another treatise. Nevertheless, it is stating the obvious that we have created our own environment by moving around, getting oriented inside our spatial bubble and, finally, choosing the location that pleases us most.

Then we uproot the forests, settle down and build our dwellings. Step by step, the location has been mutated into becoming our place, into becoming the world of *homo faber*. In the process we have drawn our horizontal lines upon which all verticals are fixed and in which all vanishing points are found (Irvine 1964: 84). We have constructed a cognitive map of living areas with the paths measured by our feet. Finally we have connected our living environment to the landscape with its own patches and corridors.[13] Only then do we feel at home in houses, which we have adapted to our way of living.

One of the questions that arose while working on this project of trying to understand how the natural environment is related to the man-made world of architecture, was the following: whether the vertical is switched off by modern architecture; and if so, what is the reason? The cautious, and still preliminary, answer is that the vertical is partly switched off because technical progress has allowed it to be.[14] Or, as Virilo, an architect before he converted to a postmodernist lamenting on speed and the acceleration of modern life, put it: 'Due to the centrifugal speed, the depth of space is abolished in modern architecture after the outbreak of the vertical in past centuries which has changed the height into cosmic distances' (Virilo 1989).

A hard-core philosopher would refer to our field of vision, as Uexküll did, emphasising the horizontal character, but to be honest, this is an even older idea than the Kantian concept. It can be found already in Plato's *Timaios*.

Our journey, which led us from the Kantian physical geometry via Uexküll's ethological interpretation to those classics of modern architecture, has ended. How can these seemingly distinct themes be connected? It would be a very simple answer if conceptual movement were allowed instead of locomotion on foot. We could have strolled around from the infinite space of reasoning via finite places, to the interior space of architecture. Perhaps we have done so, with the image of a symbiosis of ramp and spiral in our minds that intersects the architectonic horizon by its ingenious mistreating of the vertical.

NOTES

1. This is a slightly modified and enlarged version of the talk held at the Second Scandinavian-Baltic Research Workshop Uses of Nature, Tartu, May 8-10, 1998. I am grateful for all comments and suggestions.

2. In his short treatise on physical geography Kant is even more explicit: 'Sogar sind unsere Urteile von den Weltgegenden dem Begriffe untergeordnet, den wir von Gegenden überhaupt haben, insoferne sie in Verhältnis auf die Seiten unseres Körpers bestimmt sind' (Kant 1768: 995).

3. 'Sich orientieren heisst, ...: aus einer gegebenen Weltgegend (in deren vier wir den Horizont einteilen) die übrigen, namentlich den Aufgang finden. Sehe ich nun die Sonne am Himmel, und weiss, dass es um die Mittagszeit ist, so weiss ich Süden, Westen, Norden und Osten zu finden. Zu diesem Behuf bedarf ich aber durchaus das Gefühl eines Unterschiedes an meinem eigenen Subjekt, nämlich der rechten und linken Hand ... Also orientiere ich mich geographisch bei allen objektiven Datis am Himmel doch nur durch einen subjektiven Unterscheidungsgrund ... ' (Kant 1786: 269).

4. For a further discussion of how Kant applied the concepts of science to philosophy, see Friedman 1992.

5. The term 'local sign' connotates that besides biological structures indicating sensory quantities like pressure or heat, there are qualitative ones which report spatial positions of an object touching our bodies visually.

6. When he investigated the depth perception of pilots, Gibson could confirm that without a fixed and static border, i.e. invariant, it is impossible to perceive the spatial depth.

7. The danger of place theory, at least in the interpretation of Norberg-Schulz, lies in the same shortcomings as the history of mentality (cf. Burke 1994).

8. Working architects tend, however, to be critical of place theory since they argue it over-looks the main task of architecture, namely to build houses for everyday life that are comfortable for their inhabitants. For the critics, this kind of approach has fed upon a one-sided diet of examples, e.g. on palaces, temples and churches, which are, doubtless, the most exposed buildings (Scruton 1979: 43).

9. It is really puzzling that the Villa Savoye, in effect, behaves in the same way towards its environment as the Parthenon.

10. Incidently, Savoie is the French word for Le Corbusier's home county in Switzerland.

11. The idea was borrowed from a Japanese woodcut of the 17th century that Wright bought when he designed the Imperial Hotel in Tokyo.

12. A well-known historian of architecture has stated it in a more elegant way: 'The Villa Savoye suggests the light of reason unambiguously perceived, while Fallingwater impresses upon the visitors' senses the mystery of the earth and meanings that lie beyond the bounds of any strictly rational comprehension' (Crowe 1995: 11).

13. Anthropological research has coined the concept of territory when discussing how space is organised (Rapoport 1994; Lawrence and Low 1990). The difference between my approach and theirs is that they mostly deal with landscapes and how they are organised by humans. They do not explicitly discuss architecture or houses respectively in this interdisciplinary context.

14. A desideratum, as the historian of architecture Mark argues: 'Contemporary writing on architecture tends to focus on formal analysis where visual ideas dominate the discussion of the origin and meaning of style. Technology is rarely touched upon, and structure, although generally understood as necessary, is hardly seen as a legitimative giver of form, even for largescale buildings' (Mark 1996: 389).

REFERENCES

Berkeley, G. 1975. *Philosophical Works, including the Works on Vision*. London: Dent.

Besset, M. 1968. *Wer war LeCorbusier?* Genéve: Editions d'Art Albert Shiva.

Biella, B. 1998. *Eine Spur ins Wohnen legen. Entwurf einer Philosophie des Wohnens mit Heidegger über Heidegger hinaus*. Düsseldorf: Parerga Verlag.

Blake, P. 1974. *Form Follows Fiasco: Why Modern Architecture Hasn't Worked*. Boston-Toronto: Little, Brown and Company.

– 1993. No *Place like Utopia: Modern Architecture and the Company We Kept*. New York: Alfred A. Knopf.

Blier, S.P. 1987. *The Anatomy of Architecture*. Cambridge: Cambridge University Press.

Brauckmann, S. 2001. From the Haptic-Optic Space to our Environment: Jakob von Uexküll and Richard Woltereck. In Kalevi Kull (ed.), *Jakob von Uexküll: A Paradigm for Biology and Semiotics, Semiotica* 134-1/14: 293-309.

Brewer, B. & J. Pears 1993. Introduction: Frames of References. In *Spatial Representations*, N. Eilan et al. (eds.). Oxford-Cambridge, MA: Blackwell. 23-30.

Brooks Pfeiffer, B. 1987. *Frank Lloyd Wrights ungebaute Architektur*. Stuttgart: DVA.

Burke, P. 1997. *Varieties of Cultural History*. Ithaka: Cornell University Press.

Crowe, N. 1995. *Nature and the Idea of a Man-Made World: An Investigation into the Evolutionary Roots of Form and Order in the Built Environment*. Cambridge MA: The MIT Press.

Ford, E. 1990. *The Details of Modern Architecture*. Cambridge: The MIT Press.

Frampton, K. 1983. *Modern Architecture 1851-1945*. New York: Rizzoli International Publications.

Friedman, M. 1992. *Kant and the Exact Sciences*. Cambridge: Harvard University Press.

Gibson, J.J. 1966. *The Senses Considered as Perceptual Systems*. Boston: Houghton Mifflin.

– 1979. *The Ecological Approach to Visual Perception*. Boston: Houghton Mifflin.

Girsberger, H. (ed.) 1959. *Le Corbusier 1910-60*. New York: George Wittenborn.

Gölz, W. 1970. *Dasein und Raum. Philosophische Untersuchungen zum Verhältnis von Raumerlebnis, Raumtheorie und gelebtem Dasein*. Tübingen: Max Niemeyer Verlag.

Ingold, T. 1993. Globes and Spheres: The Topology of Environmentalism. In *Environmentalism: The View from Anthropology*, K. Milton (ed.). London: Routledge, 31-42.

– 1995. Building, Dwelling, Living: How Animals and People Make Themselves at Home in the World. In *Shifting Contexts,* M. Strathern (ed.). London: Routledge, 57-80.

Irvine, W. Jr. 1946/1964. *Art and Geometry: A Study in Space Intuitions*. New York: Dover Publications.

Jammer, M. 1969. *Concepts of Space*. Cambridge: Harvard University Press.

Janich, P. 1996. *Was heisst und woher wissen wir, dass unser Erfahrungsraum dreidimensional ist?* Sitzungsberichte der wissenschaftlichen Gesellschaft der Johann Wolfgang Goethe-Universität Frankfurt, Bd. 34 (2).

Kant, I. 1768. Von dem ersten Grunde des Unterschiedes der Gegenden im Raum. In *Immanual Kant, Werke in sechs Bänden,* Bd. 1 (1963). Darmstadt: Wissenschaftliche Buchgesellschaft. 993-1000.

– 1770/1968. De mundi sensibilis atque intelligibilis forma et principis. *Gesammelte Schriften,*

Band II, Preussische Akademie Ausgabe: Berlin 1900-1942, 385-420.

– 1786/1963. Was heisst: sich im Denken orientieren? In *Immanual Kant, Werke in sechs Bänden*, Bd. 3 (1963). Darmstadt: Wissenschaftliche Buchgesellschaft, 267-83.

– 1963. *Critique of Pure Reason* (2nd edition). London: Macmillan.

Langer, S.K. 1953/1973. *Feeling and Form: A Theory of Art and Developed From Philosophy in a New Key*. (5th imprint). London: Routledge & Kegan.

Lawrence, D.C. & S.M. Low 1990. The Built Environment and Spatial Form. *Annual Reviews in Anthropology* 19: 453-505.

LeCorbusier 1923. *Toward a New Architecture*. New York: Payson and Clarke.

Louck, J. 1998. Le Corbusier and the creative use of mathematics. *British Journal of the History of Science* 31: 185-215.

Majer, U. 1995. Geometry, Intuition and Experience. *Erkenntnis* 42: 261-85.

Mark, R. 1996. Architecture and Evolution. *American Scientist* 84: 383-90.

McCarter, R. 1994. *Fallingwater: Frank Lloyd Wright (Architecture in Detail)*. London: Phaidon/ Chronicle Books.

Minkowski, E. 1933. *Le temps vècu*. Paris.

Nesbitt, K. (ed.) 1996. *Theoretizing: A New Agenda for Architectural Theory*. Princeton, NJ: Princeton University Press.

Nitschke, G. 1966. The Japanese Sense of Place, *Architectural Design* 3.

Norberg-Schulz, C. 1980. *Genius Loci: Towards a Phenomenology of Architecture*. New York: Rizzoli.

O'Keefe, J. 1993. Kant and the Sea-horse: An Essay in the Neurophilosophy of Space. In *Spatial Representation: Problems in Philosophy and Psychology*, Eilan et al. (eds.). Oxford and Cambridge, MA: Blackwell, 43-64.

Pobojewska, A. 1993. Die Umweltkonzeption Jacob von Uexkülls: eine neue Idee des Untersuchungsgegenstandes von der Wissenschaft, in *Neue Realitäten. Herausforderung der Philosphie*, XVI. Deutscher Kongress für Philosophie, Sektionsbeiträge I. Berlin, 460-502.

Poincarè, H. 1946. *The Foundations of Science*. Lancaster, PA: Science Press.

Quantrill, M. 1987. *The Environmental Memory: Man and Architecture in the Landscape of Ideas*. New York: Schocken Books.

Rapoport, A. 1994. Spatial Organization and the Built Environment. In *Companion Encyclopedia of Anthropology*, Tim Ingold (ed). London-New York: Routledge, 460-502.

Richards, P. 1974. Kant's Geography and Mental Maps, *Transaction of the Institute of British Geographers* (N.S.) 11 (61), 1-16.

Scruton, R. 1979. *The Aesthetics of Architecture, Princeton*. NJ: Princeton University Press.

Scruton, R. 1994. *The Classical Vernicular: Architectural Principles in an Age of Nihilism*. New York, NY: St. Martin's Press.

Speidel, M. (Hrsg.) 1983. *Japanische Architektur. Geschichte und Gegenwart, Akademie der Architektenkammer*. Stuttgart: Hatge Verlag.

Trachtenberg, M., & I. Hyman 1986. *Architecture, from Prehistory to Post-Modernism*. New York: Harry N. Abrams.

Tuan, Yi-Fu 1976. *Space and Place: The Perspective of Experience*. Minneapolis: University of Minnesota Press.

Turner, P. 1979. *The Education of Le Corbusier: A Study of the Development of Le Corbusier's Thought 1900-1920*. New York.

Uexküll, J. v. 1920. *Theoretische Biologie*. Berlin: Gebr. Paetel.

– 1921. *Umwelt und Innenwelt der Tiere*. Berlin: Springer.

– 1922. Wie sehen wir die Natur und wie sieht sie uns? *Die Naturwissenschaften* 12: 265-71, 296-301, 316-22.

– 1934/56. *Streifzüge durch die Umwelten von Tieren und Menschen*. Hamburg: Rowohl Verlag.

Uexküll, J. v., F. Brock 1927. Atlas zur Bestimmung der Orte in den Sehräumen der Tiere, *Zeitschrift für vergleichende Physiologie* 5: 167-78.

Virilo, P. 1989. *Der negative Horizont. Bewegung, Geschwindigkeit, Beschleunigung*. München-Wien: Hanser.

Walter, E.V. 1988. *Placeways: A Theory of the Human Environment*. Chapel Hill: University of North Carolina Press.

Contributors

BJØRN BJERKLI is Lecturer in Social Anthropology at the University of Tromsø, Norway. His main interests are in circumpolar peoples, ethnic relations, identity processes, land use and indigenous rights issues.

SABINE BRAUCKMANN is a philosopher and historian of science, mainly interested in the theory construction of biomedical sciences. She is currently a research associate at the Konrad Lorenz Institute, Vienna.

NILS BUBANDT gained a Ph.D. in anthropology from the Australian National University, Canberra. He is Associate Professor at the Department of Social Anthropology, University of Aarhus, Denmark and has carried out fieldwork in the Moluccas, Indonesia.

ALF HORNBORG is Professor of Anthropology at the Division of Human Ecology, Lund University. He is the author of numerous publications on semiotics, modernity, ecology and perceptions of nature.

TIM INGOLD is Professor of Anthropology at the Department of Sociology, University of Aberdeen. His regional interests are in Finland, the Nordic countries and the circumpolar North. Theoretically, his interests include the comparative study of hunter-gatherer and pastoral societies, relations between humans and animals, language and technology, the history of evolutionary theory, and the connections between biological, psychological and anthropological approaches to culture and social life.

RANDI KAARHUS is Associate Professor in the Centre for International Environment and Development Studies at the Agricultural University of Norway. She received her Ph.D. in social anthropology from the University of Oslo in 1996. She has carried out comparative research on perceptions of environmental problems and the construction of scientific knowledge in Ecuador and Norway, and worked with developmental projects in East Africa. Recently she has focused on the role of local knowledge and community-based institutions in biodiversity conservation and natural resource management.

ARNE KALLAND is Professor of Anthropology at the University of Oslo. He has carried out research on, among other subjects, Japanese perceptions of nature, maritime resource management, and international discourse on nature protection.

LARS KROGH is Associate Professor at the Department of Geography, University of Copenhagen. His special interest is in soil science and he has carried out fieldwork in Burkina Faso. During the past five years he has participated in the multidisciplinary research project SEREIN (Sahel-Sudan Environmental Research Initiative) focusing on resource management.

TOOMAS KUKK is a researcher at the Institute of Zoology and Botany, Estonian Agricultural University.

KALEVI KULL is Professor at the Institute of Zoology and Botany in Tartu and in the Department of Semiotics at Tartu University, Estonia. Trained as a botanist, his research extends into theoretical and evolutionary biology, biosemiotics and the history and philosophy of biology. His work on the interface between the biological traditions in East and West Europe has allowed him to reintroduce works of the Baltic biologists Karl Ernst von Baer and Jakob von Uexküll and to outline a synthesis between biosemiotics, ecosemiotics and cultural semiotics.

ALEXEI LOTMAN is a biologist and Director of the Matsalu Nature Reserve, Estonia.

BJARKE PAARUP-LAURSEN is Associate Professor at the Department of Ethnography and Social Anthropology, University of Aarhus. He specialises in West Africa and has carried out fieldwork in northern Nigeria and Northern Burkina Faso.

MORTEN A. PEDERSEN is Assistant Professor in the Department of Anthropology at the University of Copenhagen. He received his Ph.D. in social anthropology from the University of Cambridge and has carried out extensive fieldwork in Siberia and Mongolia.

ANTI RANDVIIR is postgraduate student at the Department of Semiotics, University of Tartu. His main interests and recent publications concern the question of semiotics of space (cultural space, semiotics of the city), general semiotic processes and the metalanguage of semiotics.

ANDREAS ROEPSTORFF is Assistant Professor in the Centre for Functionally Integrative Neuroscience at the University of Aarhus. He is educated in biology and social anthropology and has done research on national identity in Lithuania, perceptions of nature in Greenland, and the production of knowledge in the brain imaging community. He is currently working as an anthropologist in cognitive neuroscience.

NINA WITOSZEK is Research Professor in the Centre for Development and the Environment at the University of Oslo. She has written extensively on mythologies of nature and the construction of national identity in Scandinavia, Germany and Ireland. Currently she is investigating the relation between the humanist legacy and current environmental ethics through critical appraisals of ecophilosophy and deep ecology.

Index